FRANK LLOYD WRIGHT
IN NEW YORK

THE PLAZA YEARS, 1954-1959

JANE KING HESSION
and
DEBRA PICKREL

Foreword by MIKE WALLACE

Gibbs Smith, Publisher
TO ENRICH AND INSPIRE HUMANKIND
Salt Lake City | Charleston | Santa Fe | Santa Barbara

First Edition
11 10 09 08 07   5 4 3 2 1

Published by
Gibbs Smith, Publisher
P.O. Box 667
Layton, Utah 84041

Orders: 1.800.835.4993
www.gibbs-smith.com

Designed by Kurt Wahlner
Printed and bound in China

Library of Congress Cataloging-in-Publication Data

Hession, Jane King, 1951-
  Frank Lloyd Wright in New York : the Plaza years, 1954-1959 /
Jane King Hession and Debra Pickrel. — 1st ed.
      p. cm.
  Includes bibliographical references and index.
  ISBN-13: 978-1-4236-0101-2
  ISBN-10: 1-4236-0101-7
  1. Wright, Frank Lloyd, 1867-1959. 2. Wright, Frank Lloyd,
1867-1959—Friends and associates. 3. Architects—United States—
Biography. 4. New York (N.Y.)—Civilization—20th century. 5. New York
(N.Y.)—History—20th century—Biography. I. Pickrel, Debra. II. Title.

NA737.W7H475 2007
720.92—dc22
[B]
                                              2007011257

OVERLEAF, LEFT: "A shimmering prismatic verticality. . . ."
Wright appreciated the beauty of New York at night.

OVERLEAF, RIGHT: Wright's New York Plaza Suite, 1955.

CONTENTS

Foreword
by Mike Wallace 6

Introduction 8

ONE | "Taliesin East"
At Home and At Work in New York 16

TWO | Battling the "Glass Box Boys"
The Skyscraper and the City 32

THREE | Courting the New Consumer
Foreign Automobiles and Domestic Designs 48

FOUR | In the Spotlight
A Celebrity Among Celebrities 66

FIVE | Master of the Medium
In America's Living Rooms 82

SIX | The Guggenheim Rising
The Spiral on Fifth Avenue 92

SEVEN | After Wright
A New York Legacy 110

Frank Lloyd Wright in New York City: A Chronology . .124

Acknowledgements 126

Notes 128

Bibliography 145

Credits 151

Index 152

FOREWORD

I met Frank Lloyd Wright nearly fifty years ago in New York. At ninety years of age, he was the grand old man of American architecture, as famous then for his progressive views on life and society as he was for his brilliant and revolutionary work. I was then a thirty-nine-year-old broadcast journalist hosting *The Mike Wallace Interview* on ABC, and we came face to face on the evening of September 1, 1957, when he appeared on that show.

My half-hour, single-guest program, which aired during the old black-and-white days of television, was crafted around a very simple notion: to persuade celebrated and provocative individuals whom other people were mightily interested in to sit across from me so I could ask them nosy and often controversial questions—just the kind viewers themselves would ask if given the chance.

At the time of our interview, Wright was living at the Plaza Hotel on Central Park South and working on the construction of the Guggenheim Museum on Fifth Avenue. Prior to the live broadcast, I exchanged pleasantries with the world-famous, white-haired architect, and it became apparent to me that he'd watched the show before and admired it. He knew I often tried to put my guests on the spot, but he loved the intellectual tussle of an interview. He enjoyed playing the curmudgeon, but did so with a generous measure of good humor. In fact, moments before we went on the air, he said with a twinkle in his eye, "Let's have fun." And at the end of the interview, it had gone so well and there was still so much to talk about that I asked him to sit right there for another thirty minutes. He agreed, and we taped a second segment that ran a few weeks later.

Knowing Wright was a critic of certain aspects of city living, I made it a point to ask him about life in New York. Did he find the skyline exciting . . . exalting? He replied matter-of-factly that our city was a "never-planned . . . race for rent . . . a great monument . . . to the power of money and greed." But during our conversation, he turned optimist about the future, putting his faith in the many teenagers who wrote him letters expressing interest in his architecture.

Wright died a little over a year after that interview.

Frank Lloyd Wright was many things: architect, iconoclast, and genius. His astoundingly fresh ideas came from a richly inventive and creative mind. He was then, and he remains now, a thoroughly American original.

Mike Wallace
New York City
April 2006

Wright at a 1940 retrospective exhibition of his work, Frank Lloyd Wright: American Architect, at New York's Museum of Modern Art.

INTRODUCTION

Frank Lloyd Wright (1867–1959) professed to hate all cities, but none more than New York. For decades, he lambasted the East Coast metropolis as "the greatest and greediest mouth in the world," and spurned its buildings as "cruel rat traps."[1] His relentless damnations were so widely disseminated in print and on radio and television that, by 1954, Wright's antipathy to New York was crystal clear. Yet, that same year, the world-famous architect became a citizen of the city he claimed to despise most when he established a home and office in one of its grandest Gilded Age landmarks—the Plaza Hotel (1907) at Fifth Avenue and Central Park South.

From August 1954 through January 1959, when Wright left New York for the last time, his cosmopolitan suite was "command central," the headquarters from which he negotiated— with varying measures of creativity, cooperation, and combat—an astonishing array of exchanges with the city's architects, artists, journalists, editors, publishers, designers, celebrities, power brokers, and bureaucrats. Most significantly, he shepherded the Solomon R. Guggenheim Museum (1943–1959), his New York masterwork, to near completion from his sumptuous quarters.

Although Wright's decision to become a New Yorker might be perceived as contradicting a core belief, it was actually a well-considered choice, triggered in part by professional demands. The Guggenheim was moving closer to construction, and the myriad complexities of the commission—already eleven years in the making—required his presence in the city.[2] It was becoming increasingly difficult for the eighty-seven-year-old architect to supervise the project from either of his remote architectural offices: Taliesin (begun in 1911) in Spring Green, Wisconsin, and Taliesin West (begun in 1937) in Scottsdale, Arizona.[3] Wright and his son-in-law, William Wesley "Wes" Peters, the Taliesin apprentice assigned to the Guggenheim project, needed a New York base from which to oversee the museum's planning and construction on a daily basis. And, while in the city, Wright would require a comfortable home for himself and his third wife, Olgivanna, who often accompanied him on his trips.[4]

Architecturally speaking, New York remained unconquered territory for Wright in 1954. By the time he moved into his Plaza suite, he had designed more than nine hundred projects, approximately three hundred and fifty of which had been constructed.[5] Yet he had never built a single permanent structure in the city. Although he proposed a significant project for Manhattan in the late 1920s, it did not stand in the skyline.[6] This became particularly vexing to the architect during a post–World War II building boom that benefited a host of his professional colleagues—and rivals. As their International Style buildings rose with increasing frequency along New York's most prestigious avenues, Wright remained entrenched in the battle to build the Guggenheim.

New York's Plaza Hotel (1907), 1955.

As America assumed superpower status after the war, New York became the most powerful metropolis in the world.[7] In 1946, the selection of Manhattan as the site of the new headquarters for the fledgling United Nations Organization further enhanced its international preeminence. As postwar prosperity initiated an era of tremendous growth and change in the country, demand for construction in the city reached unprecedented levels. By the middle of the twentieth century, New York had become the nation's undisputed architectural capital.[8] About 50 percent of the country's licensed architects were practicing in the city at the time, and the leading architectural journals were published there as well.[9] Taking note of this pervasive trend, the *New York Times* increased its coverage of architecture and predicted 1958 would generate more office buildings than any year in the city's history.[10] These circumstances would provide Wright with the perfect platform for promoting his own architectural principles, which stood in direct contrast to what he saw being constructed around him.

Americans looking optimistically to the future bought cars, built and furnished new homes, and launched the baby boom. At mid-century, New York was the epicenter of a consumer explosion: 25 percent of the nation's five hundred largest companies had headquarters in Manhattan; of those that did not, most had sales offices there.[11] Not surprisingly, Madison Avenue became the creative hub of a thriving advertising trade. A marketer's nirvana, New York was described by a Lever Brothers executive as "the platform from which to sell goods in America"—the company's planned center of operations would become one of Manhattan's modern landmarks.[12] Wright's professional associations would make him an active participant in this commercial wave, creating both a Manhattan showroom for elegant automobiles and lines of consumer goods targeting millions of eager purchasers.

In addition to its commercial dominance, New York was the country's media nexus. Long the center of the publishing and radio industries in America, in the late 1940s and 1950s, the metropolis became the nation's television capital as well—the majority of shows in the new medium originated in Manhattan's broadcast studios.[13] The city's literary circles and Broadway theaters virtually assured a steady supply of writers, actors, designers, and directors for the asking. This potent combination of exceptional talent, superior screenwriting, live original dramatic productions, and penetrating news programming gave rise to what would later become known as the "Golden Age" of television.[14] Capitalizing on his celebrity during his Plaza years, Wright became a persuasive television performer, effectively using its wide reach to promote his beliefs to a curious public.

In the 1950s, New York was "a world city of art," and a "center for artistic experimentation," according to art critic Jed Perl.[15] As the heart of the Abstract Expressionist movement, painters such as Jackson Pollock, Willem de Kooning, and Hans Hofmann, to name a few, all called the city home. Galleries, studios, and museums thrived in what Perl described as "the rush-hour-in-the-arts drama."[16] In its energy, intensity, size, and scale, "only New York was big enough to embrace the challenges of modern art," he said.[17] In Wright's efforts to realize his "modern gallery," as he called the Guggenheim, the architect would publicly clash with some of the field's recognized masters.

Yet, for as much as New York was changing at mid-century, one truth was immutable: the city remained a magnet for aspirants of all kinds. Luring those with dreams and ambition with a pull social reformer Jacob Riis once likened to "a lighted candle to the moth," the city remained the ultimate proving ground.[18] Writer E. B. White described three New Yorks: the first of the native-born, the second of the commuter, and the third of "the person who was born somewhere else and came . . . in quest of

Aerial view of midtown Manhattan, looking southwest, showing the United Nations Headquarters (1947–52) and Empire State Building (1931), ca. 1950s.

New Yorkers crowd Fifth Avenue's midtown sidewalks, 1948.

something."[19] The last was the greatest of the three, and the one responsible for its "incomparable achievements."[20] Of those who come to the city "seeking sanctuary or fulfillment or some greater or lesser grail," White said, "each absorbs New York with the fresh eye of an adventurer, each generates heat and light to dwarf the Consolidated Edison Company."[21] As the end of his life approached, Wright was such a New Yorker—irresistibly drawn to the city and resolved to leave a lasting architectural mark on the glittering metropolis.

———————

By the time he added the Plaza's address to his official letterhead, Wright had been traveling to New York for business and pleasure for nearly a half century, but he had always been of two minds about the city. In principle, he abhorred its unrestrained vertical growth, mushrooming population, crowded conditions, and thickening pollution. In practice, however, he enjoyed all that it had to offer. He delighted

New York's Times Square looking north, 1955.

in strolling midtown's streets with East Coast friends such as sculptor Isamu Noguchi, browsing favorite Asian art galleries, dining at "21" or other fine Manhattan restaurants, attending the theater (he was fond of musicals), and reading about himself in the New York press.[22] His relationship with the city was both contradictory and complex. As architectural critic Herbert Muschamp discerned, ". . . an observer might note a discrepancy between the tenor of these remarks and the frequent New York jaunts of their author."[23] Simply stated, when it came to New York, Wright's words were one thing, but his actions quite another.

His emotions were not conflicted when it came to the Plaza, however. He had an unabashed affection for the historic building, which he once singled out as "the only beautiful hotel . . . in all of this god-awful New York."[24] For decades, he claimed the hotel's smart restaurants and clubby bars as his own, and favored its comfortable spaces for meetings with friends, business associates, and the press, inviting all of them to "his" domain with the same proprietary phrase: "We will be in New York at the usual place (the Plaza). . . ."[25] Although Wright proclaimed in *The New Yorker* in 1952, "I've been coming to the Plaza for forty years," it would be another two years before he became an official resident.[26]

Wright had been visiting the Plaza, a hotel favored by "the smartest names in American society," for nearly as long as it had been in existence, and it never failed to serve his purposes.[27] In October 1909, the hotel provided sanctuary for the architect and his lover, Mamah Borthwick Cheney.[28] After abandoning their families (and his practice) in Oak Park, Illinois, the two stayed at the hotel before setting sail for Europe, where they planned to begin a new life together.[29] During the winter of 1926–27, the Plaza offered reassuring surroundings to the debt-ridden architect when he came to the city to find a buyer for his collection of Japanese prints. With the profits, he hoped to stave off his "ever-threatening creditors" and save Taliesin, his beloved home and studio, from foreclosure.[30] That winter, Wright and cultural critic Lewis Mumford met for the first time at the hotel. Over lunch, the two launched a thirty-year association charged with mutual admiration and political differences that often played out in the pages of *The New Yorker* and other publications.[31] During the 1940s, the architect became familiar with the seductive charms of a Plaza residence as a frequent guest in philanthropist Solomon R. Guggenheim's luxurious art-filled rooms, located directly below the ones he would later inhabit. In Guggenheim's suite, Wright and his wife were "entertained lavishly" as they discussed plans for a new museum of non-objective art that would bear their host's name and display his extensive collection.[32]

A Plaza home and office had much to offer the architect, including prestige, prospect, and refuge—an elegant perch from which to survey the city he loved to hate, and a comfortable haven within which to retreat from its insistent view. Wright's love of luxury informed his redesign of the Plaza suite, the last home and studio he would create. Throughout his life, regardless of how much he owed his creditors, Wright's personal quarters were always lavishly appointed. His Plaza suite was no exception: "Wherever he was, for a day or a year, he changed [his rooms] until they pleased his taste," his sister Maginel Wright Barney noted.[33]

In 1954, Wright issued a press release to announce, or perhaps explain, his opulent accommodations:

> He has always worked where he ate and slept and is doing so now with the air of magnificence and expense one associates with the Plaza. He has done the rooms over in the vein of the original Plaza as conceived by Henry Hardenberg [sic]—and managed at the same time to get a practicable working office, show room and sleeping quarters out of it—all pretty harmonious with Plaza elegance—with certain additions Mr. Wright thinks would have pleased Henry Hardenberg [sic], master of German Renaissance.[34]

The effect his metropolitan dwelling had on visitors was not lost on Wright, who possessed an innate gift for self-promotion. He knew the suite, like all his incomparable homes and studios, spoke volumes about its creator. "His own home was his best advertisement, the self-portrait of a man of taste and prestige," said art historian Julia Meech."[35] At mid-century, as he was about to begin construction on Manhattan's most controversial building, Wright's posh Plaza suite and fashionable Fifth Avenue address sent precisely the message he intended to convey to New York: the world-famous architect had arrived.

ABOVE: Aerial view of New York's Central Park looking north, ca. 1950. The Plaza Hotel is near its southeastern boundary.

FACING: Frank Lloyd Wright in New York with an early model of the Guggenheim Museum, 1945.

"TALIESIN EAST"
AT HOME AND AT WORK
IN NEW YORK

[
This is the Old Diamond Jim Brady suite.

It's the best part of New York.

Frank Lloyd Wright, *The New Yorker*, June 16, 1956
]

There were few finer views in New York at mid-century than the panorama from Frank Lloyd Wright's second-floor corner suite at the Plaza Hotel. Beyond its tall arched windows facing Fifth Avenue and Central Park South, the city's premier green space, Central Park, stretched north in one unbroken 843-acre swath. Along the east side of the park stood prestigious residences and great cultural institutions, including the Metropolitan Museum of Art, the Frick Collection, and "Millionaires' Row," once home to a procession of opulent turn-of-the-century mansions built by some of New York's wealthiest families. To the south, fashionable department stores and chic shops marched toward midtown. Thirty blocks to the north on Fifth Avenue, between East Eighty-Eighth and East Eighty-Ninth streets, stood the site upon which the Guggenheim Museum would soon begin to rise.

Stunning views aside, the Plaza was an ideal location for Wright's Manhattan home base. The hotel's peerless address and tradition of excellence were well suited to his rarified personal tastes and exacting standards. Above all, the Plaza was regarded by many as the finest hotel in a city of splendid hotels, and Wright had great affection for the building. "He admired its grand style and felt very much at home in this atmosphere, so very different from his own two Taliesins," noted Bruce Brooks Pfeiffer, director of the Frank Lloyd Wright Archives and a former Taliesin apprentice.[1] "It was his favorite place in New York."[2]

Aerial view of New York looking south along Fifth Avenue showing the Plaza Hotel on the southeast edge of Central Park.

Fifth Avenue and Fifty-Ninth Street, looking south. The Grand Army Plaza is bordered by the Plaza Hotel, right, and the mansion of Cornelius Vanderbilt II (1879–83, demolished 1927), center.

"THE WORLD'S MOST LUXURIOUS HOTEL"

The Plaza, designed by Henry Janeway Hardenbergh, boasts a rich and fascinating history. By the turn of the twentieth century, Hardenbergh had earned a solid reputation as the architect of elegant residential buildings and hotels for the well-to-do, notably the Dakota Apartments (1882) on Central Park West, and New York's original Waldorf (1893) and Astoria (1897) hotels on Fifth Avenue and Thirty-Fourth Street.[3] The terra-cotta-clad, eighteen-story Plaza Hotel, described as emulating a French chateau, rose from a limestone base to a distinctive green copper and slate mansard roof to create an elegant but imposing 800-room edifice. "What made it all the more grand was its size, which dwarfed all of the other buildings in the neighborhood," said Plaza historian Curtis Gathje.[4] When it opened in 1907, the Plaza claimed to be "the world's most luxurious hotel."[5]

The Plaza's urban surroundings were as distinctive as the building itself. On the Fifth Avenue side, the hotel faced Grand Army Plaza, the design of which evolved from landscape architects Frederick Law Olmsted and Calvert Vaux's original plans for Central Park, purported to be "the first landscaped public park in the United States."[6] A bronze statue of Civil War General William Tecumseh Sherman (1903, by Augustus Saint-Gaudens) and the Pulitzer Fountain (1916, by Karl Bitter and the firm of Carrère and Hastings) further distinguished the plaza.[7] To the south, at One West Fifty-Seventh Street, stood the palatial mansion of Cornelius Vanderbilt II, grandson of "Commodore" Cornelius Vanderbilt, designed by George B. Post and Richard Morris Hunt. The mansion was demolished in 1927, making way for the exclusive specialty store Bergdorf Goodman.[8] The Plaza provided unparalleled views of it all.

Conceived as a "lavish pleasure palace," the hotel reportedly became New York's most desirable address for visitors and residents alike.[9] In the tradition of the day, it did not take long for the cream of New York society to discover the advantages of establishing a fashionable in-town residence at the Plaza. Leading the way were Mr. and Mrs. Alfred Gwynne Vanderbilt, who were the first to sign the guest register on

The Palm Court at the Plaza Hotel with its original domed glass ceiling.

opening day.[10] Not coincidentally, motorized taxicab service was inaugurated in the city the same day, and Plaza patrons were offered free rides.[11]

During its first fifty years, the hotel's roster read like an international "Who's Who" of society, the arts, and industry. F. Scott Fitzgerald was a frequent visitor who took at least one impromptu dip in the Pulitzer Fountain with his wife, Zelda. Actresses Marlene Dietrich and Greta Garbo resided at the hotel for a time, as did photographer Cecil Beaton and fashion designer Christian Dior. Hotel visitors included George M. Cohan, Marilyn Monroe, the Duke and Duchess of Windsor, and presidents Harry Truman, Dwight D. Eisenhower, Richard Nixon, and John F. Kennedy with his wife, Jacqueline.[12] Its most famous fictional inhabitant was "Eloise," a six-year-old with no last name. Beginning in 1955, the irrepressible child's spirited adventures in the luxury hotel were chronicled in a series of books by Plaza entertainer Kay Thompson and illustrator Hilary Knight that popularized the hotel with a younger generation of New Yorkers.

Not only was the Plaza a highly desirable place to stay or live, it was a trendy New York dining, dancing, and entertainment venue in the 1950s. The rich and famous flocked to its enticing array of restaurants and nightspots. Among the most popular were the Edwardian Room, the Oak Room and Bar, the Palm Court, and the exotic Persian Room nightclub, where headliners included legendary vocalists Eartha Kitt, Ethel Merman, and the "Incomparable" Hildegarde.[13]

It was not surprising that the Plaza appealed to Wright, a sophisticated man of impeccable taste. However, as an outspoken critic of most architecture that was not his own, it was remarkable that he found the historicist design of the Plaza appealing. He once told a client: "Good old Henry Hardenbergh. Of course, I wouldn't do anything like it, but it is an honest building."[14] Yet he couldn't resist expounding his own colorful version of the hotel's history—"It was built by the Astors, Astorists, Astorites, the Vanderbilts, Plasterbilts, and Whoeverbilts, who wanted a place to dress up and parade and see themselves in great mirrors. So they sent for the finest master of the German Renaissance style, Henry Hardenbergh, and he did this."[15]

LEFT: The Christian Dior suite, Plaza Hotel, ca. 1949. Before Wright inhabited it, it was one of four celebrity suites created during Conrad Hilton's ownership of the building.

BELOW: Wright's Plaza suite key rests on hotel stationery that bears a sketch and signature block in the architect's hand.

Wright adopted a paternalistic attitude towards the hotel and was protective of its original décor. He did not hesitate to cross swords with anyone—including hotel management—who attempted to alter its old-world character. He protested plans to carpet the Italian mosaic floor in the lobby, he mourned the loss of the domed glass ceiling of the Palm Court, and he was saddened by the removal of the original Art Deco interior of the Persian Room, created by his friend Viennese designer Joseph Urban. On occasion, Wright even took credit for rescuing the Plaza, "a beautiful hotel," from near ruin. "They started to remodel it downstairs a few years back, but thank God, I got here in time. The little devils had already wrecked the Palm Court, but I saved the Oak Room and the dining room."[16]

Not only was Wright determined to live at the Plaza, he wanted one of its finest apartments for his home. The best suites in the house were those located on the northeast corner of the hotel, according to Gathje. These not only had two exposures, they also featured "higher ceilings and were among the largest and most spacious," he said.[17] Wright noted these advantages, and, after a thorough tour, requested combined suite 223–225 for his residence.

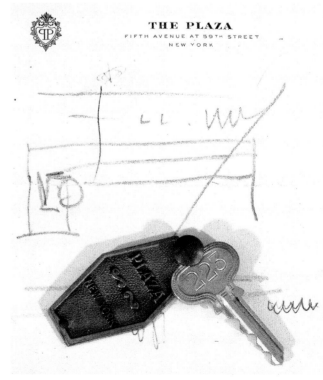

THE PLAZA
FIFTH AVENUE AT 59TH STREET
NEW YORK

The suite had an interesting past. Reputedly, "Diamond" Jim Brady, a New York financier famous for his prodigious appetite and penchant for jewels, was one of its previous residents. This was a source of amusement for Wright, who later characterized his redecoration of the space as "'Diamond' Jim Brady Modern."[18] In 1949, French couturier Christian Dior and his staff redesigned the rooms as one of four "celebrity suites" conceived by Colonel Serge Obolensky, a Russian émigré and the Plaza's public relations director.[19] The glamorous transformation was part of owner and hotel chain founder Conrad Hilton's postwar promotional efforts on behalf of his property.[20] Although the unveiling of the Dior Suite was a public relations event, its décor was short-lived. Following occupancy by film producer David O. Selznick and his wife, actress Jennifer Jones, Wright moved in and erased almost all traces of the formal French decorative scheme in favor of his own interpretation of the historic space.[21] In the tradition of famous inhabitants who preceded him, Plaza management was pleased to have Wright, a celebrity himself, redesign the suite.[22]

MAKING IT WRIGHT

Wright's decision to use the suite as both his personal retreat and professional base of operations reflected a long-standing preference for working "where he ate and slept."[23] This proclivity first surfaced in 1898, when Wright moved one of his architectural offices from downtown Chicago to his suburban Oak Park home, where he lived with his first wife, Catherine, and their six children.[24] The proximity of his living

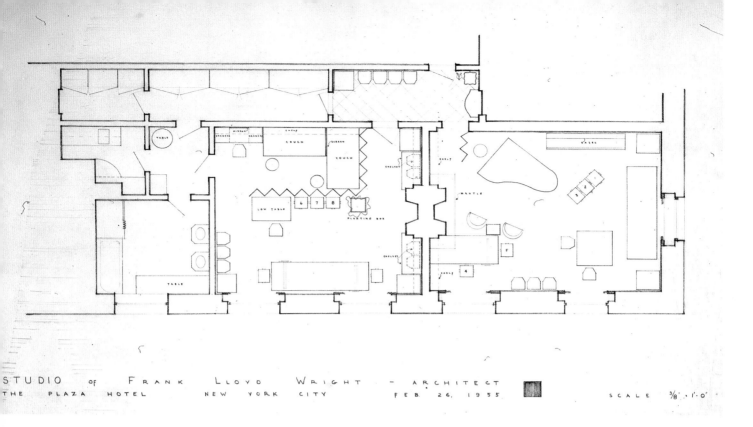

STUDIO OF FRANK LLOYD WRIGHT – ARCHITECT
THE PLAZA HOTEL NEW YORK CITY FEB 26, 1955 SCALE ⅜" = 1'-0"

quarters to his work space—the two were connected via a passageway—was a great convenience. This interweaving of residential and office spaces became the paradigm for Wright's future homes and studios, the interconnections of which became more inextricable. All would be shaped by what Wright scholar Neil Levine described as "[Wright's] vision of the unity of living and working," a concept most fully realized in his primary residences, Taliesin, and Taliesin West.[25]

The Plaza suite was not Wright's first home away from home, nor was it his first hotel residence.[26] Between 1917 and 1922, the architect made several trips to Tokyo to supervise the design and construction of the new Imperial Hotel (1913–23). In 1920, he included a "modest little nook" for himself in the annex he designed for the existing hotel.[27] The advantages, he explained, were many: "I slept there and had set up my drawing board there where I could work disturbing no one and could tumble into bed when tired out."[28] Although "the building itself wasn't luxurious," the architect's accommodations were richly appointed with Asian textiles, scrolls and artifacts, and a grand piano.[29] "We were surrounded by lovely and costly things," recalled Miriam Noel, Wright's second wife.[30] "Frank had a remarkable genius for creating an unusual and artistic environment. No family ever lived in greater luxury and splendor than we."[31]

Wright began to redesign his Plaza suite in spring 1954.[32] It was an unusual project for the architect for several reasons. Unlike most of his buildings, he was forced to work within an existing architectural framework in the space. Ceiling height, wall dimensions, and window shape and placement were all fixed elements. As a result, his vision "interpreted the old style of [the Plaza] in new terms which were sympathetic to the past," said his wife, Olgivanna.[33] The Plaza's urban setting also meant Wright could not seek design inspiration from qualities inherent in the surrounding landscape or specific characteristics of the natural environment; always creative wellsprings for the architect. Nevertheless, Wright began the process of redesign in his customary manner; he worked out his ideas on paper.

ABOVE: Floor plan of Plaza suite 223-225 (1955), showing furniture placement and room divisions.

BELOW: Wright with workmen in one of the few photos taken of the architect in the suite, 1954.

The suite, which was entered through a vestibule off the hotel corridor, comprised a corner sitting or living room (room 223) with north and east exposures, and an east-facing bedroom (room 225), hallway, bathroom, and pantry. Six tall windows and two fireplaces further defined the high-ceilinged spaces. Wright explored his ideas in annotated plans and elevations, carefully detailing furniture placement, wall color and finishes, lighting, and the desired location of plants and art objects. The drawings illustrate Wright's genius for thinking in light, color, and texture: he specified "gold" wall finish set within frames of existing decorative wall molding on the thirteen-foot-high living room walls. He also conceived round, beveled mirror insets for the upper portion of the tall arched windows, behind which he concealed a light source. The result was an up-lit effect, the rays of which he suggested with quick strokes in his sketch.

At first glance, the suite's design appears to be a departure for Wright, and, in fact, it bears many "non-Wrightian" elements including double-hung windows, decorative crown moldings, and a crystal chandelier. However, closer examination reveals Wright's aesthetic preferences, attention to detail, and masterful creative control.

"A GALAXY OF FAMOUS PEOPLE"

Wright once tried to coax the gift of a concert grand piano from the New York firm of Steinway & Sons by promising "a galaxy of famous people" would enjoy the instrument in his Plaza suite.[34] Although his entreaty failed, many celebrated personalities from the worlds of art, music, letters, journalism, publishing, Hollywood, architecture, finance, and business did meet with the architect there or in public rooms at the Plaza. Notables included:

Wright and his granddaughter, Academy Award-winning actress Anne Baxter, 1951.

Anne Baxter: Wright's granddaughter, Academy Award–winning actress

Alistair Cooke: broadcast journalist, host of television's *Omnibus* series

René d'Harnoncourt: director, Museum of Modern Art

Brendan Gill: writer, *The New Yorker*

Elizabeth Gordon: editor, *House Beautiful*

Harry F. Guggenheim: president, Solomon R. Guggenheim Foundation; client. Wife: Alicia Patterson

Maximilian Hoffman: president, Hoffman Automobiles; client

Philip Johnson: architect and curator, Museum of Modern Art

Henry J. Kaiser: industrialist and founder, Kaiser Aluminum; client

Gerald Loeb: founding partner, E. F. Hutton & Co.; client

Arthur Miller: American playwright; client. Wife: Marilyn Monroe

Marilyn Monroe: actress; client. Husband: Arthur Miller

Robert Moses: commissioner, New York City Parks. Wife: Mary (Wright's distant cousin)

Lewis Mumford: architectural and cultural critic, *The New Yorker*

Alicia Patterson: publisher, *Newsday.* Husband: Harry F. Guggenheim

Ben Raeburn: founder and publisher, Horizon Press

Baroness Hilla Rebay: curator, Solomon R. Guggenheim Foundation

Ray Rubicam: cofounder, Young and Rubicam advertising agency

Aline Louchheim Saarinen: associate art editor, the *New York Times.* Husband: Eero Saarinen

Eero Saarinen: Finnish architect. Wife: Aline Louchheim Saarinen

Carl Sandburg: Pulitzer Prize–winning poet, writer, and biographer

Leopold Stokowski: conductor, NBC's *Symphony of the Air;* director, Philadelphia Orchestra

Edward Durrell Stone: architect

Mike Todd: Academy Award–winning producer; client

Sylvester Weaver: president, NBC; client

Eric Lloyd Wright: Wright's grandson, architect

Lloyd Wright: Wright's son, architect

William Zeckendorf: real estate tycoon; president, Webb and Knapp; client

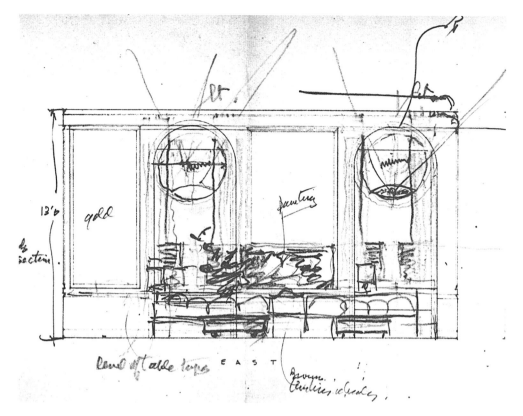

LEFT: Elevation, east wall of Plaza suite living room (1954). Wright noted wall finishes, art placement, and window treatments on the sketch.

In the living room, Wright employed a sophisticated color palette of gold, rose, deep purple/red, peach, and black. The wall surfaces, "treated as screens," were covered with Japanese rice paper flecked with gold leaf, set within frames of gilded wood molding on rose colored walls.[35] The suite's two fireplaces were painted black. He detailed the windows in four layers, adding floor-to-near-ceiling drapes in a rich purple/red velvet and the mirrored insets over preexisting sheer curtains and wooden shutters that recessed into the deep window frames.[36] To turn on the lightbulbs hidden behind the mirrors, Wright provided long pull cords weighted with crystal balls. Peach carpets covered the wood floors, and velvet chairs were upholstered in a similar hue.[37] Several contemporary upholstered armchairs by Heritage-Henredon were placed around the room. Wright brought the chairs to the Plaza from their former location in his Usonian Exhibition House (1953), a temporary structure erected on the future site of the Guggenheim Museum (see "Sixty Years of Living Architecture and the Usonian Exhibition House," page 99).[38]

Wright also designed numerous pieces of furniture for the suite, including his desk, a dozen three-legged hassocks, several tables of various heights, "tall stools to sit at the drawing boards," shelves, and an easel.[39] A team of the architect's apprentices led by R. Joseph Fabris constructed the simple plywood furniture at Taliesin in Wisconsin. Fabris then brought the pieces to the local auto body shop, where a black lacquer finish was applied.[40] Later, the exposed edges were painted Chinese red. The hassocks were topped with peach velvet cushions, which Wright specified were to be secured with "black cord tipped with scarlet balls."[41] A team of apprentices drove the furniture to Manhattan in a Taliesin van, which blocked traffic in front of the Plaza as the pieces were unloaded.[42] Other apprentices and associates living or working in New York at the time helped with additional tasks. "No sooner do they enter our apartment than their coats come off, hammers and nails appear in their hands. And they help Mr. Wright rearrange the furniture," said Olgivanna.[43]

FACING: Living room of Wright's Plaza suite, 1955. A Korean dragon jar sits on a low table, left. Contemporary chairs are by Heritage-Henredon.

A connoisseur and collector of Asian art with particular expertise in the Japanese print, Wright displayed—and frequently repositioned—favorite pieces from his art collection in the suite.[44] A Han-dynasty ceramic *hu* and a pair of bronze Chinese horses graced the living room mantel. Late-eighteenth-century Japanese prints and triptychs were arranged around the space. A large Chinese Zhou-dynasty bronze vessel and an early-eighteenth-century Korean dragon jar sat on side tables, often filled with blossoms and

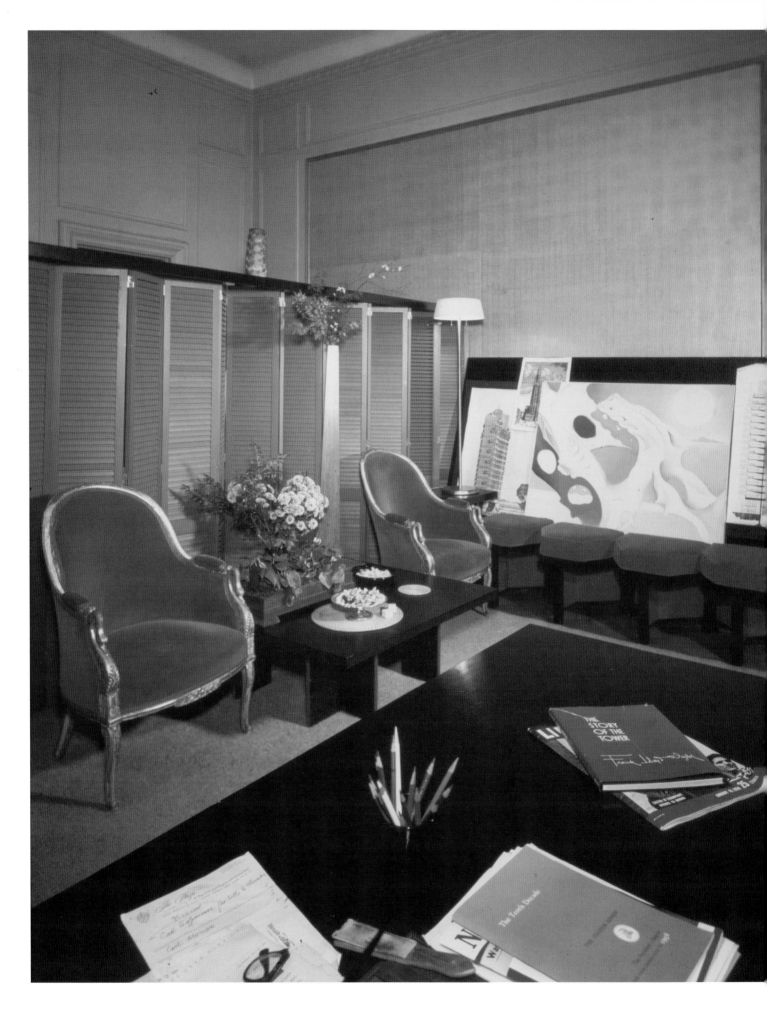

greenery. As art historian Julia Meech observed, had the architect known his dragon jar would be valued at several hundred thousand dollars in the future, he "might not have filled [it] with a top-heavy cluster of flowering branches. On the other hand, he received pleasure from his collection for the very reason that he did put everything to use."[45] A music lover, Wright made room in each of his homes for his favorite instrument. "All his life, the piano was a sort of refuge or oasis: a spring at which he could refresh himself with music" said Wright's sister, Maginel Wright Barney.[46] The suite was no exception; a Steinway grand piano assumed a place of honor in the living room.[47]

The décor of the bedroom, which Wright converted into his office/bedroom, was similar to that of the main living space. His desk stood along the east wall, surrounded by personally and professionally revealing objects including Asian art, a sixteen-volume set of *Sweet's Catalog* (an architectural reference), books he had authored, fresh flowers, and a photograph of his beloved mother, Anna. A long easel held renderings of various architectural projects in progress, as well as the painting *Pelvis with Shadows and the Moon* by Georgia O'Keeffe, a friend and fellow Wisconsinite. The artist, who called Wright "one of my favorite people of our time," offered the gift to the architect in 1947 as "a small gesture of appreciation for something I feel about you."[48] An Indian stone sculpture stood on the mantel, and a two-panel Japanese screen, depicting ducks and a lotus pond in red, green, and white tones against a dark brown background, flanked a large mirror above the fireplace. Wright purchased the screen along with several other items during an October 1953 buying spree at the Oriental Art Gallery on Madison Avenue. The room held contemporary pieces as well, notably a Heritage-Henredon wood vase with copper trim.[49]

Wright created a small bedroom for himself and his wife by screening off a portion of the west side of the office with a folding louvered screen tall enough to provide privacy, if not quiet. Olgivanna described the space as "about eighteen feet long by seven feet wide. It can just accommodate two beds lined lengthwise, and three chairs along the other wall, leaving us a two-foot passageway."[50]

Beyond the office/bedroom to the south was a cluster of small rooms. A cramped pantry/maid's room doubled as the suite's guest accommodations, and a corner of the antechamber was fashioned into a makeshift kitchen. According to Taliesin apprentice John deKoven Hill, who lived for a time in the small guest room while serving as architectural editor of *House Beautiful* magazine, the walls of the large bathroom were adorned with murals "in a very French manner" by artist Marcel Vertes.[51] The murals were vestiges of Dior's decorative scheme, as were a pair of rose velvet upholstered chairs with exposed wooden arms carved with swan heads that Wright placed in his office.[52]

Although the apartment was large, it was much smaller and more compact than either of Wright's other homes and studios. For this reason, the line between "residence" and "office" was often blurred, if not obliterated. With the exception of "the section [of the suite] which we call our bedroom," Olgivanna revealed, "every part of the rest of it is occupied by long tables with drawings, huge easels with drawings, shelves with drawings hanging from them, small tables for typewriters, and some low tables on which we have fruit or flowers."[53] Apparently, even the main living space was overrun, prompting her to qualify it as "'our so-called' living room."[54]

When completed, the suite resembled no other at the hotel, as Wright's client and friend Loren Pope witnessed firsthand. In New York on business, Pope was staying in a Plaza room with "an acre of French gray-carpeting . . . and much plate-glass mirror."[55] Upon seeing Wright's remarkable suite, Pope said, "My God, Mr. Wright! This sure doesn't look like my room."[56] Wright replied: "this guy [Hilton] . . . didn't know how to treat an elegant hotel. So a few weeks ago I called in some of the boys from Taliesin and we de-Hiltonized it."[57] Apparently, the architect was well satisfied with the results. In 1956, he pronounced in *The New Yorker* that the suite, with its spectacular view of the city, was "the best part of New York."[58]

Office of Wright's Plaza suite, 1959. A small sleeping area was behind the room divider.

SUITE DEALS:
WRITING AND RECORDING

The West Forty-Second Street office of Wright's publisher, Ben Raeburn of Horizon Press, was within walking distance of the Plaza. During the 1950s, Wright was not only a busy architect but also a prolific author who produced six books for the press: *The Future of Architecture* (1953), *The Natural House* (1954), *An American Architecture* (1955), *The Story of the Tower* (1956), *A Testament* (1957), and *The Living City* (1958).

Raeburn, "one of the legendary publishing figures in New York" known for recognizing aspiring authors before they acquired fame, became interested in Wright in the 1930s after reading his autobiography, which he regarded as "one of the great books in literature."[59] He had firsthand experience with Wright's work as well; the architect designed the Rebhuhn House (1937) in Great Neck, New York, for Raeburn's aunt and uncle.[60]

In 1952, Raeburn wrote to Wright about publishing the architect's books. A few days later, at 6:30 a.m. on a Sunday morning, Wright phoned the publisher and invited him to breakfast—thirty minutes later—at his Plaza suite. When Raeburn miraculously arrived on time, Wright asked: "Ben, can you give me one good reason why I should let you publish me instead of the big boys on Fifth Avenue with the big apparatus who are after me?" He answered, "No, but I think I know your work better than you do." Wright replied, "I believe you," and the deal was sealed.[61]

Wright, with architect Jeffrey Ellis Aronin, in the suite. Aronin holds a copy of *An American Architecture*, which Wright authored for Horizon Press in 1955. A Japanese woodblock print from Wright's extensive collection is seen on the wall to his left.

According to Raeburn, Wright was "the humblest author I have ever worked with, grateful for any criticism, full of humor, quick to consider every suggestion towards clarity—he was the very opposite of his public legend."[62] In addition to his editorial duties, Raeburn often fielded requests for interviews and meetings with the architect including a June 5, 1956, sound recording session in the Plaza suite that resulted in *Frank Lloyd Wright . . . on Record*. Raeburn posed questions to Wright during the interview for Caedmon Records, a respected producer of spoken word audio.[63] He was also protective of the aging architect, who "hardly ever said no" to requests for his time. To the best of his ability, Raeburn tried "never to let anybody tire [Wright]."[64]

Horizon published seventeen books by or about Wright during his lifetime and after his death, including a revised edition of *An Autobiography* (1977), first published in 1932 and later reissued in an expanded version in 1943.[65] Not completely satisfied with either earlier edition, Wright continued to tinker with his autobiography text for the last sixteen years of his life. Although he often read revised passages aloud to Raeburn in a process the publisher likened to "hearing him think," the architect always kept his handwritten annotations to himself. Shortly before Wright's death, Raeburn recalled: "He picked the treasure up and handed it to me, sixteen years of work, saying only, 'Here, Ben, it's yours.'"[66]

LIFE AND WORK IN THE SUITE

Whenever the Wrights came to "Taliesin East," as the suite became known, certain customs and rituals were observed.[67] "The first thing Mr. Wright usually did when arriving in New York was to go to a florist on Madison Avenue and select plants and flowers," explained Pfeiffer.[68] "I accompanied him there once, and we both had armloads . . . as we made our way on foot back to the Plaza."[69] On occasion, Hill had responsibility for the flowers: "It cost a fortune to fill the place with bouquets every time they came. And you had to be in full attendance. It required a lot of effort . . . I wouldn't have dreamed of not doing it, but it was hard."[70] Upon arrival, Wright customarily called friends and associates to invite them for breakfast or tea in the suite. Although "the invitation was for an *intime* visit, in the end there might be a few couples or twenty people," recalled Taliesin apprentice Edgar Tafel.[71]

The elegance of the suite was captured in images by two noted photographers: Ezra Stoller, an architectural specialist, who documented the rooms in black-and-white images; and Pedro Guerrero, Wright's personal photographer, who shot the spaces in color.[72] While these professional photographs caught the beauty of the apartment in moments of repose, they did little to convey the "bedlam of activity" that actually defined daily life there.[73]

Not only was the suite a busy architectural office where Wright and his apprentices worked on numerous commissions, it was also where the architect received visitors, conferred with clients, and conducted newspaper, radio, and television interviews. On any given day, it was not unusual to find clients, newspapermen, and government officials gathered in the hallway—sitting on Wright-designed stools—"patiently waiting" while a member of the press inter-

Office of Wright's Plaza suite, 1955. The velvet armchair at the desk was a remnant of Dior's earlier decorative scheme for the rooms.

viewed the architect in another room.[74] As a result, "there was pandemonium going on almost all of the time," remembered Taliesin associate Kay Schneider.[75] "The three phones in the apartment kept ringing steadily, and Mrs. Wright and I handled all of them."[76] The most intrusive circumstance was when "a TV crew takes possession of the living room," Olgivanna later remembered.[77] Yet, she added, "I am grateful that at least the telephone is shut off during these TV interviews."[78] Wright, however, thrived in the chaos. "He handled all of this activity and notoriety with ease. It was a great pleasure for him," said Schneider. "Mr. Wright was more relaxed and charming in the New York atmosphere. . . . At the Plaza [he] had all of the best of it and Mrs. Wright all of the chores."[79]

One aspect of Plaza residency the architect did not handle with efficiency was paying the bills. Wright was notorious for his elusive fiscal practices and for the legions of unsatisfied creditors he left in his wake. Not surprisingly, his financial dealings with the Plaza's accounting office were no less abstruse. His rent, which at $8,000 a year was payable at $666 per month, was nearly always in arrears. Restaurant and incidental tabs often doubled the outstanding amount.[80] Yet he remained a charming and silver-tongued debtor. Plaza Credit Manager Sheila Lee exercised diplomatic skills and persistence in her repeated dealings with the slippery architect. Over the years, she penned numerous polite notes to him (including those referencing overdue bills in excess of $4,000), in which she pleaded, "Won't you please let us hear from you?" Wright replied: "My Dear Miss Lee, Believe it or not, I had an idea that the Plaza was entirely placated as to payments . . . Hope you are as nice as ever. Affection, Frank Lloyd Wright."[81]

HOLDING COURT
IN THE OAK ROOM

There were many advantages to a Plaza residence, including the hotel's splendid public rooms and numerous amenities. From the mundane to the stylish, Wright's monthly bills suggest he availed himself of them all. He began his days with a morning elevator ride to the basement to visit the barber: "Mr. Wright hated shaving," explained Pfeiffer.[82] Room service was regularly summoned. Above all, the Wrights frequented the Plaza's superb dining facilities. "[They] usually took coffee and pastries in the Palm Court, especially if there was a guest with them," said Pfeiffer, and they often ate lunch in the Edwardian Room.[83] Once the domain of men only, the room featured wood paneling, a painted beamed ceiling, and "Spanish Renaissance" detailing, all of which Wright greatly admired.[84]

The Plaza's Oak Room. Wright favored the ornate, wood-paneled room for meetings with friends and members of the press.

As fine as the patrician dining rooms were, the Wrights sometimes tired of haute cuisine and yearned for "plain food" instead of "caviar and sauces."[85] On one such occasion, Maginel Wright Barney, an illustrator who lived in Greenwich Village, came to the rescue, smuggling "three baked potatoes and part of a cooked ham [through] the lobby of one of the world's greatest hotels" so her brother and sister-in-law could enjoy a "prosaic dinner."[86]

Of all the grand communal spaces in the Plaza, Wright's personal favorite was the Oak Room, a "German Renaissance tour de force" named for its lavish oak paneling.[87] Frescos of Bavarian castles and wine-themed décor added to the atmosphere.[88] (Adjoining the Oak Room was the Oak Bar, famous for the three impressionistic murals of old New York by artist Everett Shinn that adorn its walls.[89]) The Oak Room was Wright's preferred haunt in which to hold court with the press. Over the decades, journalists from *The New Yorker*, including Geoffrey T. Hellman, Lewis Mumford, and Brendan Gill, shared tables with him there. Over a meal, tea, or drinks, Wright would expound on whatever was on his mind, from his proposed design for a memorial on the Grand Canal in Venice ("the first new building to go up there since heaven knows when") to the evils of air-conditioning, which he claimed had "killed more good men than can be accounted for."[90] The next week, Wright's pronouncements could be read by all of New York in the pages of the popular magazine. Gill recalled the Plaza sessions as more relaxed and "less serious . . .

and less perilous" than similar encounters at Taliesin, so much so that he dared to broach difficult subjects such as Wright's "celebrated arrogance" without angering the architect.[91] However, even in the hotel's comfortable public rooms, there was one transgression that irked Wright. When he ordered his favorite spirit, Old Bushmills, neat, the waiter usually incorrectly delivered his Irish whiskey in an ice-filled glass. "Wright would pick up a spoon . . . lift the cubes out one by one, and proceed to flip them across the green-carpeted floor, to the astonishment and pleasure of the other patrons," recalled Gill.[92]

For the most part, however, the hotel's exacting standards matched Wright's own, and he derived great pleasure from playing a part in its history. "Mr. Wright was really in his element in New York City . . . He loved having an elegant suite in the Plaza," recalled Taliesin apprentice Tony Puttnam.[93] "He loved looking out over Central Park in the twilight and seeing the little lights, the very wonderful little lights that came on in Central Park. And he loved, I think, knowing how to be a nineteenth-century gentleman among people who still appreciated . . . that sort of thing."[94]

Unquestionably, Wright's suite at the Plaza was ideal for the architect's professional needs and personal gratifications. Yet, the hotel stood in a city he continued to pillory as the epitome of urban failure and architectural excess. He saw no deliverance in the sleek cityscape rising around him, evidenced by the severe modern towers beginning to proliferate just two blocks east along Park Avenue. These buildings would quickly become a focus of the architect's well-publicized wrath.

Group dinner in the Plaza's Edwardian Room, 1955. From left: Olgivanna and Frank Lloyd Wright, John deKoven Hill, Wes Peters, and Haskell Culwell, contractor for Wright's Price Tower, Bartlesville, Oklahoma (1952–56).

BATTLING THE "GLASS BOX BOYS"
THE SKYSCRAPER AND THE CITY

[
A box is more a coffin for the human spirit

than an inspiration.

Frank Lloyd Wright, the *New York Times*, May 26, 1953
]

Wright became a New York resident in a time described as "the golden age of the American corporation." During these prosperous postwar years, companies interested in enhancing their status erected towering Manhattan headquarters, and the press actively reported on the construction frenzy: *Time* featured a 1953 photo essay titled "The Great Manhattan Boom," *Business Week* called New York "the executive city" in 1956, and that same year, *Newsweek* reported on the "New New York." Midtown was the undeniable epicenter of this development and showplace of structures in the so-called "International Style," architectural symbols of mid-century establishment that Wright vehemently rejected.[1]

Inspired by *Internationale Architektur,* a 1925 book by German avant-garde architect Walter Gropius, American architectural historian Henry-Russell Hitchcock used the term "international style" in his 1929 volume, *Modern Architecture: Romanticism and Reintegration,* to describe a unique and burgeoning modernist movement. Born in Europe amidst the collapsed regimes, economies, and social revolutions that followed World War I, the style was conceived to be a twentieth-century architecture for the people. "[It] utilized and honestly expressed the materials and technologies of modern life," said historian Thomas Bender.[2]

Partly initiated by Swiss-French architect Charles-Edouard Jeanneret, widely known as Le Corbusier, the International Style developed most famously through the German Bauhaus movement, which approached building design as the solving of functional problems. Structures in the style varied somewhat in appearance, but they shared common characteristics: less massive than buildings before them, they expressed regularity rather than symmetry, and they had no applied ornamentation. Though the severe, machine-inspired qualities of these designs did not initially

Lever House (1952), 390 Park Avenue.

The new showplace of Manhattan.

New York Mayor Vincent Impellitteri quoted in the *Times*

The Soap Building . . . a box on sticks.

Frank Lloyd Wright, quoted in the *Times* and from a 1952 lecture for the American Institute of Architects

resonate in America, the energetic Art Deco and sleek Streamline Moderne styles that followed them did, paving the way for the proliferation of the International Style and the mainstreaming of modernism.[3]

In 1950s New York, box-like skyscrapers sheathed in glass curtain walls were the style's most apparent manifestations, sparkling reflections of the nation's postwar power. Following decades of representational structures such as the exuberant Art Deco Chrysler Building, the materials and details of which referenced its corporate owner's product, these stripped-down structures made no such allusions. They were easier, faster, and relatively more affordable to construct than their predecessors, and the fact that they readily accommodated modern conveniences only contributed to their popularity.[4]

The curtain wall technology of these International Style buildings was first employed by William Le Baron Jenney in his 1885 Home Insurance Building for Chicago. The cast-iron (later steel) frame system he developed that allowed buildings to reach new heights could be sheathed in a wide variety of materials.[5] For a number of years, traditional materials such as brick and terra-cotta were used for sheathing, but a German Bauhaus architect had other ideas. Thirty-five years after Jenney's innovation, Ludwig Mies van der Rohe ("Mies"), who practiced a "less is more" aesthetic that pared architecture down to its basic elements, conceived the all-glass curtain wall in two unconstructed designs. These buildings were described by the *Times* at mid-century as "the prototypes of Manhattan's new glass-walled structures."[6]

A "GLASSIFIED LANDSCAPE" [7]

When Wright moved into his Plaza suite, the city's most newsworthy examples of the International Style were the recently completed United Nations complex on the East River, and Lever House on Park Avenue, the new concourse of American commerce. Led by Director of Planning Wallace K. Harrison, the UN complex was designed by a global team of architects, including Le Corbusier, Brazilian Oscar Niemeyer, Swede Sven Markelius, Harrison's partner Max Abramovitz, and former Wright apprentice Ssu-ch'eng (Yen) Liang, who was practicing architecture in China at the time. In the end, the group adopted a scheme based largely on Le Corbusier's design concepts. The complex's thirty-nine-story Secretariat Building of 1950 (see page 10) featured glass curtain walls on two sides.[8]

Twenty-one-story Lever House was New York's first all-glass curtain wall skyscraper. Designed by Gordon Bunshaft of Skidmore, Owings & Merrill, it was the built realization of the earlier imaginings of Mies and Le Corbusier. The building's unique horizontal base was supported by *pilotis*—or slim columns—a hallmark of its style, creating a plaza that contributed to a feeling of spaciousness and an abundance of light. The first bronze-clad glass curtain wall structure, the iconic Seagram Building designed by Mies with American Philip Johnson in association with Kahn & Jacobs, would rise during Wright's final years in the city.[9]

Even though Wright was recognized as one of the world's greatest architects, he did not receive commissions for New York's major buildings for a variety of reasons. He was not asked to be a member of the UN design committee as he was determined to work alone, never bending to the will of others—"Architecture has never come out of collaboration alive," he said. When a search was conducted for an architect for the Seagram Building, Wright was rejected among the leading candidates because of his mercurial temperament. And, despite a lifetime of innovative work, some felt Wright was finally past his prime. At the least, his designs were intricate and individualized—not in step with the slick severity of corporate modernism.[10]

BELOW: Le Corbusier, second from left, discusses plans for the United Nations complex with architect Ernest Cormier of Canada, left, and other members of the international design committee. Former Taliesin apprentice Ssu-ch'eng (Yen) Liang of China is seated in the front row, second from right, ca. 1947.

FACING: Philip Johnson, Ludwig Mies van der Rohe, and Phyllis Lambert review plans for the Seagram Building. Twenty-seven-year-old Lambert, who conducted the search for the building's architect, was a student of architecture and the daughter of Samuel Bronfman, president of Seagram's Canadian parent company, ca. 1955.

Despite the popularity of the city's International Style buildings, critical reviews of them were mixed. *New York Times* Associate Art Critic Aline B. Louchheim (later Saarinen) lamented that the skyline was becoming a "mountain range of layer cakes . . . indifferent to eloquent architectural expression." John McAndrew, former head of the Museum of Modern Art's (MoMA) department of architecture, said the UN buildings seemed to "lack spiritual content." In 1957, *Times* architecture critic Ada Louise Huxtable termed Park Avenue's rapid transformation from domestic district to corporate corridor "a dramatic revolution . . . one of the most important structural and stylistic changes in the history of architectural design," but labeled most of its new edifices "stark glass boxes . . . shocking and strange . . . [creating] monotony and uniformity," reserving praise solely for Lever House and the Seagram Building, then under construction.[11]

While Wright did not object to the skyscraper in concept, he abhorred the proliferation of the International Style for several reasons: the propagation of its stark towers contributed to the city's ever-escalating congestion, and the buildings were standardized in form and showed complete disregard for their sites. He also rejected the style's prominent practitioners, a group whose work he had actually influenced decades prior but now flippantly dismissed as the "glass box boys."[12] The roots of Wright's intense objections were established many years earlier, when the architect formulated his singular design philosophies and dynamic ideas for building tall.

"THE ARCHITECTURE OF NATURE"[13]

Brought up in a Unitarian family in agrarian Wisconsin, Wright worked his family's land as a teenager and was immersed in the philosophies of Transcendentalists Ralph Waldo Emerson and Henry David Thoreau. This experience left him with deep impressions that would significantly impact his future career—"Nature was [his] constant preoccupation," says Wright scholar Neil Levine.[14]

Defining his self-described "organic architecture" as "the free architecture of ideal democracy"—"the architecture of nature, based upon principle and not upon precedent"—Wright's design ethos incorporated a number of specific qualities: dimensional character that expressed a building's purpose, form equal to a building's function, modular schemes based on nature's geometries, a kinship to site, a preference for natural local materials and colors, shelter provided by cantilevered roofs, structural continuity (interrelated elements that strengthen the building), and breaking the "specious old box," as he described the plans of traditional structures, to create a "third dimension" that resulted in free-flowing spaces and connectivity between inside and outside. Wright's famous "Prairie houses," many of which were constructed in and around Oak Park, Illinois, his town of residence in the early twentieth century, were the first fully developed examples of these philosophies.[15]

These "organic" standards formed the basis of an even greater goal for Wright. Historically, architectural styles in the United States were derived from those created and propagated in Europe. Even the country's vernacular interpretations fell largely under foreign influence, and the nation, in Wright's opinion, had no style it could specifically call its own. Pursuant to the bold, simplified forms developed by American architect H. H. Richardson, and expounding on the work and principles of his employer and "Lieber Meister" Louis Sullivan, Wright set out to change this circumstance by creating a uniquely "American architecture" based on his own stated beliefs. Just as it was to Sullivan, the

Seagram Building (1958),
375 Park Avenue.

concept of individuality as the basis of building design was especially important to Wright, as it mirrored the individuality of man, the essence of independence on which the country was founded and developed. Distinctive designs, delivered with his fresh sense of space, symbolized true "democratic freedom" to him. "Principle is the only safe tradition," he said.[16]

Wright was a proponent of modern materials and an early advocate of the machines used to shape them. However, in his process of designing "from the inside out," such materials were to be used as structural support for a building's form, not as visible expressions of it, as reflected in the International Style. He advocated what he called "plasticity"—"the total absence of constructed effects as evident in the result . . . with the quality and nature of materials to be seen as 'flowing or growing' into form instead of built up out of cut and joined pieces."[17]

The concept of plasticity evolved to become one of "continuity" for Wright—form and function as intrinsic and symbiotic elements in a building. "I have bones in my system," he said. "And what are the bones for? To activate the form, aren't they? Now if I take the bones out . . . is that [still] true? . . . The International Style . . . has left out what is beauty and what is human. . . . We want [them] together. We want the poetry of the thing." Deeply committed to the spirituality he believed to be inherent to his craft, Wright felt that, without it, "architecture . . . would just be plain lumber." His designs for the skyscraper, developed over an entire career, would demonstrate these sentiments in addition to the architect's closely held organic philosophies.[18]

The apex of Mies van der Rohe's career.

Writer Thomas W. Ennis in the *Times*

The Whisky Building . . . but the best of its kind.

Frank Lloyd Wright, quoted in the *Times*

In a series of photographs shot at the Plaza Hotel for his book *The Future of Architecture* (1953), Wright used his hands to demonstrate the differences between "nineteenth century" post-and-beam architecture (left) and his own organic designs (right), 1953.

"TALL BUILDING IS FASCINATING"[19]

Wright began to consider the skyscraper early in his career, and the resulting designs would stand in sharp contrast to the austere glass boxes of 1950s New York. Inspired by Sullivan's 1890–91 design for the Wainwright Building in St. Louis, the first skyscraper created in a unified artistic form, Wright conceived two early towers that remained unexecuted. In the 1920s, however, a time when skyscraper construction was proliferating and the architect was eager for work, his hope was renewed when he received two new urban tower commissions.[20]

In 1924, Wright designed a glass curtain wall structure, the National Life Insurance Company, for a Chicago client, and his plan for the building was remarkable in many ways. The entire structure was to be sheathed in iridescent sheets of copper and glass. Its windows could be adjusted to control ventilation, and its copper screens acted as blinds to reduce glare—a problem intrinsic to Mies's original glass curtain wall designs and to mid-century's International Style edifices to come. Most significantly, the building negated the steel frame in favor of Wright's novel "taproot" structural system, which would become more apparent in his later skyscraper designs. The system was based on the organic form of a tree—a central concrete core formed the "trunk" of the building, which supported cantilevered floors, or "limbs." Based

GLASS BOXES GOING UP . . .

In addition to the Seagram Building, a number of significant International Style skyscrapers rose on and around Park Avenue while Wright was a New York resident.[21]

1954

- National Distillers Building: 99 Park Avenue; Emery, Roth & Sons
- Colgate-Palmolive Building: 300 Park Avenue; Emery, Roth & Sons
- Manufacturers Trust Company: 510 Fifth Avenue; Skidmore, Owings & Merrill (Charles Evans Hughes III and Gordon Bunshaft)
- 424 Park Avenue (completed in 1957); Kahn & Jacobs

1955

- Union Carbide Building: 270 Park Avenue (completed in 1960); Skidmore, Owings & Merrill (Natalie DuBois)

1956

- Pepsi-Cola Building: 500 Park Avenue (completed in 1960); Skidmore, Owings & Merrill (Gordon Bunshaft and Natalie DuBois)
- Corning Glass Building: 717 Fifth Avenue (completed in 1959); Harrison, Abramowitz & Abbe

1957

- 666 Fifth Avenue; Carson & Lundin
- 410 Park Avenue; Emery, Roth & Sons (incorporating Chase Manhattan Bank (completed in 1959); Skidmore, Owings & Merrill)

1958

- 277 Park Avenue (completed in 1964); Emery, Roth & Sons

on the National Life design, termed a "work of art" by Sullivan, Wright staked claim to conceiving the first "sheltered-glass tower-building." The building would go unconstructed, however, as the conservative client abandoned the project.[22]

The architect's second skyscraper commission was for a New York City clergyman. In 1927, William Guthrie, rector of New York's St. Mark's-in-the-Bouwerie, wrote to Wright, a longtime friend, requesting a design for an apartment tower to generate rental income for his church. Wright responded by designing three eighteen-story edifices for the site's park-like environment and another for a lot to the south across the street. The identical structures were based on his National Life taproot concept and were also sheathed in glass and copper, but their plan was prismatic (or multifaceted) rather than rectilinear in form. Employing modern materials and prefabricated construction, the unusual buildings were designed with light, space, and privacy in mind.[23]

Wright called the structures "modern—not modernistic," and *Architectural Record* agreed: "[The designs realize] some of the most advanced aims professed by European architects, without attendant anomalies. The uninterrupted glass window is achieved without either unprotected steel or rooms cluttered with interior posts."[24]

On October 19, 1929, the *Times* announced the church's plans for the towers, calling them "odd-type buildings." Ten days later, the stock market crashed, and Guthrie and his vestry members became increasingly skittish about Wright's unusual and unproven design. The project was shelved in May 1930, but its taproot plan would provide the model for the architect's freestanding tall buildings to come.[25]

Two decades would pass before Wright's taproot tower scheme would be realized—in a midwestern factory town. Conceived in 1944 and completed in 1950, the Johnson Wax Research Tower was constructed in Racine, Wisconsin, adjacent to the company's Wright-designed administration building of 1936. The fourteen-story streamlined structure had a skin of brick and glass tubing with alternating mezzanine floors that seemed to "float" within it.[26]

FACING: Wright's glass tower for the National Life Insurance Company (1924) was designed for Chicago's North Michigan Avenue overlooking Water Tower Square.

ABOVE: In 1929, Wright proposed St. Mark's-in-the-Bouwerie, a series of replicated towers to surround a historic church (1799) located at 131 East Tenth Street in Manhattan.

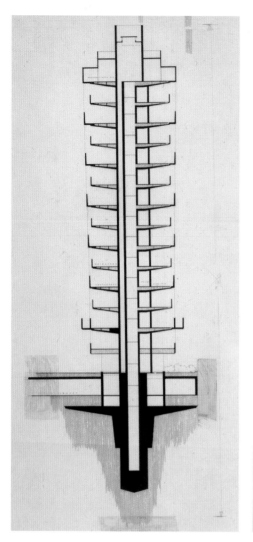

LEFT: Wright's taproot structural system, first realized in his Johnson Wax Research Tower (1944, Racine, Wisconsin), employed a steel-in-concrete core embedded deep in the ground to support multiple cantilevered floors above it.

RIGHT: The curved lines, alternating horizontal brick banding, and glass tubing of the Johnson Wax Research Tower were reminiscent of the Streamline Moderne style, which reached its peak as the adjacent Johnson Wax Administration Building (1936) was constructed, 1950.

"THE TREE THAT ESCAPED THE CROWDED FOREST"

In 1953, as International Style skyscrapers began to multiply in midtown Manhattan, a second Wright tower, more diminutive than its New York counterparts, began to rise on the plains of Oklahoma. The nineteen-story Price Tower, adapted from the St. Mark's design, was constructed in the oil industry town of Bartlesville. Reduced in scale from the original and revised to accommodate both business and residential spaces, the dynamic building was the tallest Wright edifice ever erected.[27]

Price Tower's relatively rural site was no doubt as pleasing to the architect as the realization of the building itself. Respecting the urban skyscraper's form yet negating its social aspects and implications, Wright began to promote the idea of placing the tall tower in open spaces in the 1930s, when he reconceived the modern metropolis with his Broadacre City project: "The skyscraper is indeed the product of modern technology, but not suitable if it increases congestion," he said. "It inevitably would unless it could stand free in the country."[28] (See "The Tall Tower in the City Reimagined," page 42.) The architect's first Oklahoma commission would satisfy this vision.

Wright's Bartlesville client, Harold C. Price Sr., was the wealthy owner of the Price Company, an oil pipeline enterprise. His sons suggested that Wright should be commissioned to design the company's headquarters. Unlike New York's rectilinear corporate glass boxes, the cantilevered Price Tower was conceived on an intricate pinwheel plan—every side of the building was different. Wright described its key

characteristics in his 1956 book, *The Story of the Tower*, published to commemorate the structure's opening: "The central steel enforced masonry shaft extend[s] well into the ground. . . . The supporting members stand inside, away from day-lighted space and carry elevators and the entrance hallways well within themselves," he said. "The building [offers] complete standardization for prefabrication; only the concrete core and slabs need be made in the field."[29]

The edifice's smooth exterior surfaces were counterpointed by pressed copper cladding with patterning that echoed its angular forms. Like the St. Mark's design, the structure was sited to best capture light, its "mellow tinted glass" shaded by copper louvers—vertical versions for the apartments and horizontal iterations for the offices. These controlled natural illumination, reduced the use and cost of air-conditioning, and added lively dimension to the building's appearance.[30]

The interior spaces of Price Tower were as varied as its exterior features. The ground level featured separate entrances for workers and residents, a newsstand, and a retail shop, with covered parking nearby. An adjacent two-story wing housed the tenant firm of the Public Service Company of Oklahoma, where visitors could pay bills, buy appliances, and enjoy home economic demonstrations in a double-height auditorium. A mezzanine included an extension of the shop and the auditorium's balcony.[31]

ABOVE: The Price Tower (1952, Bartlesville, Oklahoma) stands singularly tall in its prairie setting. This photograph shows the residential side of the building (identifiable by its vertical louvers), covered parking, and attached wing, ca. 1956.

BELOW: This plan of Price Tower's intricate pinwheel design (1952) shows Wright's space-efficient organization of a typical floor, right, comprising three offices and a single dwelling. The plan of the dwelling's mezzanine level is shown, left.

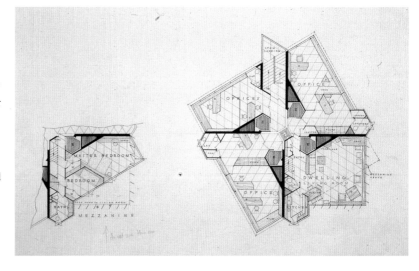

A view of "Broadacres Countryside" from Wright's 1958 book, *The Living City*. The St. Mark's-in-the-Bouwerie Tower design appears prominently.

In 1958, as New York experienced its second building boom of the twentieth century, Wright published his final book, *The Living City*. A culmination of his ideas about decentralizing cities to enhance man's quality of life, it revised and expanded on thoughts first proffered in his 1932 volume, *The Disappearing City,* and on more developed concepts presented in his 1945 book, *When Democracy Builds*.[32]

Combining agrarianism with industrialization, Broadacre promoted autonomous, decentralized communities as appealing alternatives to dense urban living. Among other theories, Broadacre City publicized Wright's romantic belief that the skyscraper should be placed "out in the country where it belongs," not adding to the "metropolitan misery" of crowded sidewalks and escalating traffic. Instead, "Bring the country to the city and take the city to the country—and I believe there is the city of the future," he said.[33]

In this idealized, siteless society, residents would enjoy one acre of land on which to live and to farm. Prefabricated housing reduced individual costs, services were centralized, government was localized, and the ubiquitous automobile provided mobility. Siting the skyscraper within this context eliminated the need for commutation altogether, according to Wright. No longer feeding congestion and casting ominous shadows on narrow city streets, it would be surrounded by light, space, and air to enhance the worker's day. Most significantly, it would stand on its own as a dignified building among Broadacre's other agricultural, industrial, civic, and residential buildings, a key component of a spacious, democratic whole. To demonstrate this effect, the architect included his St. Mark's-in-the-Bouwerie Tower (as well as other unbuilt designs) on a

twelve-foot-square model of Broadacre. Constructed with his apprentices, the model went on display in 1935 at Rockefeller Center in the heart of congested Manhattan.[34]

More than two decades after he conceived the Broadacre plan, Wright was still advancing its theories as he prepared for the publication of *The Living City*. Increasingly mindful of the freedom-enhancing and time-saving benefits of modern transportation, he designed innovative "Road Machines" (with one wheel in front and two in back to enhance flexibility in traffic) and "Aerotors" (helicopter taxis that required no landing field), adding them to the book's illustrations.[35]

In some ways, it might be said that Broadacre's concepts indeed mirrored the nation's advancing suburbanization and even forecast mid-century sprawl. In a 1959 review of *The Living City,* author John Peter said: "Whether the form of settlement our crowding planet will take will correspond to Wright's vision is open to serious question . . . [however, nearly everyone] will agree that the problem of our exploding cities and their suburban fall-out has reached the critical stage. Most would also agree that Frank Lloyd Wright's abiding respect for nature, love of enrichment and, above all, sense of human scale are badly needed in any solution."[36]

While Wright's vision for the tall tower set in bucolic surroundings would remain largely unrealized with the exception of Price Tower, Broadacre's principles of decentralization provided a platform that the architect, primarily an outsider to building in cities, could and would promote until the end of his days.

Above these levels, the tower rose skyward. Its triangular plan permitted "flexibility of arrangement not afforded by the rectangle," according to Wright. "Three offices and one double-decked apartment [are on] every alternate floor; each apartment is unaware of the other or the offices, as all look outward." The compact offices, which varied in size, featured built-in Philippine mahogany desks reflecting the building's geometric scheme and lightweight partitions that divided office areas. The dwellings included living, dining, and kitchen spaces on the first floor, with two bedrooms on a mezzanine above. The architect designed wood, cast aluminum, and copper furnishings for the structure.[37]

The floors that culminated in the building's crown—sixteen through nineteen—varied in appearance from those below them. They contained the company's commissary, the Price's executive apartment (used occasionally by the couple or for guests), and Harold Price Sr.'s corporate office. A television antenna spire reflected the latest technology and added drama to the skyscraper's pinnacle.[38]

Completed in 1956, Price Tower was quite costly to construct. Final estimates ranged to over $2 million at the time, an amount exceeding $15 million today. Yet, the building was remarkably distinctive. *Architectural Forum* reflected: "Here is an office building that is all flowering ornament . . . Here is a tower whose surfaces have depth, whose form is manifestly intended to 'transcend function and be touched with poetic imagination.'"[39]

Calling his prairie tower "the tree that escaped the crowded forest," Wright enticed Americans to "witness this release of the skyscraper from the slavery of commercial bondage to . . . human freedom. . . . Democracy builds . . ."[40] Located far from congested Manhattan in distance and even farther from its glass boxes in form, Wright's prairie skyscraper was a remote work of art.

PROTESTING THE PARK AVENUE PRACTITIONERS

Compared with Wright's tall towers, which he designed with respect for individuality and the elevation of the human spirit in mind, the architect termed the cookie-cutter forms of International Style structures "neither international nor a style." Instead, he believed they represented a return to the constrained post-and-beam construction of the previous century, which his organic architecture had superseded. Four months after Price Tower opened, Wright joined CBS television reporter Newt Mitzman in a New York hansom cab for a mobile interview titled "The Changing Face of Park Avenue." As they traveled down the transformed avenue, Wright raised his cane toward its new edifices in public protest: "These buildings are . . . poetry-crushers . . . posters, probably, for some kind of business or other, but for God's sakes, don't call it architecture . . . call it modern, but don't call it new."[41]

But mounting congestion and severe box forms were not all Wright objected to about these skyscrapers—he reserved perhaps his greatest ire for the practitioners of the International Style. The majority of these architects, many of whom were extolled in MoMA's seminal 1932 Modern Architecture: International Exhibition, were European (see "On Exhibit: The Museum of Modern Art and the International Style," page 45). Flying in the face of his "America first" proclivities, their place of national origin fueled Wright's resentment against them, and the attention they were receiving only compounded his negative opinions of their work. Lashing out, he described them as "an old totalitarian cult made new by organized publicity . . . who didn't understand the nature of materials or human beings." He said their "Nuremberg Fascist Modern" style cast a "communistic shadow" over his country's democratic tradition of individuality, powerful words in the Cold War years. Undeniably rancorous, his wrath can be viewed as somewhat ironic, as the ordered simplicity and abstraction of his own early-twentieth-century designs actually influenced the work of the very architects he criticized, some of whom he knew personally.[42]

Wright's 1910 *Ausgeführte Bauten und Entwürfe von Frank Lloyd Wright* (more commonly known as the "Wasmuth monograph" or "portfolio") inspired Europe's early modernists. This drawing shows the imposing verticality of the 1903 Larkin Company Administration Building, Buffalo, New York.

"There is plentiful documentation of the inspiration that . . . Wright . . . provided for the work of Gropius, Mies, and others," says Bauhaus historian Margret Kentgens-Craig. "Wright's 1910 visit to Berlin on the occasion of the first German exhibition of [his] drawings in the Academy of the Arts reinforced this exchange. In that year and thereafter, the Berlin publishing house of Ernst Wasmuth published a comprehensive two-volume monograph of Wright's work . . . [allowing it to reach] a broader audience."[43]

The European architects themselves confirmed this connection. Gropius acknowledged that Wright's work "'interested [him] very much' in his formative years." On behalf of his professional associates, Mies said: "The more we were absorbed in the study of [Wright's] creations, the greater became our admiration for his incomparable talent, the boldness of his conceptions, and the independence of his thought and action. The dynamic impulses emanating from his work invigorated a whole generation."[44]

Wright recognized his connection with Europe—"Holland was the first . . . to wake up to my work. Then Germany, England, France, and others"—but rejected how his clean lines, open spaces, and natural geometries were severely translated. He reflected: "A style which I had some influence in forming has become false in their hands and lost its meaning and accordingly has appeared 'new-fangled.'" Bruce Brooks Pfeiffer explains: "What came back to the United States [from Europe] as a result of [Wright's] early influence were machine-governed buildings that had absorbed the [streamlined] effects but not the [organic] principles of [his] early work."[45]

ON EXHIBIT:
THE MUSEUM OF MODERN ART
AND THE INTERNATIONAL STYLE

Though Wright did not build in Manhattan until the 1950s, his work was frequently on exhibit there starting in 1930, when the Architectural League of New York mounted the architect's first retrospective—Frank Lloyd Wright: Work from 1893–1930. Over the course of twenty-eight years, more than twenty exhibits or exhibitions, three of which were retrospectives and at least ten that showed Wright's work alone, were presented in the city (see "Frank Lloyd Wright in New York City: A Chronology," page 124). Over half of these were featured at the fashionable Museum of Modern Art (MoMA), an institution dedicated to actively showcasing the austere aesthetics of modernism.[46]

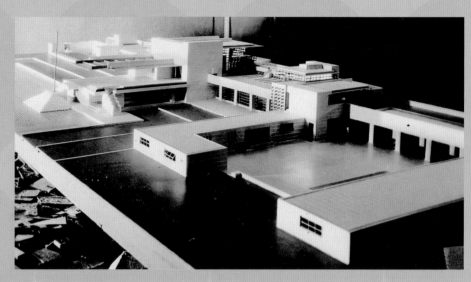

Wright submitted this model of his House on the Mesa (project, 1931, Denver, Colorado) for MoMA's Modern Architecture: International Exhibition. The design reflected the streamlined aesthetic of the European modernists.

Wright often criticized MoMA and its directors, yet, understanding the museum's societal import, he could not ignore its promotional power in relation to his own career.[47] Perhaps no other architectural exhibit was more controversial or culturally significant than one of the earliest in which the architect was included—the 1932 Modern Architecture: International Exhibition. During his time as a New York resident, Wright would come face-to-face with its personally objectionable implications once again.

The Modern Architecture exhibit and an accompanying book, The International Style: Architecture Since 1922, promulgated the term "International Style" in America. Respectively curated and coauthored by Hitchcock and MoMA newcomer and curator Johnson (who would later practice architecture himself), the exhibition provided the country's first public platform for the masters of modernism. "Heavily influenced by the German Bauhaus, it defined Modernism quite specifically, even narrowly, celebrating industrial materials and methods and demanding purity of form," says historian Thomas Bender.[48]

Conceived to showcase the future of architecture as a unified style burgeoning on both sides of the Atlantic, the exhibit actually focused primarily on the work of Europeans, including Le Corbusier, Gropius, and Mies. The work of these practitioners was complemented by the designs of American architects who advocated their International Style aesthetic, including Raymond Hood, the firm of Howe and Lescaze (George Howe and William Lescaze), and Richard Neutra. Wright's inclusion was cast in more of a "historical" or influential role.[49]

Mired in a career low compounded by the Depression, some believed the sixty-four-year-old architect to be representative of architecture's past, not its future. Johnson termed Wright "the greatest architect of the nineteenth century," describing his inclusion in the exhibit as a "courtesy" to acknowledge his earlier contributions to modern design, a sentiment that raised the architect's ire.[50]

Modern Architecture: International Exhibition did not set attendance records, nor did the press flock to cover it. Skeptical Times reviewer H. I. Brock vicariously echoed Wright's sentiments about the European modernists, describing the "functionalist" architects as those "who build merely for maximum use at minimum cost [and are] not concerned with beauty." Addressing Wright's inclusion in the show, he said the architect "really counts only as the greatest and most incorrigible of the individualists," observing: "Discipline is a watchword of their school, whereas Wright is a rebel to all discipline."[51]

In 1932, Wright's most productive years actually lay ahead of him. Reflecting on the effect the exhibit had on the architect's work to come, Wright scholar Neil Levine said: "When he began to see clearly that he was no longer the most advanced thinker in architecture, that these younger Europeans had been doing things that he really had not been aware of and had not been able to accomplish in his own work, what's fantastic is that he was able to take up that challenge and completely remake himself." The results would include such remarkable structures as Fallingwater, the Johnson Wax Administration Building, and New York's own Solomon R. Guggenheim Museum.[52]

Beginning in the 1930s, Wright first met several of his mid-century architectural adversaries but, predictably, became close friends with none. Rebuffing requests from both Le Corbusier and "Herr Gropius" to visit Taliesin, he later mended fences somewhat with Gropius, conversing with him at a 1938 MoMA opening and subsequently visiting the émigré's self-designed house in Lincoln, Massachusetts. Considering Mies more of an individualist than his European contemporaries, Wright initially fostered a cordial relationship with him, inviting him to stay at Taliesin. However, their friendship abruptly ended in 1947 when the elder architect visited a major MoMA exhibition of the German's work and publicly assailed his "less is more" design philosophy. Wright had the most ongoing interaction with Philip Johnson, Mies's Seagram Building compatriot. The two first became acquainted during the contentious planning of the 1932 MoMA exhibit, and, for mutually beneficial reasons, they continued to see each other and correspond sporadically over the course of Wright's life.[53]

Facing the popularity of these architects and their International Style works in the 1950s, Wright defended his position: "I defy anyone to name a single aspect of the best contemporary architecture that wasn't first done by me!" Modern architect and Swiss emigrant William Lescaze, among others, found fault with Wright's perceived forked-tongued rhetoric: "He claims credit for the entire modern movement both here and in Europe, though vilifying [it]."[54]

Perhaps Wright's indignation was magnified by the fact that the majority of his twelve tall tower designs were unbuilt, largely due to economic concerns and client uncertainty about his unorthodox ideas. Despite any Broadacre proselytizing to the contrary, Wright was unable to ignore the fact that he remained shut out from building in America's celebrated cities. He, the world's greatest architect, became determined to define the urban tower of the future, glass box boys be damned. The Mile-High "Illinois," Wright's last gesture for a skyscraper scheme, was the result.[55]

Wright presented his last skyscraper design, the Mile High "Illinois," to reporters at a 1956 press conference.

MILE-HIGH ASPIRATIONS: THE "SKY CITY" [56]

In 1956, a Chicago commission for a television antenna grew to epic proportions in Wright's hands when he decided to place it atop the 528-story Mile High "Illinois," a structure far bigger and bolder than anything his contemporaries might dare to conceive. "I detest seeing the boys fooling around and making their buildings look like boxes. Why not design a building that really is tall?" he said, boasting that his "cloudscraper" would make the Empire State Building look like "a mouse by comparison." [57]

Designed to hold one hundred thousand workers, the colossal tetrahedron taproot tower was supported by steel-in-tension cables. Wright said the structure, which "[spiraled] to a point like a huge sword," represented "the future of the tall building in the American city," and reflected on how it might work in New York: Manhattan could be leveled "to one large green" with a few such well-spaced buildings erected and surrounded by serene parkland. "All you would have to do would be to sweep New York into the Hudson and build two of them in Central Park and that would be the city," he said. Ten buildings would probably "be enough to rehouse almost the entire office population" of the island, he estimated. [58]

Acknowledging that no one could afford to build the $60 million Mile High at the time, Wright, ever the futurist, said that in years to come, "no one can afford NOT to build it." While the utopian structure would go unrealized, author Donald Hoppen describes it in prophetic terms: "Like a great space marker heralding the twenty-first century, it is a haunting image that heralds a technology and culture yet to come." [59]

THE INTERNATIONAL STYLE WANES IN POPULARITY

At mid-century, as New York reached ever skyward and most of his own urban tower imaginings lay dormant, Wright predicted that the lack of human respect demonstrated by the "pretentious shells" of the International Style would wane in time, and that his own organic principles would experience a renaissance. Expressing confidence about the future based on the volume of affirming correspondence he received from young people, he said: "I'm only pessimistic concerning the present fellows on the bandwagon, that's all." [60]

In 1956, Aline Saarinen suggested that through the International Style, architecture had realized a "violent therapy of stripping down to essentials in order to see freshly and find contemporary design." However, with results beginning to appear stark and monotonous on the skyline, she felt it was time for variety once again. Her observations proved prescient, for even as New York's mid-century moguls settled into their glassy new headquarters, fresh architectural trends were beginning to emerge. The "New Formalists," including Wright's friend Edward Durrell Stone and an evolving Johnson, would start to explore ways to decorate or elaborate the box in order to restore a sense of beauty to modern buildings. And soon, the dynamic shapes of Expressionism, including Wright's own kinetic Guggenheim Museum, would redefine "modern" altogether. [61]

Even though Wright did not contribute a corporate tower to New York's architectural mix, he would engage in the city's commercial supremacy in other ways, including the creation of a showroom for foreign automobiles along the very corridor where the glass box boys were making their mark.

COURTING THE NEW CONSUMER
FOREIGN AUTOMOBILES AND DOMESTIC DESIGNS

[
The machine in the hand of culture
could be an enormous blessing.

Frank Lloyd Wright, Taliesin Fellowship talk, August 24, 1958
]

Following World War II, New York City became the heart of a megalopolis that extended from northern Virginia to southern New Hampshire—and a primary nucleus of the suburban sprawl that proliferated nationwide.[1] The result of this unparalleled development was a "happy-go-spending" society insatiably eager for goods to suit their new lifestyles, and an economic boom based on the rise of corporate industry would work to satisfy their every desire.[2]

In the 1950s, the concept of "Populuxe"—fashionable and luxurious goods that were also affordable to many—fueled "one of history's greatest shopping sprees." Americans spent five times as much for home furnishings and decorations in 1951 as they did in 1940, a trend that would prevail for most of this prosperous decade. As manufacturing jobs slowly gave way to managerial positions in the nation's largest metropolis, influential real estate developer William Zeckendorf called the shift "magnificent," heralding "higher paid, higher educated administrative personnel that make New York an unparalleled consumer's market."[3]

Wright may have expressed disdain for New York's unrivaled commercial persona but, terming it ". . . the most important market place of the world," he was undeniably lured by its seemingly endless offerings. Famous for admitting that he was willing to forgo the necessities of life so long as he had the luxuries, Wright frequented a number of favorite shops and galleries when in Manhattan, readily acknowledging that his philosophy "kept the butcher, the baker, and the landlord always waiting"—for payment.[4]

Wright designed a variety of retail spaces over the course of his long and prolific career. In his early years in and around Chicago, he created interiors for a bookstore, an art gallery, and an

A 1950s crowd anticipates store-opening at New York's Macy's Herald Square.

interior decorating shop, as well as a multi-merchant arcade; his first design for New York was commerce-based—a 1910 trade fair sales booth for the Universal Portland Cement Company. While none of these works survive, most of his later retail designs are extant and still function as commercial spaces.[5]

By the time Wright became a New York resident, leading retailers were extending their reach beyond major cities, building branch stores in burgeoning suburbs across the country, a trend the architect had predicted years earlier in his *Autobiography*.[6] Offering individual mobility and accessibility around the clock, the family car provided ready transportation to and from these convenient shopping destinations. Perhaps more than any other single factor, the car fueled the go-to-work-and-get-the-goods dynamic of this consumer-driven era.

A SHOWROOM ON PARK AVENUE

Located in the heart of corporate modernism, the 1954 Hoffman Automobile Showroom at 430 Park Avenue and Fifty-Sixth Street was Wright's first permanent work in New York, his first constructed automotive design, and one of his very few interior-only projects.[7] Commissioned by Austrian emigrant and luxury automobile importer Maximilian Hoffman as a space to display Jaguars, the showroom was conceived with floor-to-ceiling windows on two sides of its corner site. A low ceiling compressed the space, but mirrored interior walls and building columns enhanced its visual impact.[8] The sales area's central feature was a kinetic combination of a rotating turntable and spiral ramp on which six automobiles could be displayed. The spiral, a signature element of several of Wright's automotive and retail designs, would be used most famously for the Guggenheim Museum, which would rise thirty blocks north on Fifth Avenue before the end of the decade.[9]

By the 1950s, the showroom had become the standard-bearer of product merchandising in New York, taking full advantage of the alluring shop window, a nineteenth-century invention described by mega merchant John Wanamaker as "eyes to meet eyes." Acting as a consumer magnet, the glass expanses of these retail spaces removed the visual barrier between consumer and merchandise, creating a tempting see-but-not-touch dynamic.[10] The Hoffman Automobile Showroom was one of only a small number of well-designed automobile sales venues in Manhattan, further enhancing the prestige of Wright's already-prosperous client.[11]

The automotive industry was in Hoffman's blood, and his business sense was exceptionally acute. His affluent father was the Rolls-Royce dealer of Vienna, and Hoffman himself was a racecar driver before World War II. Arriving in New York just six months before America joined the conflict, he made a living manufacturing costume jewelry until the war was over and he could work his way back to the business of fine cars.[12]

Maximilian ("Max") Hoffman was one of mid-century New York's most influential automotive executives, ca. 1950s.

Initially importing the French Delahaye and limited assortments of other French, British, and Italian automobiles, Hoffman's first important contract was with Jaguar. He persuaded the British company that their cars could be successful in the United States, and that he should have their exclusive franchise. Jaguar agreed, and the make was a stateside sensation. Adding BMWs, Porsches, and Volkswagens to the mix, Hoffman quickly became the city's leading importer of prestige cars at a time when consumer interest in them was just beginning.[13]

Lacking advertising funds following the war, Hoffman opened his first showroom in 1947 on prestigious Park Avenue. A Jaguar showroom along Broadway's "automotive row" followed in 1951, then a second Park Avenue space for Mercedes-Benz in 1953.[14] As business continued to escalate, Hoffman began a hunt for an architect to design a house for him outside the city. He first turned to his friend Philip Johnson, but when Hoffman judged his designs as too austere, Johnson (somewhat ironically, given their mercurial relationship over the years) suggested the auto magnate contact Wright. When the two titans met, they "got along very well," according to Hoffman. Singularly focused, exacting, and determined, Hoffman and Wright shared a mutual passion for hard work, blunt honesty, and the design of fine automobiles.[15]

In December 1953, with discussions about his residence underway with Wright, Hoffman asked him to design a Jaguar showroom to be housed in a new building at 430 Park Avenue.[16] While the architects of No. 430 described it as stylistically similar to the UN Secretariat, a structure Wright abhorred, the Hoffman showroom commission proved too tempting for him to resist for a number of reasons.[17] First, there was the allure of a New York City site, proposed to him by an established and potentially lucrative client. Second, as Wright had been passed over for other plum commissions in this celebrated area of town, this project would proffer him the opportunity to make his own design statement, however limited, in the center of the city's architectural action. Finally, the commission would allow Wright to showcase his personal passion for the automobile at last.

The Hoffman Automobile Showroom (1954) was Wright's singular design on New York's Park Avenue, 1955.

Wright witnessed the car's invention and development during his lifetime, and was fascinated by this purveyor of individual freedom.[18] Throughout his career, he was at the vanguard of creating "strategies, forms, and building types" for the automobile, but most were never realized. He invented the carport in the 1930s, and twice tried his own hand at car design.[19]

Given a choice, Wright preferred the sleek silhouettes of foreign automobiles to Detroit's "ferryboats coming down the street," and he owned a constant stream of them throughout his life.[20] When Hoffman offered imported vehicles to his architect as compensation for services rendered, Wright immediately accepted. Ever the charmer, he told Hoffman that his ownership of Porsches would be "good for the appreciation of this fine foreign car" as there were none "within hundreds of miles of Madison, Wisconsin," adding: "My daughter, Iovanna, still clamors for the Citroen."[21]

On April 6, 1954, the *Times* announced Wright's commission to design Hoffman's new showroom. Like so many of the architect's undertakings, the process from client contract to project completion would be

fraught with delays. Several times that June, Hoffman prodded Wright regarding the "need to get to work," no doubt believing that the architect's decision to open a New York office might expedite construction.[22] Originally scheduled to open in January 1955, the space did not debut until May. By this time, however, resenting Hoffman's exclusive power and ongoing partnership with Mercedes-Benz, Jaguar had bought back his franchise, and Porsches, BMWs, and Alfas filled the new showroom instead.[23]

Despite its professional import for Wright, the Hoffman Automobile Showroom received little notice in the press. *Architectural Forum,* an influential architectural journal of the day, was an exception, covering it as a "small commercial installation." Likening the showroom's atmosphere to a garage—"congested, but flattering to the cars"—the magazine praised its warm color palette and surfaces that "contrast and complement the steely shine of the beautifully detailed but unrelenting industrial products." It also admired the rotating turntable, but noted that customers were reluctant to mount it without a salesman's invitation, and that viewing additional models required scaling a sloping ramp. The space clearly "emphasiz[ed] the circulation of cars, not people."[24]

Five months after its opening, Wright wrote to Hoffman saying he'd heard reports from the "big-city" that the showroom was "over-crowded [with] decorations . . . cheaply and badly done" with displays including "a big chassis vehicle plus one too many cars on the turntable and ramp." Blaming Hoffman's assistants for the "short-sighted policy and poor salesmanship," he implored the auto mogul to "spend a little more time and money . . . on the novel show-room. . . It is a bijou—not a wholesale," the architect

Hoffman compensated Wright for his architectural services with gifts of imported automobiles, including the Mercedes shown here with the architect in front of Hillside Studio at Taliesin in Spring Green, Wisconsin, 1956.

THE HOFFMAN HOUSE
RYE, NEW YORK
1955

On November 10, 1952, Max Hoffman wrote to Wright: "[I] would like to have my house designed by you." While he had not made a final site selection, he asked Wright for photographs of his recent houses "similar [to what] you have in mind for me."[25] Apparently, Hoffman was unfamiliar with Wright's work and its site- and client-specific nature, but was willing to commission him based on Johnson's recommendation and the master's professional eminence.

Two more years would pass before the auto mogul purchased a 2.2-acre lot on Manursing Island on Long Island Sound for his three-bedroom house. Wright made several visits to the property, driven there by Hoffman in a small Porsche at rapid speed, much to the architect's delight. Wright sent his client plans for a "seaside cottage" before the end of that year—a grand scheme featuring a large circular swimming pool adjacent to a living room with a soaring, cathedral-like roof. Hoffman, a man of small stature, objected: "But it is too big for me, Mr. Wright! Just too big!" Wright created a second design based on a diamond-shaped module incorporating condensed proportions and a different roof. After a second rejection, the architect created a third design substantially reduced in size from the first two—a square-grid, in-line plan including a basement and air-conditioning—which Hoffman approved.[26]

Wright suggested "warm and domestic" brick for the residence, but Hoffman chose the finest of materials, including Philippine mahogany and hand-chipped granite, a physical embodiment of his professional success. When Hoffman queried Wright about an appropriate interior designer, the architect fired back that he had "never yet built a building where an inferior desecrator was employed. The success of my work would be in danger," but relented by suggesting John deKoven Hill, "who knows the nature of the house you are going to live in." Hoffman complied.[27]

Karl Ludvigsen, author of a biographic piece on Hoffman, said his "elegant and richly-detailed home of tailored opulence" cost about five times its original estimate of $100,000.[28]

The facade of the Hoffman House shows the fine materials and attention to detail that characterize its design.

admonished. Wright's candid comments, along with the length of time it took to complete the show-room, did not deter Hoffman's desire for a Wright home. In 1955, he accepted, and proceeded to con-struct, the third of the architect's designs for his residence[29] (see "The Hoffman House," page 53).

The Hoffman Automobile Showroom—a gleaming space in the heart of the nation's most bustling city—established Wright in New York and granted him an active role in the decade's bustling consumer culture. The static "glass boxes" of his architectural rivals may have received praise as the new monoliths of modernism, but now when the critics spoke about contemporary architecture on Park Avenue, the name of Frank Lloyd Wright would be in the mix.

PROMOTING "DEMOCRATIC LIVING" IN POSTWAR AMERICA

The expensive automobiles featured in Hoffman's showroom were tantalizing but out of reach for the middle class that fueled mid-century's spending boom. For this burgeoning societal sector, comprised largely of millions of returning GIs with new wives and growing families, affordability was a key consid-eration. Deprived of material needs during the war, these citizens now had shiny new tract houses to fur-nish top to bottom, and the product-churning machine of American industry, led by trendsetting New York–based companies, raced to accommodate.[30] Wright, however, was an unlikely participant in this process. While he wanted to spread his ideas for affordable living far and wide, feeding the hungry mouth of mass consumption would be new to him in practice.

Believing the machine's production advantages to be "the modern emancipator of the creative mind" capable of making life more beautiful, Wright tried his hand at designing for the masses in 1930, creating an unexecuted line of crystal and dinnerware for a Dutch company.[31] However, his long career had been built upon highly customized, client-specific commissions. Rooted as it was in his exacting "organic" principles, the architect's work was never fully embraced by the general public, despite promotion in a number of reputable magazines.[32] However, Elizabeth Gordon, the headstrong editor of *House Beautiful,* would singularly work to change this—partly through her editorial coverage of Wright, and also by inspiring him to reach out to the masses through his own signature products—the first concerted com-mercial effort of its kind by an American architect.[33]

A midwesterner like Wright, Gordon took the helm of her venerable publication in January 1941, begin-ning a twenty-three-year reign as its editor.[34] Headquartered in New York—the nation's magazine pub-lishing hub since 1825—*House Beautiful* was owned by Hearst Magazines, one of the city's periodical powerhouses.[35] "Shelter" magazines, historically a highly popular industry category, would become partic-ularly appealing to a postwar population hungry for home-enhancing ideas and information. Gordon believed this audience was ripe for Wright. Swept up in a spirit of optimism and opportunity, the nation was in an expansive mood, and the architect's open-plan homes and democratic ideals seemed particularly relevant. Gordon also had a built-in competitive advantage—since its inception, her magazine had had close ties with Wright.[36]

The 1896 book *The House Beautiful,* designed by Wright and produced with his client William H. Winslow, reproduced a sermon by Unitarian minister William C. Gannett, a supporter of the Arts and Crafts move-ment. Its key message was that "the home was the most deserving focus of creativity," which Wright trans-lated as the "rescu[ing] of American houses from Victorian excess," providing a new sense of spatial freedom and individuality. Inspired by the book, Chicagoans Eugene Klapp and Henry Blodgett Harvey created a magazine of the same name based on the guiding principle that "a beautiful house furthered the good life." *The House Beautiful* magazine first covered Wright's work—his Oak Park home—in its third issue, February 1897, and continued to periodically cover his designs and ideals for more than sixty years.[37]

In 1912, the progressive magazine with the egalitarian motto, "taste goes farther than money," moved its offices to New York, dropping "the" from its title in 1925. While *House Beautiful* did not cover European Modernism's rise in the early 1920s, it did introduce its readers to the giants of "stark white planes, ribbon windows, and glass brick"—including Marcel Breuer, Walter Gropius, and Le Corbusier—in the final years of the decade.[38] By the end of the 1930s, however, the publication was promoting "American Modernism . . . neither barrenly mechanistic nor oversentimental." Any residual praise for the severe International Style would not survive the editorship of Gordon.[39]

Known for a commanding sense of taste and unrelenting curiosity, Gordon called her magazine "a propaganda and teaching tool," and she was determined to define her editorial curriculum around the democratic philosophies of Wright, who had experienced a career renaissance in the 1930s. Praising him as the magazine's "ideological founder," Gordon was on a crusade to spread the architect's organic message. Her uniquely prolific and in-depth coverage of Wright's work would succeed in keeping him in the public eye while most critics—and other magazine editors—were focused on the news-making modernists.[40]

As *House Beautiful*'s fiftieth anniversary issue (December 1946) approached, Gordon made plans to feature Taliesin West and to acknowledge Wright as "The Most Influential Design Source of the Last 50 Years" on its pages. A spring interview with the architect at his desert home also resulted in a short June issue piece, "Meet Frank Lloyd Wright," in which she termed him "the greatest architect alive—oh, why not say it, the greatest architect who ever lived." Gordon's words sparked a lifelong relationship of mutual admiration: "Perhaps the closest ever between an American architect and a popular magazine," according to author Diane Maddex.[41]

Just as Wright's hated "glass boxes" began to infiltrate the area around her 572 Madison Avenue office, Gordon became his implicit partner in an ongoing campaign against them. Her anti–International Style sentiments reached a crescendo in *House Beautiful*'s April 1953 issue, when she published a highly controversial editorial, "The Threat to the Next America," flatly rejecting the style.[42] The piece's bias shocked New York's design community and prompted members of her staff to resign.[43]

Gordon's 1946 interview with Wright at Taliesin West marked the beginning of a professional relationship that lasted until the end of the architect's life. The editor continued to feature and promote Wright's work and principles until she left *House Beautiful* in 1964.

Firing a verbal barrage at photographs of Mies's Tugendhat House (1930, Brno, Czechoslovakia [now Czech Republic]) and Le Corbusier's Villa Savoye (1930, Poissy, France), both constructed more than twenty years earlier, Gordon railed "something is rotten in the state of design," terming the International Style a "school boy's exercise in cubes and rectangles" with comfort sacrificed "in order to achieve serenity." She criticized the style's "cult of austerity" based on "stripped down emptiness" promoted by a "self-chosen elite who would dictate not only taste but a whole way of life." And she implied that the style threatened "cultural dictatorship" virtually equal to communism in a time when Cold War concerns weighed heavily on the nation's mind. Mocking Mies's famed design philosophy, she punctuated it all by saying, "less is *not* more . . . it is simply less"—the antithesis of the better living made possible by the material abundance of the postwar years.[44] Speaking at a New York Home Fashions League meeting one month later, Gordon expounded on her thoughts about design's social significance, emphasizing the importance of "democratic architecture for a democratic society." When it came to living spaces, the editor said, Americans could choose either individualism or collectivism and totalitarian control.[45]

Regardless of how real the "threat" of the International Style may or may not have been to the country's new domestic bliss, Gordon viewed Wright as the personification of democratic modernism—the architect who could combine sensible architecture with the comforts of appropriate embellishment—and she became his unwavering apostle.[46] When Wright read her controversial editorial, he telegrammed:

"Surprised and delighted. Did not know you had it in you. From now on at your service. Godfather." Offering her "first crack at publishing his new work," Wright also urged Gordon to hire staff from Taliesin to help develop stories for the magazine.[47] Their professional relationship flowered.

When the architect visited the "Big Market," as he termed New York, he would often meet his good friend "Beth" at her office to take her to lunch, or they would meet for dinner or art gallery visits. "[Mr. Wright] was fun to be with . . . a very good conversationalist," Gordon reflected at the age of ninety. "He would make comments on window displays and what people wore, and he always liked my hats."[48]

In the spring of 1953, when architectural editor James Marston Fitch left *House Beautiful*, Gordon asked Wright to suggest a suitable replacement. The architect sent John deKoven Hill to fill the position for a year, but Hill remained with the publication for a decade, eventually becoming its editorial director.

Over time, he was joined on the masthead by several other Wright apprentices. "The architecture department was an extension of Taliesin," Gordon later reflected.[49]

Wright himself became a contributor to the magazine when Gordon invited him to pen his own critique of the International Style for her July 1953 issue, followed by a related statement in October. That same month, the Usonian Exhibition House, an example of Wright's affordable, quality-driven designs for the middle class, opened on the future site of the Guggenheim Museum, and *House Beautiful* created its interior décor (see "Sixty Years of Living Architecture and the Usonian Exhibition House," page 99).[50] The following year, Gordon's reverence for Wright reached full bloom when she dedicated her entire November 1955 issue to the architect: "Frank Lloyd Wright: His Contribution to the Beauty of American Life." Its intensive, singular dedication to Wright's concepts for living was a first for a mainstream magazine. A *Times* advertisement announced "Leadership Recognized," alluding to the two-pound, 388-page periodical's theme as well as to its publishing milestones: first million-dollar issue, biggest circulation distribution (835,000 copies), and largest number of advertising pages (247) in the history of shelter magazines. When Wright saw the groundbreaking issue, he telegrammed Gordon: "Your valiant spirit shines through the whole encyclopedia and honors us both. . . . We are all very happy."[51]

ABOVE LEFT: *House Beautiful* staff members and contributors visited Wright at Taliesin in 1954. Left to right: Ann Parker, wife of Maynard Parker (second from left), photographer; Carolyn Murray, Gordon's assistant; Wright; Jean Lawson, gardening editor; Dr. Joseph Howland, technical editor; and former Taliesin apprentices Robert Moser, building editor; and John deKoven Hill, architectural editor.

ABOVE RIGHT: The cover of *House Beautiful*'s November 1955 issue.

DESIGNS FOR THE NEW DOMESTICITY

In addition to more than twenty features on the master architect, *House Beautiful's* special issue introduced the Taliesin Ensemble, an array of mass-produced home furnishings products designed by Wright but orchestrated by Gordon herself. Conceived to appear equally at home in a New York high-rise or a New Jersey development, the collection included fabrics and wallpapers by F. Schumacher & Company, furniture by Heritage-Henredon, paints by the Martin-Senour Company, rugs by Karastan, and exotic wood accessories by Minic. Editorial features and advertisements promoted the lines, including an exuberant twelve-page piece—"And Now, Frank Lloyd Wright Designs Home Furnishings You Can Buy!"—in which the products were called a "development that is logical and long overdue." [52] The writer emphasized

Wright's belief that "[furnishings] should be sympathetic to each other and to the architecture of the house," while explaining that the new products were "intended to transform, as much as possible, an *existing space* according to [his] principles for creating a unified, organic whole." [53]

The adaptability of the furniture line was praised as a key benefit—distinctive geometric pieces created to "go together" offered "group and regroup" options (early examples of today's modular furniture). Designed without hardware, the pieces featured integrated carved molding instead. Implying that this sense of "wholeness" may not be for everyone, the magazine defended both the line and Wright's architecture in general: "both are Wrightian—and that is saying a great deal." [54] The feature also promoted the color, individuality, richness, and texture of the fabric designs, underscoring how they worked in ensemble with the furnishings, as well as Wright's rugs and accessories (ultimately not produced), to provide "luxury at reasonable prices, perhaps a new system of furnishing an entire room." [55]

While Wright's furniture and fabric lines were represented as "designed" by the architect, the Martin-Senour interior paint colors were described as "selected" by Wright and his wife in partnership with William Stuart, the company's president. Twenty-seven wall colors and nine accent colors including

Promotional stills of Wright's 1955 Heritage-Henredon lines were styled to appeal to the mid-century cult of domesticity.

"Cherokee Red" and "Spring Green" were chosen to work harmoniously with the other Taliesin Ensemble lines. Wright's products became available to the public in November and December 1955 through department stores and decorators.[56]

THE GENESIS OF THE ENSEMBLE

The Taliesin Ensemble was the eventual outgrowth of a meeting Gordon had with her close friend and business associate René Carrillo, Schumacher's director of merchandising, to show him some fabrics for production consideration. The "fabrics" were actually dance performance costume materials created by Taliesin apprentices.[57] "They were nice designs . . . but they weren't commercial at all," Carrillo reflected years later. "I said to her if we could ever get anything done by Mr. Wright—if he'd let us use his name—we'd be terribly interested."[58] The editor replied that Carrillo would have to visit Wright and get permission, which would be a challenge. Hill arranged for the merchandising director to take a train to Taliesin West to pitch the idea. There, Wright told Carrillo that he had never heard of F. Schumacher & Company, yet years earlier, he or his associates had ordered fabrics from the prestigious company for his Robie House (1906, Chicago) and Coonley House (1907, Riverside, Illinois).[59] Carrillo succeeded in persuading Wright to agree to a licensing partnership on one condition: "It's going to cost you a lot of money," the architect said, requesting a $10,000 fee before further conversation. Schumacher's senior executives rejected the request, but Henry Rose, the company's sales manager, convinced them of the value of the investment. A deal was struck with the architect based on the fee and handsome royalties. Carrillo said Wright also agreed to design wallpapers, but wanted licensees to produce carpet and furniture too. As the architect quickly executed an entire set of pattern drawings for the fabrics, Gordon began to approach other appropriate manufacturers.[60]

Like Wright, Schumacher believed that America's middle class should have access to good design. Wright's "Taliesin Line" was one of several product partnerships the company had with prominent twentieth-century designers, including Paul Poiret, Raymond Loewy, and Dorothy Draper, but Richard E. Slavin, author of *Opulent Textiles: The Schumacher Collection,* calls it the "most famous" and one of the "most important" for its prominence and longevity.[61]

According to Carrillo, Wright preferred geometrics, plain materials, and bright colors. The final Schumacher line comprised thirteen fabrics (seven woven and six printed), some of which invoked the architect's early art glass creations, produced in a variety of fibers. Wallpapers, set to launch in the spring of 1956, were created to complement three of the fabrics. The architect and the textile company worked collaboratively on product concepts and colors, but Schumacher determined final hues.[62]

The 1955 Martin-Senour paint sampler for the Wright line featured thirty-six colors.

TALIESIN PALETTE IN MARTIN-SENOUR PAINTS

Wright designed three furniture lines for Heritage-Henredon: "The Honeycomb," based on triangular shapes; "The Burberry," on circular forms; and "The Four Square," on rectilinear geometries. Author and curator David Hanks says the designs were rooted in "the furniture vocabulary that Wright had developed in the Prairie years and expanded in the 1930s," attributing their use of molding to the architect's furniture designs for the Husser House (1899, Chicago, Illinois) and Bogk House (1916, Milwaukee, Wisconsin). In the end, only "The Four Square" was produced. Incorporating elements of the other two lines, it was renamed "The Taliesin Line." Hanks suggests that "The Four Square" may have been selected for a number of reasons, including ease of manufacturing and sales appeal as the "quietest and most conservative" of the three collections. Approximately sixty-six of Wright's individual furniture designs were created, each featuring his burned-in signature hidden in an inconspicuous spot. Hill reported that the architect was pleased with the line but regretted that it was more conservative and conventionalized than his original schemes.[63]

Schumacher's elegant 1955 trade portfolio showcased Wright's fabric designs. Quotes from the architect and photographs of houses he designed were also featured.

INTRODUCTIONS TO THE PRESS

"The advance word is that the stuff is simply super and revolutionary in the best Wright tradition," gushed the *Chicago Daily Tribune* about the architect's furniture prior to its introduction. But when the line debuted in October 1955 at the Chicago Furniture Mart, complemented by the architect's Schumacher products, it was met with mixed reviews. The *Tribune* reported "the biggest furor in the industry in years." The *Chicago Daily News* praised Wright's initiative but implied confusion and misunderstanding about the furniture's design intentions—how might the pieces work in with other styles? The same month, the fabrics and the furniture went on display to decorators and their clients in New York's National Republican Club at 54 West Fortieth Street, next door to, and at the expense of, Schumacher.[64]

Covering the exhibition's opening, the *New York Times* heralded "an enormous new venture" for Wright but called the mahogany furniture "fairly conventional . . . not noticeably different from much of the

Schumacher's

"**TALIESIN LINE**"

of Decorative Fabrics and Wallpapers

When the world famed designing genius of FRANK LLOYD WRIGHT turns to decorative fabrics and wallpapers one has every reason to expect a significant new contribution to the art of interior decoration. The "Taliesin Line," masterfully reproduced and presented by SCHUMACHER'S, *is just that* Never has there been a collection so refreshingly original in design and color concept . . . so wonderfully adaptable to traditional or contemporary decors

On view at your decorator or decorator department of better stores displaying the authorized emblem

designed by FRANK LLOYD WRIGHT

F. SCHUMACHER & CO. 60 W. 40th St. New York, N. Y.   •   Fabrics   •   Carpets   •   Wallpapers   •   Waverly Fabrics

modern furniture currently available," terming the fabrics "somewhat more distinctive." The reporter pointed out discrepancies between Wright's long-held design convictions and his new products, such as his belief that furniture should be integral to a house—not added later—and his disdain for anything that might mar the beauty of natural materials by covering their inherent qualities: "I have never been fond of paints or wallpaper or anything which must be applied to other things as a surface," he once said.[65] Yet, he was now producing furniture, wallpaper, paints, and more for the mass market.

The Wright display vignettes—two bedrooms, a dining room, and a living room—filled an entire floor of the National Republican Club and were designed by Virginia Connor Dick, who created the room settings featured in *House Beautiful*'s piece on Wright's products. The fabric selection was made by Carrillo. The *Times* said the spaces seemed "completely unrelated to the strong, linear, masculine interiors Mr. Wright has put together himself in the past"—and Wright's own reaction to them almost cost Carrillo his job.[66]

During a walk-through of the exhibition prior to its opening, Wright lashed out at the merchandising director: "You can't put my name on this stuff, you've had a decorator do this.... I won't be associated with an ... 'inferior desecrator' ... I'm through!" Olgivanna, who had accompanied her husband to the preview, calmed him and told Carrillo to proceed. Unsatisfied, Wright then wrote to Carrillo: "The spirit of my work has been reduced to the usual tripe, decoration à [*sic*] la mode [not reflecting] the harmonious unique character of what I did for Schumacher." The architect requested that the company "kindly refrain from connecting my name with the exhibit."[67]

Four days later, Carrillo fired back, explaining that his company catered to a mass market and had a responsibility to its customers: "the great majority ... cannot start from scratch." He explained that the model rooms "attempt[ed] to show [them] ... how they can rehabilitate their homes ... even ... though they can't afford a Frank Lloyd Wright house, [they] can afford a bit of your genius through the use of our products styled by you." He underscored that the display rooms did not claim to be "Frank Lloyd Wright interiors, nor are they promoted in that way." The line launched as planned, although weeks passed before the two spoke again. *Architectural Record* quoted a diplomatic Carrillo describing the development of the program: "a wonderful if exhausting experience."[68]

WRIGHT AT RETAIL

Press reviews—and the architect's own critiques—implied that the Schumacher display rooms lacked his customary creative brilliance and masterful control, but his comprehensive vision for his lines would only further unravel once the products reached the floors of New York's leading department stores.[69] B. Altman & Company and Bloomingdale's effused about the new lines. Brooklyn's Abraham & Straus heralded "signed masterpieces ... [the] same type of furniture Frank Lloyd Wright designed only for his personal clients." Yet, these retailers sold the lines only in their flagship stores, and advertised them in the *Times* solely at their launch.[70] Altman's said the furniture created "an atmosphere that will add to any decorating scheme, whether it be modern, Oriental or Early American!" but sold it in their eighth-floor modern galleries. Bloomingdale's offered the Schumacher fabrics on the fourth floor, but sold the architect's "meets all budgets" Heritage-Henredon furniture in fifth-floor modern furnishings.[71] Thus, Wright's imaginings for the cohesive display of his lines in-store went largely unrealized, diluting his synergistic design message.

House Beautiful's feature on the Taliesin Ensemble optimistically forecasted that the new products were "only the beginning," with "more ... sure to follow with these five [and other] manufacturers." Concurring with the other licensees, Martin-Senour's Stuart wished for "a continuing program over a number of years." However, only Wright's paint and fabric lines would continue for more than two.[72]

Schumacher's Wright line launch advertisement in *House Beautiful*'s November 1955 issue showed the products featured in display rooms designed to replicate the home environment.

What might be called "brand clarity" today was missing from the Wright product program, contributing to the public's cherry-picking of its offerings and to its mixed results. Nationwide, variances in public communications, promotional programs, limited points of sale in an age of proliferating suburban shopping centers, and weak marketing and merchandising strategies stood in contrast to Wright's idealized vision for the lines and to Gordon's published bet on their success.

The furniture line proved to be the most problematic. Donnell Van Noppen, vice president of Henredon Furniture at the time, said the endeavor was discontinued because furniture buyers "were not familiar with Wright's designs, [and] the repeat orders from the stores were insufficient," but there were other contributing factors.[73] The company's decision to offer the collection only through its own franchises limited its exposure. Additionally, Hill said the line "mystified department store shoppers," confused by splintered merchandising and indistinct classification at point of sale. (Even *House Beautiful* recognized this dichotomy when it spoke of "richness that recalls some of the fine English furniture of the past" while dually praising its contemporary qualities.) Wright knew the furniture wasn't doing as well as expected and futilely suggested that the company try "do[ing] some of the designs as I made them."[74] In the end, the sale of Heritage Furniture Industries (one sector of Heritage-Henredon) to Drexel Furniture Company in fall 1956 may have sealed the line's fate. Textile and design expert Virginia T. Boyd believes Wright's furniture was ahead of its time: "It would take the general public several decades to understand and incorporate the innovative ideas he introduced. Coffee tables, TV tables, modular furniture, and entertainment centers were yet to come."[75]

While slow to start, the Schumacher products fared much better. They were less expensive, more adaptable, and well promoted through an elegant portfolio that designer representatives were required to buy in addition to a certain allotment of fabric. After making amends with Carrillo, Wright frequently purchased from the company, but only his Rayward House (1955, New Canaan, Connecticut) featured fabrics and wallpapers selected solely from his own line.[76]

In 1956, Schumacher's Rose, the executive who had secured the fee for Wright that cemented their agreement, effused that the "Taliesin Line" was "the most outstanding success of any fabric and wallpaper promotion we have ever undertaken."[77] The Wright licensing agreement with F. Schumacher & Company remains active today.

APPEALING TO THE MASSES

While it is easy to understand why Wright-smitten Gordon would be actively engaged in the development and promotion of her idol's consumer product lines, it is more challenging to understand why Wright, "the arch enemy of . . . the merely marketable," according to *Architectural Record,* would agree to them. Hill explained their premise simply: "The war was over, people were starting . . . families, and suddenly there was a big audience eager for ideas. The idea of the licensing program was to take a plain little house or an empty New York apartment and give it architectural character without great expense." However, the lines were clearly unrelated to Wright's primary profession and contradictory to some of his core principles.[78]

On more than one occasion, Wright had made it clear that he abhorred the concept of interior design and all who practiced it, and he actually disagreed with the uses of several of his products. Furthermore, while the architect embraced the potential of machine production for delivering quality design, he may have struggled to reconcile this with a career based on designing for the individual that offered him complete customization and control. "Often, his clients did not know whether the house was really theirs or his," his son John Lloyd Wright once commented.[79]

THE CASS HOUSE
STATEN ISLAND, NEW YORK
1957

During World War II, prefabricated structures were rapidly erected to meet emergency housing needs for troops and defense workers. After the war, more attractive versions supplied a ready solution to the affordable housing demand generated as multitudes of veterans returned home. Quick to construct—as their standardized sections could be assembled on-site—the homes were sold to the public through builder-dealers nationwide.[80]

By 1955, the sales of prefabricated dwellings reached an all-time high of ninety thousand houses, or one out of every twelve residences in the country. Riding the crest of this growing trend, Wright introduced his own line of prefab homes in 1956, produced in partnership with Marshall Erdman & Associates of Madison, Wisconsin. (Erdman had been the builder of Wright's 1947 Unitarian Meeting House in Shorewood Hills, Wisconsin.) Staten Island's Cass House, named "The Crimson Beech" for a centuries-old tree on its site, was one of only eleven of these houses ever constructed. It was the first Wright prefab in the eastern United States and the architect's sole New York City residential commission.[81]

Erdman's vision was to qualify builders in all fifty states to build Wright's prefabs, but the Cass House was one of a limited number realized, 1959.

By the mid-1950s, William Cass, an employment agency owner from Corona, Queens, had grown tired of living in his pedestrian row house. Contrary to his wife Catherine's wishes, he believed a change of location would be good for his growing family. In fall 1957, Cass saw Wright discussing the need for affordable housing on *The Mike Wallace Interview* and decided the couple should contact the architect about a design for a new home—an idea Catherine called "crazy." Cass wrote a letter anyway, informing Wright of a lot he had purchased on Lighthouse Hill and his construction budget of $30,000 to $35,000. The architect replied that based on such limited funds, Cass should contact Erdman about the new Wright prefab home program.[82]

The program was not Wright's first attempt to address what he termed "America's major architectural problem . . . houses of modest cost." Throughout his career, he had tried his hand at creating solutions for affordable housing, but most of his concepts did not succeed for a variety of reasons, including expense. Criticizing standardized buildings of the day for their lack of "grace, proportion and distinction," the architect's challenge would be to create designs that were distinctively "Wright" but also employed stock materials to contain costs. To this end, he produced three designs for Erdman's company, the first model of which was constructed in Madison in 1956.[83]

Wright required that the purchasers of his prefabs be screened and approved to make sure his design, not the buyer's desires, would be carried out on-site. Following this process with the Casses, the parts for their home were shipped to their lot and erected under the unpaid supervision of Morton Delson, a former Wright apprentice. Catherine objected to the purchase of the residence: Wright "doesn't stop to think about the All-American dollar," she told her husband. Indeed, while the $20,000 price for the house was within the range of prefab market offerings at the time, once the cost of the lot and contractors' fees were included, the final bill climbed to $62,500.[84]

Cass House living room.

Based on Wright's 1956 "Prefab 1" design, the exterior of the split-level, Prairie style–inspired, 3,750-square-foot structure featured sand-textured masonite walls with horizontal redwood battens, standard doors and windows, and a terne (lead and tin alloy over sheet steel) roof. Mahogany walls with horizontal banding and plasterboard ceilings painted with sand-colored, sand-textured paint finished the interior.[85] The home included four bedrooms accessed off of a "gallery" (or hallway), a living room with fireplace, an open dining area, a combination family room and kitchen, two bathrooms, a powder room, a terrace, and a carport, as well as abundant storage space and a basement, which were anomalies for most Wright homes. A forced-air heating system also accommodated air-conditioning. The use of texture in the dwelling and its functional room arrangements were described by the *Times* as a "contradiction to current practices in popular home development." Furnished by Macy's department store to Wright's exacting specifications, the Cass House was showcased in a July 1959 open house before the family moved in that August.[86]

In a 1956 interview, Wright described his prefabricated home program as a pilot effort that would be expanded if successful: "I am casting bread on the waters," he said. But his intentions would go largely unrealized. Regardless of his desires to the contrary, the issue of cost would once again prove the primary culprit in the demise of Wright's final "affordable" housing initiative.[87]

Financial gain was a sure factor in Wright's decision to proceed with the Taliesin Ensemble. In 1954, he announced to his apprentices: "So, we're now in the fabric industry for the royalty for the designs, and I insisted on a retainer before we would accept."[88] Aside from monetary reward, the lines also offered the architect the opportunity to expose a broad sector of the public to his ideas in familiar forms, perhaps inspiring them to explore and then adapt his principles for democratic living. If he could not build homes for everyone, perhaps he could furnish their existing houses with products that provided the spatial arrangements and sense of design his architecture so readily supplied, with *House Beautiful* as his perfect press partner.[89]

While his lines were not the success he had hoped for, and whatever his motivations for creating them, Wright was a socially conscious, active participant in the consumer explosion of the 1950s. The cars rotating serenely in the Hoffman Showroom were too costly for most Americans, but the glittering space certainly paid homage to the automobile, a symbol of personal freedom in a suburb-focused decade. And, although the architect's attempt to create comprehensive organic décor for the nation's new homes may not have come to full fruition, beaming housewives were able to show off their Wright drapery fabrics and speak proudly of their "Spring Green" living room walls. The architect's contributions to mid-century consumerism conclusively demonstrate that the octogenarian was an of-the-moment creative force, adeptly using the nation's largest metropolis as his promotional stage.

Wright discusses his Martin-Senour paint line with the press, 1955.

IN THE SPOTLIGHT
A CELEBRITY AMONG CELEBRITIES

[
I don't mind the fame, but I hate the notoriety.

Frank Lloyd Wright, *Look*, September 17, 1957
]

Frank Lloyd Wright was not a man to get lost in the crowd—even in the anonymous crush of midtown Manhattan. On his city strolls or following his New York lectures or public appearances, reporters, photographers, and autograph-seekers often trailed the silver-haired architect, who, well into his eighties, remained "a fantastically distinguished figure," in the opinion of *The New Yorker*.[1]

For years, Wright had been an object of fascination for the press and public alike. His long storied life was characterized by measures of genius, artistry, arrogance, success, failure, scandal, tragedy, and rebirth—all vicariously alluring topics for the average American. But by the 1950s, Wright had attained true celebrity status. In 1953, at the age of eighty-six, he was the subject of more books and articles in the architectural and general press than at any other time in his life.[2] Indeed, as the result of a spate of commissions, awards, and intense publicity during his final decade, Wright became, "in effect, the first superstar architect of the twentieth century," according to Neil Levine.[3] "He was recognized everywhere, even by New York cab drivers," said a friend.[4]

In at least one respect, Wright's stardom was surprising: he was not in a field such as politics, television, or the film industry in which professional success was linked largely to image and visibility. On the contrary, in his business, an architect's name and work might be renowned, but his face and form were generally unfamiliar to anyone other than the architectural cognoscenti. Wright, however, was well known beyond professional circles and was conceivably the only architect recognizable to the general public based on physical appearance alone. A primary reason for this was his distinctive and unforgettable public persona, an identity he carefully crafted—and astutely marketed via every available avenue—for most of his life. Wright bore the mantle of fame easily and, in fact, was galvanized by the attention he aroused.

Wright surrounded by students at New York's Columbia University, 1956.

Wright honed his public image over decades and, like his architectural philosophies, it was firmly rooted in American culture rather than European aesthetics. Sartorially, he cut a dashing figure, if not always a contemporary one. Observers likened his distinctive style of dress and ample charisma to that of other American originals, including Mark Twain and W. C. Fields.[5] New York playwright and Wright client Arthur Miller thought Wright evoked "a great romantic . . . a theatrical type of the old school who Orson Welles would love to have played."[6]

Wright's clothes were impeccably—and expensively—tailored. Over well-cut suits, he often sported a long flowing cape or topcoat draped dramatically over his shoulders. Although he wore ties, he fashioned them in knots "of his own invention," noted his biographer Meryle Secrest, or placed a silk scarf around his neck.[7] Even in his later years, he boasted an impressive mane of hair, which he often topped with a cap or his favored porkpie hat. He always carried a cane, not because he required one for walking, but because "he wanted it for gesturing purposes," or to bat at something for emphasis.[8] As a result of his elegant but unorthodox style of dress, the architect always stood out in a crowd—particularly in the sea of gray flannel suits that swarmed New York's thoroughfares in the 1950s.

Wright's personal style, supreme confidence, and architectural stature had a magical effect on people, including those who were highly accomplished in their own rights. Miller, describing his first encounter with Wright, said he was "tall and theatrically handsome," yet the playwright was at least half a foot taller than the architect.[9] "So powerful was the impression Frank made on [Miller], that he remembered him as being a tall man," observed Brendan Gill.[10]

Wright's Plaza address, which he often mentioned in media interviews, bolstered his prestige, and, commensurate with his VIP status, Wright attracted many notable clients. When in Manhattan, there was no finer place in which the celebrated architect could receive the rich, powerful, and famous who sought his time and talent than in his own sophisticated suite.

Wright signs an autograph at the Sixty Years of Living Architecture retrospective exhibit of his work on the future site of the Guggenheim Museum, 1953.

THE HOLLYWOOD ACTRESS AND THE NEW YORK PLAYWRIGHT

Marilyn Monroe first met Wright at the Plaza in 1956. The screen siren, who had recently married Miller, approached the architect about designing a country retreat for herself and her new husband. She wanted to make "a gift to [Miller] of a unique home," for the two-hundred-acre farm the couple owned in Roxbury, Connecticut.[11] Miller termed his wife's action a "royal impulse," but it may not have been as impetuous as he implied.[12] At least twice before, her path had crossed—tangentially—with the architect's. In 1950, Monroe appeared in the film *All About Eve* with Wright's granddaughter, actress Anne Baxter. In 1953, Monroe and her husband at the time, baseball legend Joe DiMaggio, honeymooned at the Imperial Hotel in Tokyo, one of the architect's most magnificent creations.

Miller knew something of Wright as well and, from the beginning, had serious doubts about being able to afford a house designed by him, particularly in view of the architect's reputation for having "little interest in costs."[13] He was equally concerned that Monroe, who viewed money as something "to be spent as it came in, and rather grandly at that," did not share his unease.[14] Nonetheless, they forged ahead.

The Millers, who kept an apartment on East Fifty-Seventh Street, met with Wright more than once at the Plaza to discuss the project. The first consultation, to which Monroe came alone, was held in the

Newlyweds Marilyn Monroe and Arthur Miller in Roxbury, Connecticut, 1956.

architect's suite. Although the actress arrived at the appointed day and time, Wright had kept the particulars of the meeting to himself. When apprentice Wes Peters responded to the ringing doorbell, he "was astonished to find Marilyn Monroe standing alone at the door."[15] He didn't see her for long, he recalled, as Wright appeared and "immediately spirited her into the living room of the suite."[16] Peters was more fortunate than most: Taliesin apprentice John Rattenbury, who was in the apartment when Monroe arrived, was not permitted to meet the Hollywood star at all. Wright "wanted to interview her alone and wouldn't let anyone else in," Rattenbury remembered.[17] Wright was equally covetous of his access to the Millers as a couple. Kay Schneider, who was serving as Olgivanna's secretary at the time, remembered another meeting with the famous pair in the suite: "Mr. Wright sent me and Mrs. Wright out shopping. He just wanted to have any beautiful woman to himself."[18]

Wright's wife had a slightly different take on the situation. With regard to the Millers, she observed: "something strange went on with Frank."[19] Olgivanna admired Monroe as an actress and had looked forward to meeting the celebrated couple when they came to the suite. She was "quite shocked" by her spouse's adamant refusal to allow her to do so during their visits.[20] He relented once and allowed her to greet the pair for a brief moment before he planned to join them for dinner. "Marilyn looked as lovely as she did in the moving pictures, but I felt very sad that I couldn't go with them," Olgivanna remembered.[21]

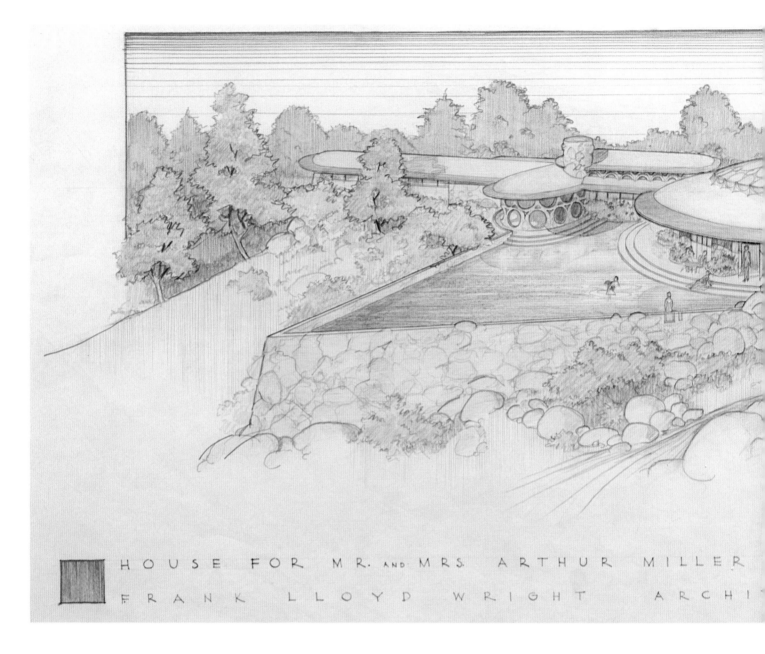

HOUSE FOR MR. AND MRS. ARTHUR MILLER

FRANK LLOYD WRIGHT ARCHI

Perspective, House for Mr. and Mrs. Arthur Miller (1957).

Wright was equally guarded about the Millers when it came to the press. On *The Mike Wallace Interview* in September 1957, when the architect was asked about the "dream home" he was designing for the couple, he responded, "I'd be very happy to design a house. But they haven't asked me in so many words yet."[22] He was more forthcoming when Wallace asked his professional opinion on Monroe "as architecture." Smiling, he replied, "I think Miss Monroe as architecture is extremely good architecture."[23] In an article published in *Look* magazine in October of the same year, Miller was similarly vague about the details of the project. Although he announced the pair's plan to build "an absolutely modern, stark-raving mad house with a view of mountain ridges that would make you faint," on their property, he did not mention Wright's name in connection with "the place where we hope to live until we die."[24]

In fall 1957, the Millers met Wright at the Plaza and drove him to Connecticut to show him their "old rundown farm."[25] When he saw the interior of the existing farmhouse, Wright said: "Ah yes, the old house. Don't put a nickel into it."[26] Miller recalled that the ninety-year-old architect, who had napped on the two-hour drive from New York, then energetically and without pause marched up a long steep

ECT

incline of at least half a mile to the designated site for the new residence. "His vitality was amazing," the playwright noted.[27] On reaching the summit, Miller explained to Wright that he and Monroe did not want "some elaborate house with which to impress the world," but rather a home that reflected their desire to live simply.[28] Miller observed: "this news had not the slightest interest for him."[29]

The scheme Wright proposed for the Millers was neither simple nor new. In fact, it was a reinterpretation of two of his earlier unbuilt designs: the Windfohr House (1949, Fort Worth, Texas), and the Bailleres House (1952, Acapulco, Mexico). Wright proposed placing the Millers' house atop sloping terrain that was flanked by a brook. A huge circular living room, which included a fireplace, projection booth, and a retractable movie screen, dominated the plan. Sizable piers of local fieldstone supported a roof constructed of "thin concrete domes covered with gold aluminum."[30] A massive chandelier and a round skylight provided illumination from above, and a glass wall encircled the living space. Two wings angled off the central area: one contained the kitchen, dining room, card room, conservatory, pavilion, and servants' quarters; and the other housed a library, guest bedroom, and chauffeur's accommodations. The second floor comprised separate bedrooms for the Millers and, poignantly, a children's suite. A large triangular swimming pool, built into the side of the hill, projected from the rear of the house.

The couple first viewed Wright's "watercolor fantasy" drawings for their home in his Plaza suite.[31] Miller immediately deemed the design much too ostentatious for their lifestyle and inappropriate for the rustic site. He objected to the grand size and scale of the residence, citing the sixty-foot diameter of the living space and the seventy-foot length of the swimming pool to support his contention.[32] Although Wright estimated the cost of the house to be in the neighborhood of $250,000, Miller had his doubts. Noting the massive swimming pool retaining wall, which he guessed would require "heavy construction on the order of the Maginot Line" to achieve, he feared the pool alone would cost that amount.[33]

While cost concerns and the extravagant nature of the design contributed to the couple's abandonment of the project, their overwhelming personal problems were also a factor.[34] By 1958, their marriage had begun to crumble, and Monroe's health and career were in serious decline.[35] There would be no "dream house" for the Millers, by Wright or anyone else.[36]

Old friends Wright and Sandburg also met in 1957 on television's *Omnibus*, hosted by Alistair Cooke.

"MEETING OF THE TITANS"

Carl Sandburg and Frank Lloyd Wright were American originals. In April 1957, the Pulitzer Prize–winning poet, historian, and biographer (and later a Presidential Medal of Freedom honoree) joined Wright in his suite for a discussion about architecture, literature, and each other. Alicia Patterson, publisher of Long Island's *Newsday*, which she founded with her husband, Harry Guggenheim, moderated the session. Although the text of the interview was published in her newspaper under the headline "Meeting of the Titans," the gathering was actually a reunion of old friends. Sandburg and Wright, who met as young men in Oak Park, Illinois, had been close for nearly half a century. And both were intimates of Patterson and Guggenheim, who was Wright's client on two projects at the time (see chapter six).[37] Although Sandburg had visited Taliesin in the past, the Plaza interview marked the first time the friends had seen each other in twenty years.[38]

Unlike many of Wright's media exchanges, the tone of the session was convivial, and the men's mutual admiration was freely expressed. Patterson probed broad areas of thought: "Which will live longer in time: architecture or literature? What makes genius?" but also questioned each man about the other's work.[39] When Sandburg was asked to name his favorite Wright building, he mentioned two in Oak Park: the architect's home and studio, and Unity Temple. Sandburg observed about Wright's former residence: "There was something about that house that intrigued me. I would go out of my way to see it. . . ." Wright's favorite among Sandburg's writings was not his "biggest . . . hardest work," a six-volume biography of Abraham Lincoln, but rather "the easiest . . . quickest," and the one Sandburg once read aloud to the architect: "*The People, Yes.* I think it was great," Wright simply said.

The session concluded when Patterson asked, "What do you think of each other?" Wright spoke first: "I wouldn't have any one of my friends improved. . . . I like Carl as he is." Sandburg answered: "I think I will [write] a Frank Lloyd Wright poem and it will have music and it will have dimensions in it." When Wright asked: "Third dimensions?" Sandburg cleverly replied: "I will even suggest a fourth one."[40]

"BRAINS, MONEY, AND IMAGINATION"

Wright's draw as a celebrity and the marketability of his name led to a 1957 collaboration with an improbable triumvirate of men, each a giant in his respective field: theater and film producer Mike Todd; steel, ship building, and aluminum industrialist Henry J. Kaiser; and former NBC president Sylvester "Pat" Weaver. All had offices in Manhattan, and they met to discuss the development of an innovative building prototype—the aluminum domed theater—at a single gathering in the architect's suite.

At the time, Todd was a brash show business impresario with an impressive string of New York theater successes. In 1957, he enhanced his status considerably when he married actress Elizabeth Taylor and won an Academy Award for best picture for producing *Around the World in 80 Days*. To celebrate, he hosted "the biggest party for the biggest people" at New York's Madison Square Garden.[41] According to television journalist Walter Cronkite, who covered the eighteen thousand–guest bash for CBS News, "in 1957, they didn't come any bigger than Mike Todd. [He] was an amiable self-promoter whose charm was as oversized as it was irresistible."[42] *Around the World in 80 Days* was a hit with moviegoers largely because it was filmed in Todd-AO, a groundbreaking new widescreen film and projection system that Todd pioneered, but also because his shrewd and creative marketing plan maximized its exposure.[43] Breaking with the tradition of premiering movies in established theaters in downtown cultural districts, he booked many of its first-run engagements in "new shopping center theaters" located on the outskirts of large and small cities nationwide.[44] These financially lucrative bookings led Todd to conclude that suburban shopping venues, which offered easy access and an abundance of parking, would be ideal locations for a chain of Todd-AO movie theaters.

Taylor with husband, Todd, next to *The Liz,* Todd's private plane, February 1958.

Todd began to assemble a team of powerful players who could make his plan a reality. His first call was to Kaiser, founder of Kaiser Aluminum. Todd knew the tycoon had recently built the Kaiser Aluminum Dome—a one thousand–seat auditorium based on the pioneering geodesic dome designs of architect R. Buckminster Fuller—on the grounds of his new Hawaiian Village Hotel complex in Honolulu.[45] Todd seized on the idea of adapting this versatile dome to the specific needs of a fleet of theaters designed to accommodate Todd-AO projection. "I'll get twenty of them; twenty of them around the world. My own domes," he enthused.[46] He told Kaiser the concept would "revolutionize the theater business."[47]

Weaver, an acquaintance of Todd's, was the third person to join the team. In addition to being a consultant for Kaiser Aluminum, Weaver was the programming genius responsible for the creation of such signature NBC shows as *Today* and *Tonight*.[48] That fall, the three men met in Hawaii and announced the formation of a company with Weaver at the helm that would "design and build a pilot aluminum dome as the fore-runner of multi-purposed aluminum theaters."[49] They planned a chain of two thousand–seat auditoriums that would only take "a day or two to build and could be used for theater, community, or the spectacu-lar."[50] As one onlooker observed, "It'll be something like Howard Johnson's—only with movies."[51]

With the framework of their plan in place, they needed the right architect to design the theater proto-type. Although Fuller was the inventor of the geodesic dome and a brilliant structural innovator, his was not a household name. The moguls wanted a high-profile architect who was well known to the American public to draw up the plans.[52] Not only was Wright arguably the only architect who could make that claim, he was "flamboyant and always attracted attention," Mike Todd Jr. explained later.[53] In short, he was just the man they needed. Todd, with Taylor in tow, first approached Wright about the commission in December 1957 on a visit to Taliesin West.[54] He asked the architect to create a theater using the Kaiser dome as the roof, to be supported by a new "under-structure" of his own design.[55] In an article on the proposed theater titled "Brains, Money, and Imagination," one magazine reported that "the gifted quartet of showmen" planned to build the structures in "fifteen or twenty major suburban centers, where there is lots of parking, lots of shopping, and lots of opportunity for smart showmen."[56]

Following Todd's visit to Taliesin West, the four titans, along with Todd's attorney Herman O'Dell, con-vened in Wright's suite to discuss the project. Existing architectural drawings and a model of the Kaiser Aluminum Dome were brought to the session. According to O'Dell, "from the start, Wright held center stage. He demanded total autonomy in designing the settings and décor for the domes."[57] Kaiser was dis-appointed with the architect's dominance of the conversation, and Todd, who tired of Wright's "flowing descriptions of what he would create," dubbed the architect "the biggest ham actor in the world." Nonetheless, the men signed a memorandum of understanding to build and operate "multipurpose theatres utilizing the Kaiser Overhead Aluminum Dome."[58] On December 11, the *New York Times* announced that production would begin immediately for "world-wide use of the domes," with the first theater planned for California.[59]

LEFT: Weaver, Wright, Todd, and Kaiser discuss ideas for the Mike Todd Universal Theater in Wright's Plaza suite, 1957.

ABOVE: Perspective, the Mike Todd Universal Theater, 1958.

Despite his outspoken wishes to the contrary, the contract specified that . . . Wright would be responsible solely for the design of the understructure of the dome. He explored various options for the walls, but favored using precast concrete shells to raise and support the roof.[60] However, in a departure from the agreed terms, which required that the Kaiser dome be used in its "present structural form . . . without modification," Wright altered its arc, resulting in a "gentler line of curvature" to the roof.[61] He justified this breach in a note to Todd, jotted on one of the existing dome drawings provided by Kaiser's engi-neers, explaining that he cared "to do nothing" with the original scheme, finding the two thousand–seat

interior space "far out of human scale" and the perspectives "twisted and elaborate."[62] He reasoned, "Why not do something with less bunk . . .?"[63] To address the scale issue and "to create a place in which to see a picture that is more human," he proposed two schemes for smaller theaters—one with six hundred seats and a second with 1,550.[64] Other additions and alterations included a thrust stage, cross aisles for ease of access, integrated planters, and reflected ceiling lighting under the dome. Wright called the project the "Mike Todd Universal Theater."[65]

Over the next three months, Wright exchanged brief notes and telegrams with Weaver and Todd that touched on design, timing, and possible building sites for the theaters. By mid-January 1958, he had prepared a set of presentation drawings that he planned to share with the men at their next meeting. Although Wright kept the drawings under wraps, he hinted at the virtues of his design in a March 7 telegram to Todd. Comparing the attributes of his schemes to the impresario's stunning wife, Wright wrote, "Love to Elizabeth, but the new Michael Todd [theater] is almost as beautiful and will last longer."[66] Todd replied he would "stop in Phoenix" to see Wright's plans on an upcoming trip to the West Coast.[67]

Sadly, Todd never saw the drawings.[68] Two weeks later, on his way east to attend a Friars Club Roast in his honor at New York's Waldorf-Astoria Hotel, he perished when his private plane, *The Liz,* crashed in New Mexico.[69] Although the surviving partners made some attempt to pursue the project, and informally added Todd's son, Mike Jr., to the team, in truth, any hope of realizing the Mike Todd Universal Theater died along with its colorful conjuror.[70]

ON THE INTERNATIONAL STAGE: A DESIGN FOR BAGHDAD

On May 2, 1958, six hundred invited guests, including members of the UN diplomatic corps, gathered at the Iraqi Consulate on Manhattan's Upper East Side. Although the occasion marked the twenty-third birthday of King Faisal II of Iraq, Wright and his designs for a Grand Opera and Civic Auditorium, part of a $45 million cultural center for Baghdad, made the headlines.[71]

A year earlier, Wright had been one of a group of internationally prominent architects (including Le Corbusier, Walter Gropius, and Finland's Alvar Aalto, among others) invited by the Iraqi Development Board to design a series of new buildings for Baghdad. The initiative was part of the oil-rich country's

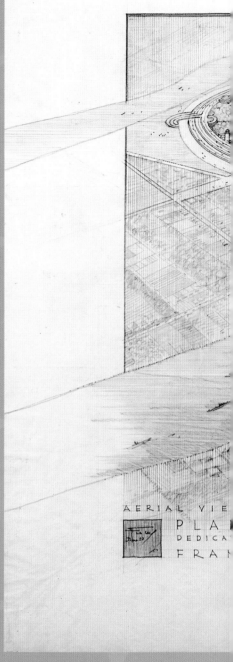

AERIAL VIE
PLA
DEDICA
FRAM

"billion-dollar, nine-year public works project" to improve its infrastructure and cultural resources.[72] Although Wright was specifically assigned the design of the opera house, he expanded his focus to include a master plan for the city comprising two museums, an art gallery, a grand bazaar, a casino, a post and telegraph building, a university, and a monument to Haroun al-Rashid, an eighth-century caliph of the city.

Wright first met King Faisal in 1957 when he flew to Baghdad to study the city and the scope of the public works project. Although another site had been selected for the opera house, on his descent into Baghdad, Wright spotted a location he preferred: a small island in the Tigris River owned by the royal family. He requested an audience with the young monarch in the hope that he would designate the island as the site for the opera house and expanded cultural center. The king acquiesced: "The island, Mr. Wright, is yours."[73]

Wright had been interested in the art and culture of the Middle East since boyhood, when *Thousand and One Nights* was a favorite book. He admired Islamic architecture, which he believed to be "the work of an enlightened people," and he was pleased to have a commission in Iraq.[74] "I would not give a hoot to

LEFT: Wright explains his concept for the Grand Opera and Civic Auditorium for Baghdad (1957) to diplomat Hashim Hilli during a reception at the Iraqi Consulate in New York, 1958.

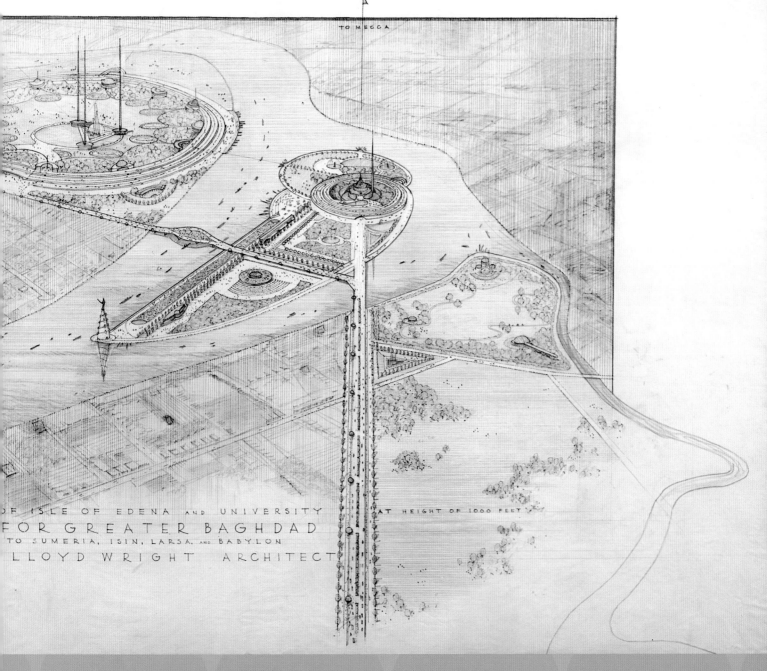

Within the illustration: TO MECCA · AT HEIGHT OF 1000 FEET · ...OF ISLE OF EDENA AND UNIVERSITY · ...FOR GREATER BAGHDAD · ...TO SUMERIA, ISIN, LARSA, AND BABYLON · ...LLOYD WRIGHT ARCHITECT

build an opera house in New York or London . . . but Baghdad is a different story," he explained.[75] Wright's designs referenced his respect for the city's rich civilization and "sought to combine solutions to modern problems with characteristics of Middle Eastern architecture."[76] Such adaptations in his plan included King Faisal Esplanade, a boulevard of merchant kiosks on axis to Mecca, as well as the use of ziggurat-inspired forms derived from the ancient Mesopotamian stepped tower, which provided spiraling access ramps and parking for nearly two thousand cars.[77]

The project was tragically short-lived. On July 14, 1958, King Faisal II was assassinated in a military coup. Less than two weeks later, a new minister of development announced that "houses for villagers instead of a palace for the king" would be built.[78] The new government planned to review "all projects not under contract," including Wright's cultural center. Although none of the architect's projects would be realized in Baghdad, Wright's design for the opera house served as inspiration for another building completed shortly after his death: the 1959 Grady Gammage Auditorium at Arizona State University in Tempe, located approximately twenty miles from Taliesin West.

ABOVE: Wright's plan for Greater Baghdad (1957).

THE REAL ESTATE TYCOON

During his years in New York, it was perhaps predictable that Wright, an outspoken detractor of cities, would cross swords with William Zeckendorf, a powerful real estate tycoon who was an aggressive proponent of the city's exponential growth and development.

As president of Webb and Knapp, a New York real estate development firm, and former owner of the Chrysler Building, Zeckendorf was a legend in his field by mid-century. In physical bulk and with cigar-wielding swagger, "the over-sized, bulldog of a man [was] a caricature of the jowly big-bellied real-estate operator."[79] As a former colleague summarized, he was "a great planner, a dreamer, but he was overenthusiastic, over zealous, over-everything."[80] Zeckendorf was a genius at sniffing out overlooked and undervalued properties and crafting multimillion-dollar commercial deals that totaled more than $3 billion over the course of two decades.[81] His most breathtaking transaction, and the one that would have enduring, international significance, occurred in 1946. The United Nations Organization was about to select Philadelphia as the home for its new headquarters when Zeckendorf offered a parcel of land along the East River between East Forty-Second and East Forty-Ninth streets to the fledgling organization" for any price they wish to pay."[82] A host of powerful players quickly crafted a viable deal. In the end, John D. Rockefeller Jr. purchased the property for $8.5 million and donated it to the UN for the project.[83]

Wright and Zeckendorf first met as adversaries when they were pitted against each other in a televised debate on the future of cities on NBC's *American Forum of the Air*. In his autobiography, Zeckendorf revealed he had read Wright's speeches and writings prior to the April 22, 1956, broadcast and had "discovered the man made profound good sense. As a result, during the show we sang in duet and had a great time," he later recalled.[84] Yet in fact, during the lively debate, the men struck few, if any, harmonious notes, as Wright persistently made a case for the obsolescence of American cities, and Zeckendorf doggedly proposed their revitalization through urban renewal. Philosophical differences aside, the combatants emerged from the studio without rancor and proceeded to Zeckendorf's estate in Greenwich, Connecticut, to continue their conversation over cocktails and dinner.[85]

Their inauspicious beginning notwithstanding, the two men fostered a warm and loyal friendship. In her 1960 memoir, *The Shining Brow*, Olgivanna Wright said her husband liked "big generous William Zeckendorf with his earthy sense of humor."[86] Professionally, however, Wright was not above firing inflammatory volleys his crony's way. Their unlikely camaraderie thrived because each was able to keep his personal affection for the other separate from their public wrangles. In this regard, Zeckendorf faced the greater challenge, because Wright was often on the attack. He accused "Brother Zeckendorf" of killing cities through investment and overbuilding, then profiting from their deaths.[87] He even used "zeckendorfs" as a derogatory term for big-city realtors and developers who were "building bigger towered skyscrapers to get more rent while the getting lasts" to sell to "fools . . . [who] don't know where they're going."[88] Yet, in a personal note to the mogul, Wright praised his friend but contradicted himself: "You are built on a large scale, Zeck, and have a heart accordingly. Never have I thought of you as a 'realtor.'"[89] In reply, Zeckendorf made his admiration clear: "Nothing gives me greater pleasure than looking forward to working with you."[90]

In 1957, the two would work together as client and architect when "Zeck" asked his friend to design a motel for a twenty-five-acre plat in New York.[91] Wright proposed two designs for the project. The first, a variation of an unrealized 1956 design for the Motor Hotel for Bramlett Enterprises in Memphis, Tennessee, featured three multistory cylindrical towers of ninety-six rooms each, linked by sky bridges. The second, based on a 1955 unbuilt design for the Wieland Motor Hotel in Hagerstown, Maryland, comprised twelve low cylindrical structures arranged in a hemicycle; the largest housed the office, kitchen, and dining facilities, while the rest contained guest rooms. The structure wrapped around a garden with a circular combination swimming pool and fountain at its center. A filling station/garage was

New York realtor William Zeckendorf, 1964.

provided for motorists' convenience. Wright enthused about the project for the better part of a year and repeatedly dunned Zeckendorf for a specific site, but the scheme never came to fruition. That same year, Wright also unsuccessfully tried to interest Zeckendorf in building a version of his 1956 Golden Beacon, a fifty-story apartment building sheathed with gold-anodized aluminum that was originally designed for a Chicago client, cajoling: "Why not clean up a block at 'the Battery' and show your city something?? OR save up a block in Chicago and plant it there. We will call it the 'Zeckendorf Beacon' topping everything in every way."[92]

Wright was likely aware that Zeckendorf might have a site available in Chicago. In 1957, the firm of Webb and Knapp was overseeing a major urban renewal effort in the Hyde Park neighborhood just north of the Robie House, a Prairie residence designed by Wright in 1906. The house was at the center of a heated, international preservation battle because its owner, the Chicago Theological Seminary, wanted to demolish it and build a dormitory in its place. It was the second time the seminary had threatened to destroy the house—the first was in 1941. Wright went on the offensive and, with what biographer Brendan Gill described as the architect's "incomparable gift for making enemies," publicly lashed out at the seminary board: "It all goes to show the danger of entrusting anything spiritual to the clergy," he charged.[93]

As he had done with great success in the case of the UN, Zeckendorf once again stepped into the fray. On December 21, the *New York Times* announced that the developer had purchased the Robie House for $125,000. He planned to use it for "about four years" as Webb and Knapp's local office during its urban renewal efforts, eventually deeding the property to the appropriate organization.[94] The gesture marked an important victory for architectural preservationists and was a generous personal benefaction to Wright. The appreciative architect wrote to his friend: "I feel the warmth of your great heart in this gift to the endeavor of my lifetime in Architecture," adding: "Our country has good cause to thank you but how much greater cause have I?" Zeckendorf replied: "If anything I have done gives you gratification I consider myself already richly rewarded."[95]

Wright appreciated the enormity of Zeckendorf's gesture, and wanted to recognize his friend's contribution in a public, permanent way. He proposed setting a bronze plaque with "well-designed lettering" on the brickwork of the rescued house to commemorate the deed. In the ultimate compliment he would ever pay a "realtor," he suggested the inscription read in part: "Saved from destruction . . . by William Zeckendorf, American-Builder [sic]."[96]

Wright's debate with Zeckendorf on *The American Forum of the Air* was only one of many broadcast appearances by the architect during the 1950s. While living in New York, he would take full advantage of the popular new medium of television to spread his architectural ideas to an increasingly tuned-in American audience.

BELOW: The Frederick C. Robie House (1906, Chicago, Illinois). Zeckendorf's financial intervention saved the Wright-designed Prairie house from destruction in 1957.

FACING: Plan for the New Motor Hotel for William Zeckendorf (1958).

THE NEW MOTOR HOTEL
FRANK LLOYD WRIGHT ARCHITECT

SCALE - 1/16"=1'-0"

MASTER OF THE MEDIUM
IN AMERICA'S LIVING ROOMS

[
I have never sought publicity of any kind.

I've yielded to it . . .

Frank Lloyd Wright, *The Mike Wallace Interview*, 1957
]

Television and Frank Lloyd Wright were perfectly suited to each other. Despite an age disparity—television was a young industry at mid-century and Wright was an elderly man—both were brash, bold purveyors of experimental ideas. The popularity of television was exploding, and TV sets were rapidly replacing radios in the hearts and homes of most Americans. Much of the power of the fledgling medium derived from the fact that TV was literally inventing itself—often in live broadcasts—as millions of viewers tuned in. Because the industry was so new, there were few confining prototypes or protocols to dampen creative impulses. This proved particularly invigorating for those behind the scenes and helped to shape the character and content of many of the early shows. "You didn't know what you couldn't do, so you did it," explained veteran television journalist Mike Wallace.[1] The booming industry was simply a "revolution," and its nerve center was New York, the undisputed television capital of the world.[2]

The industries of radio and television had deep New York–area roots. In 1933, the Radio Corporation of America (RCA) moved its headquarters, including corporate offices and radio broadcasting studios, into the RCA Building, a component of the soaring new Rockefeller Center in midtown Manhattan, thereby establishing the complex as "Radio City" in the eyes of the world.[3] However, RCA already had its sights set on dominating the emerging television industry as well. Two years earlier, in 1931, the National Broadcasting Company (NBC), an RCA subsidiary, had begun transmitting experimental television signals from the top of the Empire State Building.[4] By the end of the decade, most of the cutting-edge research related to the development of television in the United States had been consolidated under RCA's patent control.[5]

New Yorkers peer through a Rockefeller Center display window to watch the 1953 coronation of Queen Elizabeth II on television.

Prior to his small-screen debut in the United States, Wright appeared on BBC Television in London in 1939.

The first demonstration of this mesmerizing medium occurred on the opening day of the 1939 New York World's Fair in Flushing Meadows, Queens, when NBC transmitted President Franklin D. Roosevelt's dedication of the fair.[6] Soon, television sets, including those produced by RCA, went on sale to the public. Ten years later, 3.6 million of them had been sold; in 1950 alone, sales doubled. By 1954, twenty-six million, or 55 percent of American households owned televisions.[7]

FRANK LLOYD WRIGHT IN BLACK AND WHITE

Before he made his American television debut, Wright honed his broadcast interview skills on a variety of live and recorded radio shows. Among the earliest was a 1930 broadcast during which Wright discussed the "New" in architecture with Hugh Ferriss, an architect best known for his ethereal renderings of tall buildings, published in his 1929 book *The Metropolis of Tomorrow.*[8] Wright's other New York radio engagements included multiple appearances on two of NBC's most popular interview shows: *The Mary Margaret McBride Show,* hosted by one of radio's pioneering female journalists, and *The Tex and Jinx Show,* anchored by the husband-and-wife team of Jinx Falkenburg and Tex McCrary.[9] He was also invited to appear on a number of the network's signature radio productions, including *NBC Lecture Hall,* "a series of lectures by outstanding figures of our time," and *Monitor,* a highly successful and profitable weekend news and variety show.[10]

On one occasion in 1954, Wright was a guest in the Rockefeller Center offices of the man who dominated the broadcast industry in New York—"General" David Sarnoff, president of RCA. A subsequent letter from the architect to Sarnoff reveals the subject of their meeting as well as the punster in Wright: "Dear General: It was nice seeing you in your remarkable tower offices—the best place for a 'general' in general I've yet seen."[11] Getting down to business, Wright lamented the condition of Taliesin's antiquated film projectors and expressed his desire to replace them with new "RCA equipment which our investigation seems to assure us is the best in the world."[12] He asked Sarnoff for two 35mm projectors and enclosed a copy of the charter of the Taliesin Fellowship and documentation of its tax-free, nonprofit status, implicitly suggesting the equipment be donated—an invitation Sarnoff declined.[13]

Although he would continue to be in demand as a radio guest, Wright soon added television to his broadcast repertoire.[14] A natural in front of the camera, his clear, well-modulated voice, calm demeanor, sartorial elegance, and ability to provide provocative answers to probing questions made him an ideal on-screen guest. The twinkle in his eye and his dry sense of humor added to his on-air charm. He quickly demonstrated his ease on the small screen in a range of televised appearances—from live to scripted and edited.[15]

One of Wright's earliest appearances was on a nationally telecast segment of NBC's *Conversations with Elder Wise Men* (a series that would later be expanded and rebroadcast as *Wisdom*) on May 17, 1953.[16] The series was the brainchild of network president Sylvester "Pat" Weaver, who later became a client of Wright's (see chapter four). The noble concept for the show, according to Weaver, was to "find the world's greatest thinkers and achievers, put them on camera, and let them tell us what they were doing or thinking, where mankind stood at the moment, and where we were going."[17] In the process, Weaver hoped to "raise the cultural level of American television."[18] Among the "great thinkers and achievers" featured were Bertrand Russell, Carl Sandburg, Jawaharlal Nehru, Herbert Hoover, Edward Steichen, and Igor Stravinsky.[19]

From the beginning, the production team thoughtfully considered how to best elicit "wisdom" from the august participants. They committed to a relaxed interview format that would, in tone and physical surroundings, suggest the interviewer was a "guest" in the elder wise man's home, a listener rather than a cross-examiner.[20] In truth, each segment was a thirty-minute edited sound-on-film crafted from ninety minutes of raw footage. Wright's segment, produced by NBC's Ben Park, was nearly nine months in the making. The outline of the interview, including specific questions to be asked and responses to those questions, was developed during meetings and communications between Park and Wright in the months preceding the session. According to Park, the goal of the show was to reveal "Mr. Wright's generalized thinking," through the understanding of "particulars" such as "accomplishments, specific hopes, and disappointments." For his participation, Wright received $1,000 plus expenses.[21]

NBC executives David Sarnoff, Weaver, and Robert Sarnoff, 1953.

At the age of eighty-five, Wright had the distinction of being the oldest, yet "one of the most youthful-minded" *Conversations* subjects, and the first architect invited to appear.[22] His "guest," or interviewer, for the segment was Hugh Downs, a thirty-two-year-old NBC staff announcer. Filmed on a studio set in Chicago, the broadcast began when Wright, who was already seated, beckoned Downs to join him: "Come in, lad."[23] Downs took a seat on a very low chair to the left, while Wright commanded a much higher position to the right, effectively establishing, at least in the visual sense, the architect's stature as the elder, wiser man. As Downs explained, his goal was to get a clear picture of "the essence of your thinking about American architecture and American life," to which a puzzled Wright replied, "In a half hour?"[24]

During a discussion that moved smoothly from Wright's early influences through the structural differences between his organic and other "conventional" architecture, Wright identified his greatest disappointment as the "imitation of imitation by imitators" that prevailed in American architecture of the day.[25] When asked to name "the most satisfactory achievement" of his long life, he responded: "Oh my dear boy—the next one, of course, the next building I build!"[26]

The questions, which were carefully crafted to evoke the most informative and insightful responses, also invoked Wright's ironclad opinions and robust self-esteem. At one point Wright explained, "You see, early in life I had to choose between honest arrogance and hypocritical humility. I chose honest arrogance, and have

AT THE PUBLIC PULPIT

For most of his life, Wright preached his own gospel of nonconformist beliefs, a tendency he came by genetically. On his mother's Lloyd Jones side of his family, he was descended from a long line of Welsh clergymen whose nontraditional, some might say heretical, canons often required defense.[27] According to Meryle Secrest, the architect's forebears demonstrated "a consistent, stubborn insistence on their renegade opinions and a melancholic pride in being persecuted for them."[28] This dogged determination was reflected in the family's defiant motto, "Truth Against the World." "No one ever accused the Lloyd Joneses of deserting their principles," Secrest added.[29]

Like his ancestors, Wright was quick to proclaim his views. No matter how much outrage his comments provoked, he was seemingly impervious to rebuke. Although architectural principles were at the heart of his "truth," the scope of his opinions was much broader. He was not afraid to assail people ("a bureaucrat is a short man, however long his legs may be"), places ("Pittsburgh . . . abandon it"), or institutions (the AIA, or American Institute of Architects, as the "Arbitrary Institute of Appearances") to make a point.[30] From the media's perspective however, this was Wright's greatest strength. "Mr. Wright is always news," *Harper's* magazine declared in December 1953. "Outrage is his stock in trade and he is a reporter's delight."[31]

Unlike his forefathers, who for generations prose-lytized from pulpits from Wales to Wisconsin, Wright ingeniously spread his doctrine through secular means—and was phenomenally successful at doing so. "Early in his career, [Wright] began the life-long task of developing and disseminating his own ideas through every available forum," said architectural historian Robert L. Sweeney.[32] In the late nineteenth and early twentieth centuries, his vehicles included lectures, books, newspapers, and magazines. Over time, however, Wright added sound recordings, radio, and finally television to his impressive communications repertoire. He proved to be equally effective in all media because, among his talents, he was not only "the most articulate of modern architects. He was also his own best publicist," said Sweeney.[33] By the time he established a residence at the Plaza in New York—a city that, in 1954, supported thirty newspapers and was the center of the nation's publishing, radio, and television industries—Wright was an expert in the art of self-promotion.[34]

Wright with reporters in 1955.

Downs and Wright on the set of the NBC broadcast *Conversations with Elder Wise Men,* May 1953.

seen no occasion to change even now."[35] Recalling Wright's confident unflustered demeanor on screen, Downs said, "It's hard to imagine him saying, 'Well, I am not sure about that. I'll have to look that up.'"[36] Years later, reflecting on his encounter with the architect, Downs made two observations: Wright "did not waste a lot of effort on the lubrication of tact," and "he was a genius, no doubt about it."[37]

Conversations was well received by Jack Gould of the *Times,* who found Wright to be "an engrossing and stimulating figure on screen," whose presence was enhanced by good humor and "engaging wry wit."[38] Gould noted the elderly architect's youthful spirit, observing, "in his thinking and mode of expression there is a freshness, pungency and originality that belie his years." He perceptively observed both the muse and the steel in Wright, describing him as a poet and "not one to give ground easily."[39]

On May 15, 1953, two days before his *Conversations* interview aired, Wright was a guest on NBC's *Today* show in New York.[40] The show originated from the network's unique street-level, glass-fronted studios in Rockefeller Center. The large picture windows not only allowed pedestrians to peek into the fascinating arena of live television but also afforded home viewers a glimpse of the bustle of Manhattan just beyond the set.[41] Wright's segment began with such a city-to-studio connection. As Dinah Shore and Tony Martin crooned "I'll Take Manhattan," the television camera slowly tilted down from the skyline to the crowd gathered on the sidewalk.[42] It then zoomed in on the front-page headline of the previous day's *New York Herald Tribune:* "Says Frank Lloyd Wright: Grass in the Streets of N.Y. in 25 Years."[43] In the piece, Wright predicted that in the near future, urban centers would disappear while decentralized communities would flourish. "The city is going to the country . . . in twenty-five years, grass will grow where least expected now and flowers will bloom in the concrete," he prophesized.[44]

The show's host, Dave Garroway, repeated the provocative headline, and then launched into an accolade-laden introduction of the man responsible for the brash statement. Garroway was interrupted when Wright interjected, "Don't make me blush, please. You wouldn't get [the color] on television," demonstrating his astute grasp of the limitations of the black-and-white broadcast medium, as well as his quick wit and firm upper hand in the verbal exchange.[45]

Calling Wright one of the most "fearless and original thinkers of our time," Garroway pressed the architect to elaborate on his prediction. Wright explained his vision for the future: decentralized self-sufficient communities located outside of urban areas (see "The Tall Tower in the City Reimagined," page 42). The automobile, which he identified as the "great *desideratum* in our civilization," would be a key to their success, he argued. "For the first time in history, we can step into something and go places ourselves, without asking anybody's permission." A car was also, he presciently noted, "the dearest possession any family can have. Ask the children."[46]

Despite the fact that he was sitting in the heart of it, Wright verbally pummeled New York, calling it an "antiquated scrap pile," populated only by people who "are stranded here, who must be here. By choice, they would not live here." With a smile he added, "unless it was in a penthouse," of which, he realized, there were few. The architect predicted the exodus from the city would accelerate quickly because "twenty-five years is like a century now." He gave Robert Moses, the controversial New York City parks commissioner who was his distant cousin by marriage, credit for facilitating decentralization through his aggressive and widely debated highway and bridge building program. In classic Wright expository style, he explained, "Once upon a time, Moses led his people out of captivity, but [Robert] Moses is making a way of people getting away from New York as well as getting into it. And the more Moses works and the better he works, why, the sooner will come decentralization."[47]

Unquestionably, Wright's most curious television appearance occurred June 3, 1956, on "Everybody's Favorite Guessing Game," *What's My Line?* The format of the popular CBS show, which was broadcast from New York, featured a panel of celebrities who attempted to deduce, through rounds of questioning, the occupation or identity of assorted guests. In the case of a famous visitor such as Wright, panel members donned blindfolds to prevent instant recognition. That evening, when host John Daly asked "our mystery guest to enter and sign in please," a dapper Wright, complete with cane, walked onstage, picked up a piece of chalk, and carefully signed his name on the blackboard.[48] To further identify him, the words "World Famous Architect" were superimposed on the screen.[49] Wright, who indicated he understood the scoring system because he had "watched one of the shows with interest," was identified only as "self-employed" to the blindfolded panelists: actress Arlene Francis, ventriloquist Paul Winchell (with dummy Jerry Mahoney), journalist Dorothy Kilgallen, and actor Peter Lawford. Noting his "impressive voice," the panelists posed questions in an attempt to deduce both his profession and identity:

Wright appeared on NBC's *Today* show three times in the 1950s. He is seen here with host Dave Garroway in a May 1953 broadcast.

Question: "Do people come to you [for your service]?"
Wright: "They must. I have never gone to them."

Question: "Do these people come to you more than one at a time?"
Wright: "Frequently two at a time."

Question: "Does what you do have to do with the law?"
Wright (humorously): "Unfortunately, yes."

Wright was having trouble hearing the panelists' questions and ultimately gave himself away when he noted, "the sound goes out and does not come back." Host Daly quickly said, "Oh, don't worry about that. We have a bit of an acoustic problem." Ever the professional, Wright replied: "You do have. Never mind, we'll overcome it." Based on this extemporaneous remark, Kilgallen identified the architect. Prior to leaving the set, the nearly eighty-nine-year-old Wright was asked if he was "active" in any new design work. He replied, "Did you say active? I'm in harness! I just built a new tower on the western prairie," referencing his recently completed Price Tower. As he shook hands with the panelists and prepared to exit the stage, he remarked, "Such an extraordinarily intelligent panel!" Wright was not the only mystery guest that evening; Liberace, the flamboyant pianist, also appeared.[50]

Of all of Wright's television appearances in the 1950s, the most famous and provocative was *The Mike Wallace Interview*, which originally aired in two parts in September 1957 on ABC.[51] At the time, "interview shows were pap," said Wallace, but *The Mike Wallace Interview* was different, the renowned journalist reflected, because "it dug into things that people ordinarily would not have heard in prime time."[52] His penetrating questions, the guest's candid responses, and the camera's unsparing close-ups set the show apart from others and resulted in arresting television that grabbed viewers' attention.

Wallace invited Wright to appear on his New York–based show because "he was a stormy petrel . . . an object of great admiration [and] his ideas were fresh."[53] Wallace's approach to the interview was equally fresh. He sought to engage not only Wright the architect, but Wright the social critic as well: "his architecture was social criticism."[54] Unlike many other shows of the day, *The Mike Wallace Interview* was unrehearsed, uncensored, and unedited. There were no ground rules, nor were questions provided in advance. According to Wallace, none of this fazed Wright, because he thrived in intellectually challenging situations.[55] "Wright's trenchant opinions on life and art came from a richly original mind," the journalist later observed.[56]

LEFT: In 1952, blindfolded celebrity panelists prepare to identify the evening's "mystery guest" on *What's My Line?*

RIGHT: Wright, with host Daly, was one of two mystery guests on the June 3, 1956, episode of the CBS show.

The look of the show, from the stark logo and strident music to the bare black set animated only by wafting cigarette smoke, suggested part tough, hard-hitting journalism and part minimalist aesthetic of New York's 1950s beat culture. On screen, battle lines were quickly drawn: Wallace, thirty-nine, perched edgily on a stool and leaned over a desk replete with notes, a pack of Philip Morris cigarettes, and an ash-tray; Wright, ninety, elegantly attired with a silk scarf draped around his neck, sat with an erect regal bear-ing in a chair; Wallace, who was off camera for much of the interview, was on his home turf; Wright, almost constantly on camera in harshly lit close-ups, was on the spot. Although everything about the on-screen atmosphere suggested imminent conflict, the mood off camera was congenial. As Wallace noted, Wright "came to rassle and to play," and he knew he would be treated fairly.[57]

Wallace set the stage for the interview by eliciting Wright's "capsule opinions" in three potentially volatile—and decidedly non-architectural—topic areas: organized Christianity (Wright: "Why organize it?"); the American Legion (Wright: "I never think of it if I can help it."); and mercy killing ("If it's mercy killing, I'm for it."). Wallace admitted he chose the subjects because he knew they were "going to get [Wright's] heart started, so to speak."[58]

The two men verbally jousted on a wide range of topics, including organic architecture, the American press, modern art and music, arro-gance, the opinions of the common man, Charlie Chaplin, teenagers, democracy, freedom, and sex. Wright delivered his opinions thoughtfully and without apology, never losing his composure.

At one point, in the midst of Wallace's grilling, Wright turned the tables when he asked his inquisitor if he felt like apologizing for "that thing you have in your mouth," referring to the cigarette provided by the program's sponsor, the Philip Morris Company.[59] As he was, in effect, "doing commercials for the cigarette," Wallace remembered it as an awkward moment.[60] Wright spared his interviewer any further discom-fort: "Let's leave the cigarette smoker his solace," he said.[61] Later, remembering Wright's merciful retreat, Wallace noted, "He was a very kind fellow—who led us around by the nose."[62]

On September 1, 1957, ABC aired the first of two Wright segments on *The Mike Wallace Interview*. The men debated many issues, including Wallace's smoking habit.

Among those who watched Wright's appearance on *The Mike Wallace Interview* with interest was Lawrence Spivak, producer and moderator of NBC's *Meet the Press*. Spivak, who found the program "fascinating," wrote to Wright: "You did a truly superb job in every way. Your answers hit a new high for literate television, and I could have taken anoth-er hour of what you had to say on a variety of subjects."[63] In the same letter, he expressed a desire to interview Wright on his show. In late 1958 and early 1959, the two men attempted to zero in on a date and location for the interview. Spivak hoped the session would occur on June 8, 1959, which he, like many others, erroneously believed to be Wright's ninetieth (rather than, correctly, his ninety-second) birthday.[64] Although Wright did not address the birth date error, he suggested a venue for the broadcast in his last letter to Spivak on February 28: "Since television interviews can now be made anywhere at any time—why don't we do this one some time when I am in New York at the Plaza? Will be there a number of times before June 8th and will notify you accordingly, if satisfactory."[65] One can only imagine the stimu-lating exchange that might have occurred between the two men; Wright died two months prior to the scheduled session.

If Wright understood the promise and power of television, he also recognized its flaws. He once dismissed television as "chewing gum for the eyes," censuring it for being "merely a form of entertainment" rather than "the cultural agency" it could be.[66] In his opinion, the major stumbling block to "the rescue of this great medium" was its dependence on advertisers prone to constantly "interrupting and demoralizing the whole better element of television."[67] Why should culture "be at the mercy of . . . candle wax, toothpaste, Bufferin, cigarettes, or what have you?" he asked.[68] Presciently, he believed that "emancipation" of the medium would come in the form of subscription television.[69] His criticisms notwithstanding, Wright claimed television to be "a great medium, and if organic architecture could possess itself of the television, it could go very far, very soon."[70] The proselytizer in Wright instinctively understood the medium's vast promotional reach, and during the last decade of his life, he astutely availed himself of its expanding sphere of influence. He knew New York, television's capital, was the ideal place from which to disseminate his views to the largest possible audience.

As his collected broadcast images reveal, Wright was a savvy television performer who delivered his message with equal measures of certitude and charm—a potent combination of which he must have been aware. He was "an early master of the sound bite," observed architectural historian Hilary Ballon.[71] Although he stated on *The Mike Wallace Interview* that he had "never sought publicity of any kind" but merely "yielded to it," he in fact submitted to a remarkable array of televised appearances and remained a popular guest until the end of his life. In truth, "he adored publicity, [and] sought it continuously all his life long," noted Brendan Gill.[72]

Wright displayed "such conviction in front of the camera," according to Terence Riley, former curator of architecture and design at MoMA, because, during broadcasts, he was essentially "doing what he [had] been doing his whole life . . . giving a sermon, thumping the Bible and letting all of us in the audience, the congregation, know what he was thinking about."[73] Yet, he wryly added, there were benefits for the architect as well: "One of the reasons for Wright's longevity is that he refused to die until they invented television."[74] Despite his intractable determination, however, Wright would not live to see the opening of his most important and controversial New York project—the Solomon R. Guggenheim Museum.

THE GUGGENHEIM RISING
THE SPIRAL ON FIFTH AVENUE

[*This eleventh-hour building is a thoroughbred.*]

Frank Lloyd Wright, the *New York Times,* September 22, 1957

In 1954, the *Times* reported that Frank Lloyd Wright was opening an office in Manhattan to supervise the construction of the Guggenheim Museum. More than a decade had passed since the building's commission, yet ground had not been broken, and the museum was still another five years from completion. What began in 1943 as an eccentric curator's plea to Wright for a "temple of spirit" to showcase a philanthropist's collection of avant-garde art became an interminable waiting game for its architect, fraught with deepening controversy.[1]

The complex process of the project, which spanned sixteen years from World War II to the Pop Art era, engaged many sectors of New York's citizenry: city officials, the museum's board and staff, the modern art community, the media, and the increasingly curious public were all intertwined in the continuing saga of the spiral on Fifth Avenue. In his determination to see the building rise, Wright confronted a host of obstacles, including the death of his client, a thorny relationship with the museum's curator, and the dictates of a new director with divergent views. Rising costs, contract disputes, scores of building code infringements, several redesigns, and a constant flow of opinions from critics of all kinds further complicated the process. While Wright never backed down from his resolve to construct the great "archeseum," as he creatively termed the structure, the struggle to build the Guggenheim "pressed down unmercifully hard upon him" at times, recalled Director of the Frank Lloyd Wright Archives Bruce Brooks Pfeiffer. In the end, after designing for New York for nearly fifty years, the Guggenheim Museum, which alone required six complete sets of plans, would become Wright's first major building in New York.[2]

Wright at the Guggenheim Museum construction site, ca. 1957–58.

A DECADE OF
DESIGNS AND DELAYS

"Could you ever come to New York and discuss with me a building for our collection of non-objective paintings?" queried Baroness Hilla Rebay in a 1943 letter to Wright.[3] Born and educated in Europe, Rebay was curator of the Solomon R. Guggenheim Foundation, an organization founded in 1937 for "the promotion of art and education in art and the enlightenment of the public."[4] Since the 1920s, she had guided the mining magnate and his wife, Irene, in the acquisition of non-objective art, which she defined as "painting[s] that represents no object or subject known to us on earth . . . simply a beautiful organization of colors and forms to be enjoyed for beauty's sake."[5] For a number of years, Guggenheim displayed his art in his Plaza Hotel suite, at Trillora Court (his palatial estate on Long Island's North Shore), and in temporary quarters at 24 East Fifty-Fourth Street known as "The Museum of Non-objective Painting."[6] By the early 1940s, however, the aging philanthropist's expanding collection needed a permanent home.[7]

Irene Guggenheim suggested Wright as the designer of her husband's museum. Rebay, who had initially "assumed the seventy-year old architect was dead," studied his work and became convinced he was the right candidate to craft the transcendent space she envisioned: "I need a fighter, a lover of space, an originator, a tester and a wise man . . . and your help to make it possible," she wrote to him. Wright agreed, confidently replying: ". . . of course I should have no difficulty in giving the Foundation what it desires and needs." Less than a month after receiving Rebay's letter, Wright and Guggenheim signed an agreement for the construction of the museum, including a stipulation that its site be secured within a year, with total cost not to exceed $1 million.[8]

In their quest to identify a site, Guggenheim and Wright were assisted by one of the most commanding and contentious men in New York: Robert Moses. As parks commissioner, city construction coordinator, and a member of the city planning commission (among many other positions during his long career), Moses had for decades driven the massive urban renewal and building programs that would forever change the face of New York—little of consequence was constructed within the city without his say so.

Non-objective paintings adorned the walls of Solomon R. Guggenheim's suite at the Plaza Hotel, ca. 1930s.

THE MODERN GALLERY
MUSEUM FOR THE SOLOMON R GUGGENHEIM FOUNDATION
FRANK LLOYD WRIGHT ARCHITECT
HOLDEN AND McLAUGHLIN ASSOCIATES

Wright realized from the beginning that his "cousin Bob's" good will and assistance would be critically important to the success of the Guggenheim project: "He can do more than anyone in New York to help get this building built," he explained in a letter to Rebay. Moses knew of and suggested several possible sites for the new museum, but, for various reasons, none of them were selected.[9]

In March 1944, Guggenheim made a decision to purchase land at the corner of Fifth Avenue and Eighty-Ninth Street (which would expand incrementally to eventually encompass the entire block front between Eighty-Eighth and Eighty-Ninth streets) as the location for his new museum. Wright, who had optimally hoped for a site outside crowded Manhattan, was at least pleased that the spot bordered Central Park, commenting that it ensured "light, fresh air and advantages in every way but one . . . congestion." On March 21, the *Times* announced Wright's commission to design the "ultra-modern museum," with construction to begin following the war.[10]

ABOVE: Drawing of Wright's concept for "The Modern Gallery," 1951.

BELOW: Wright with Moses, 1955.

PRESS CONFERENCES
AT THE PLAZA

Wright, curator Hilla Rebay, and Solomon R. Guggenheim with a model of the Guggenheim Museum in New York, 1945.

The Plaza became the unofficial headquarters for a series of 1945 presentations to the press regarding the architect's developing plans. At the hotel in July, Wright showed preliminary drawings of his design, based on the Assyrian ziggurat, the verticality of which was well suited to a constricted (and expensive) Manhattan lot.[11] The spiral form had long interested Wright; in 1924, he proposed such a design for the Gordon Strong Automobile Objective and Planetarium, an unusual project for an expansive site on a Maryland mountaintop. Although he developed ziggurat schemes of varying geometries for the Guggenheim, he ultimately inverted the form to generate a structure that widened as it rose from the ground. The museum's exterior was a direct expression of its interior, where the spiral functioned as one continuous gallery that rose six stories along an inclined ramp. After taking an elevator to the top floor, visitors would embark on a slow, winding descent through time, space, and art.[12]

That September, accompanied by Guggenheim and Rebay, Wright unveiled a model of the building at the hotel. In contrast to the Metropolitan Museum, which he described as an "undemocratic, outdated stone

quarry," Wright believed his building represented "pure optimism." "The thing you can't get anymore in church you ought to get here . . . the health, vitality and beauty of the human imagination," he said, announcing that construction would begin when wartime restrictions were lifted—but this was not to be.[13]

Guggenheim had initially delayed construction because he felt inflated wartime building costs would soon fall, but numerous other factors would now impede progress. Site expansion and changes in the building program would require Wright to redesign the museum several times. And the complex structural requirements of the spiraling "monolith of reinforced concrete" proved to be difficult and time-consuming for even the most experienced engineers to bid. The cost of the museum soon exceeded, and eventually tripled, contracted limits. Delays, fee disputes, and numerous disagreements between Wright and Rebay further complicated matters.[14]

In 1948, with Wright's proposed building no closer to realization, the Museum of Non-objective Painting moved into its second temporary quarters at 1071 Fifth Avenue, a six-story mansion on the museum's future site. As Guggenheim's health began to decline, the project was officially put on hold. *Architectural Forum* concluded that Wright's building, which evoked reactions ranging from "fright to enthusiastic approval," might be built "someday."[15]

The Metropolitan Museum of Art on Fifth Avenue, ca. 1960. Wright argued that the Guggenheim would stand in dramatic contrast to the building.

The site of Wright's Guggenheim Museum on Fifth Avenue between East Eighty-Eighth and East Eighty-Ninth streets, 1951.

A CHANGING OF THE GUARD

On November 3, 1949, Solomon R. Guggenheim died at the age of eighty-seven, bequeathing his art collection and a $6 million endowment fund to his foundation. He left an additional $2 million solely for the museum's construction, a figure agreed upon shortly before his death, but did not specifically name Wright as its architect. In addition to these monetary designations, the magnate's will also established a board of trustees comprised primarily of members of his family.[16] As the new board moved forward with plans for the museum—and financial concerns continued to escalate—Wright's status as the project's architect was far from secure.

Rebay's position was becoming progressively precarious, as well. The museum's board members were less tolerant of the idiosyncratic curator and her narrow artistic focus than was their founder. Trustee Harry F. Guggenheim, Solomon's nephew, grew increasingly skeptical of her usefulness. The matter went public in a 1951 *New York Times* feature in which Aline B. Louchheim (later Saarinen) censured Rebay for her "doctrinaire attitude" and "addiction to non-objective art" as contrary to the foundation's wider mission and also criticized the trustees for delaying construction of Wright's "critical[ly] acclaimed" design. Facing mounting opposition and citing ill health, Rebay resigned in March 1952 and was appointed "Director Emeritus."[17]

Rebay's departure marked the beginning of major change at the museum. That fall, Guggenheim and the trustees announced that the Museum of Non-objective Painting would broaden its focus and be renamed "The Solomon R. Guggenheim Museum." James Johnson Sweeney, the former director of MoMA's Department of Painting and Sculpture, was hired as Rebay's replacement.[18]

Wright continued to press toward the goal of seeing the museum built, revising his scheme when the board of trustees purchased the remaining piece of block-front property for the building's site in 1951, while at the same time working to stay within the allotted budget. His revised plans were approved by

SIXTY YEARS OF LIVING ARCHITECTURE AND THE USONIAN EXHIBITION HOUSE

In 1953, before construction on the Guggenheim began, Sixty Years of Living Architecture, an exhibition of Wright's work, was mounted in a pavilion of his own design on the museum's site. A full-scale, completely furnished Usonian Exhibition House accompanied the show. Both opened in late October, attracting 30,241 visitors in fifty-two days.[19]

Sixty Years included more than eight hundred drawings and artifacts. It was not only the largest exhibition of Wright's work to date, it was also the largest architecture exhibition on record devoted to one man.[20] Conceived by Arthur Kaufmann, Gimbel's chief executive and cousin of Fallingwater client Edgar Kaufmann Sr., and Philadelphia architect Oskar Stonorov (who also designed and organized the show), it debuted at Gimbel's Philadelphia department store in 1951. Afterward, the exhibit began a three-year European tour with a stop in Italy, where it visibly redressed a rising tide of communist propaganda that America lacked any real culture aside from the worship of money.[21]

In New York, Wright's custom-built exhibit pavilion was adjacent to the exhibition house. "I've never had a building in New York," he proudly told The New Yorker, "This little pavilion is my first." But the magazine termed the exhibit structure a "rakish affair of red brick, canvas, and steel poles," acerbically adding: ". . . we got the impression, listening to Wright, that he wouldn't consider the insertion of 'the Only' before 'Living' in the exhibit's title a misstatement of historical fact."[22] Harper's magazine defended the integrity of the show, describing Wright's work on display as ". . . all along, a lover's quarrel with the world, and he has never pretended otherwise."[23]

Exhibition houses allowed Wright to promote his ideas to those who might never see his residential designs or read his extensive writings.[24] The New York house gave him the opportunity to bring his vision for democratic suburban living to the biggest city of all, perhaps to convince its residents that this is the lifestyle they would *truly* prefer, if they just had the chance to experience it.[25]

In "Concerning the Usonian House," an essay by Wright in the exhibit's souvenir booklet, the architect explained the "spirit of democracy" apparent in his domestic designs as early as 1900: "[I] took off the attic and the porch, pulled out the basement, and made a single spacious, harmonious unit of living room, dining room and kitchen . . . the sleeping rooms were convenient to baths approached in a segregated, separate extended wing and the whole place was flooded with sunlight from floor to ceiling with glass." This transformation delivered an "open plan" in which the housewife played the new role of "'officio,' Wright said, "operating in gracious relation to her home, instead of being a kitchen-mechanic behind closed doors."[26]

On the eve of the house's opening, Wright hosted a preview tour for the press. Waving his ubiquitous cane, he exclaimed: "I think this has the old Colonial on the run." Editorial coverage of the house in the November 1955 issue of House Beautiful spread Wright's message for better living to a broader national audience.[27]

Wright's Sixty Years of Living Architecture retrospective exhibit employed large-scale photographs as well as models to represent the architect's work.

ABOVE: The living room of the Usonian Exhibition House (1953) featured a Japanese screen from Wright's personal collection, armchairs from Heritage-Henredon (later moved to Wright's Plaza suite), and dining area furniture of the architect's design.

LEFT: The Wrights attended the opening of the Usonian Exhibition House, October 1953.

the museum's board and filed with the New York Building Commission in early 1952. When a permit was denied because of thirty-two building code violations, aggravation mounted for Wright. As he made the necessary concessions to address fire, safety, and other issues, cost concerns loomed large. In December 1953, Wright revoked the permit application and advised Guggenheim he was "work[ing] out a good revision that saves one third present cost yet gives plenty of space and distinction."[28]

The expense and difficulty of dealing with the project's complex mix of personalities, organizations, and issues from his remote offices spurred Wright's 1954 decision to establish a New York base. But, as he prepared to move into his Plaza suite, his problems were far from over: he was the last of the project's originators to remain involved; the building commission had not yet issued a permit; and Sweeney, the museum's new director, was about to become an assertive challenger.

THE NEW GUGGENHEIM REGIME

As the chairman of the foundation's board of trustees, Harry Guggenheim was now running the show. He was an improbable candidate to spearhead the effort to construct one of the century's most controversial cultural institutions. Unlike his uncle, he was not an art connoisseur or collector but was a well-educated man of wealth, diverse interests, and abilities. Beyond his associations with the family's business, he was an early promoter of America's aviation industry and a close friend of Charles Lindbergh, who was a frequent visitor at Falaise, Guggenheim's secluded estate on Long Island's North Shore. A staunch Republican, Guggenheim served as ambassador to Cuba in the late 1920s during the Hoover administration.[29]

Harry's third wife was Alicia Patterson, daughter of Joseph Medill Patterson, founder of the *New York Daily News*. Moses credited the pilot and sportswoman with inheriting her father's "strength, his energy, [and] his colorful nature." Successful in her own right as publisher of *Newsday*, Patterson was an admirer of Wright and his work. Guggenheim and Patterson each brought encouragement and support to the museum project, and they became close friends with the Wrights. The couples frequently entertained each other in their lavish homes.[30] Under Patterson's aegis, *Newsday* critically praised the Guggenheim Museum when it finally opened in October 1959 (see chapter seven).

Alicia Patterson and husband, Harry Guggenheim, at Falaise, their estate on Long Island.

From the outset, Harry Guggenheim made his loyalties clear: by constructing the new museum, he and the trustees would be carrying out their "obligations to the benefactor [Solomon Guggenheim] and our duty to the public."[31] Without Guggenheim's patient negotiations, diplomatic talent, and unflagging commitment, Wright's controversial vision might not have been realized. Generally speaking, the two men enjoyed a cordial, respectful, professional relationship. In correspondence, Wright addressed his client as "*Lieber* Harry," an affectionate descriptor once reserved for Louis Sullivan. Even when pushed to the limit by Wright's intractable stances, Guggenheim addressed the architect as "*Carido Francisco,* who tries me sorely but for whom I have a very great affection."[32]

For the duration of the museum project, Guggenheim would walk the difficult line between Wright's desires and opposing demands made by Director Sweeney, while simultaneously endeavoring to represent the best interests of a largely apathetic board. Guggenheim was successful because he maintained a clear position on the responsibilities and duties of all parties, and, when boundaries were crossed, he firmly stepped into the fray. However, as capable as he was, he could do little to solve the stalled building permit application. For that, Wright sought the help of his commanding "cousin."

THE IRON FIST
OF ROBERT MOSES

Although Moses was not a fan of modern architecture, and his differences with Wright would surface both in the press and face-to-face, the architect knew "Cousin Bob" would be indispensable in negotiating bureaucratic red tape. "Let me assure you that *our* permit will not be one we will get by standing in line at the City Hall—but a special permit with Moses' help and the good will of the Building Commission," he wrote Rebay.[33] His supposition proved correct.

Citing a construction delay of two years, rising building costs, and being "myself, no spring chicken," Wright appealed to Moses in October 1955 for help in securing the elusive permit and "shortening the devastating waste of time." "I don't personally like either the Museum or what's going into it," Moses wrote to Guggenheim, but he offered assistance in the matter, nonetheless, "to help some good friends in a dubious enterprise because they are friends and for no other reason." Guggenheim responded: "Many thanks for your note. . . . Both Frank and I have appreciated your very friendly interest in the Frank Lloyd Wright building even though the building and the Foundation's objectives did not conform to your personal tastes. . . . The Museum, I now very sincerely believe, will be a great addition to the culture of the City of New York."[34]

In total, it would take four years of negotiations and an iron-fisted ultimatum by Moses to the building commission—"Damn it, get a permit for Frank. I don't care how many laws you have to break."—before a permit was issued in March 1956. Described as "long heralded and long deferred" by the *Times,* the structure was now estimated to cost $3 million and construction was projected to take eighteen months to two years. The newspaper, which withheld critical commentary until an official sketch of the structure was published on May 7, ran an editorial the next day reporting that its editors were "somewhat aghast." They felt that Wright had "overshot the mark," likening the building to "an oversized and indigestible hot cross bun." As groundbreaking neared, George N. Cohen, owner of Euclid Contracting Corporation, who wisely told Wright at their initial meeting that he was not an expert but had "come to learn from him," was employed as builder. William Short, an architect in the office of Holden, McLaughlin & Associates, was hired as "clerk of the works," responsible for interpreting Wright's drawings and keeping a close eye on thousands of minute construction details.[35]

On August 16, 1956, thirteen years after Rebay first contacted Wright, ground was finally broken for the monumental museum. Although the building was still three years from completion, Wright imagined the finished structure from the start. Shortly after work began, he visited the site with his publisher, Ben Raeburn, and descended to the deepest point of the excavation. Waving his cane across the sky above, Wright enthused: "A magnificent building, isn't it, Ben?"[36]

THE GUGGENHEIM EMERGES

For several years, the massive building site would be a maze of formwork, scaffolding, and workers as the concrete spiral slowly began to rise. When in residence at the Plaza, Wright frequented the site "in all

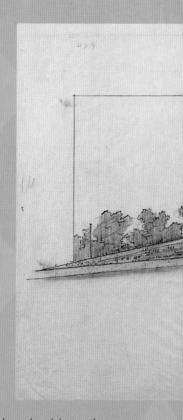

Wright explored the tensile strength as well as the delicate appearance of steel cables in his design for the New Sports Pavilion for Harry F. Guggenheim.

THE NEW SPORTS PAVILION
BELMONT, NEW YORK, 1956

Harry F. Guggenheim had a passion for thoroughbred racehorses. At one time, he was an active and successful breeder who maintained Cain Hoy Stables in South Carolina. In 1953, his horse Dark Star won the Kentucky Derby.[37] Closer to home, Guggenheim was also instrumental in the formation of the New York Racing Association (as it later became known), a nonprofit corporation created to assume ownership of four New York thoroughbred racetracks (Belmont, Aqueduct, Jamaica, and Saratoga) and to "pour millions of dollars into [their] modernization."[38] In 1956, as construction on the Guggenheim Museum began, Guggenheim offered Wright a second commission: the design of the New Sports Pavilion at Long Island's Belmont Park, home of the annual Belmont Stakes.

Conceived primarily for horse racing, the project was also adaptable for other sports, including football and baseball, the fields for which were

radiant heating was planned for the floors.[41] An admirer of the delicate appearance yet remarkable strength of steel cables, which he described as ". . . this beautiful material that spins like a spider and produces a tension so perfect that you can balance a monolith on a pinpoint," Wright used the material integrally in the project's design.[42] Two tall concrete towers supported a translucent roof "suspended on a lacework of slender tensile steel cables," eliminating the need for "pillars of any kind" under the span.[43] Wright liked Guggenheim's suggestion that the roof be retractable, but proposed that in lieu of canvas, a "new plastic we have used at Taliesin West" be used as its construction material.[44]

Dr. J. J. Povlika, a structural engineer who consulted with Wright on several projects, assessed the structural system of the pavilion in 1957. Humorously calling it "Pro-Bono-Publico-Belmontis," Povlika wrote that it was "a revolutionary but very practical and economical build-

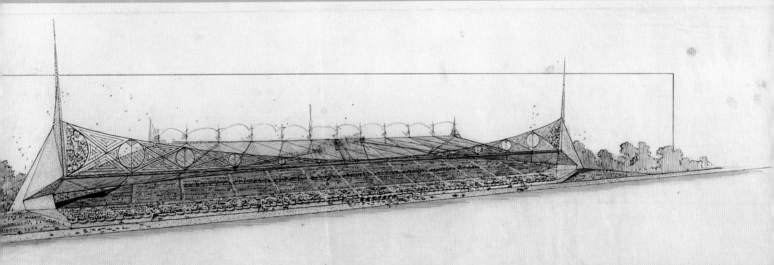

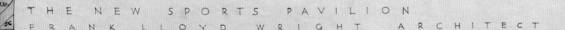

THE NEW SPORTS PAVILION
FRANK LLOYD WRIGHT ARCHITECT

reflected on Wright's plans. The dominant feature of the scheme was an enormous grandstand "with total visibility for 75,000 to 80,000 people" and parking for up to five thousand cars.[39] A tunnel connected the stables to the track, and seating was accessed by a series of escalators that rose from the area surrounding the grandstand. Wright packed the proposed facility with amenities, including a clubhouse with shops, a grand ballroom, and "a broad mezzanine for diners overlooking the race-track [sic]."[40]

The architect's design for the pavilion was structurally daring. A "massive concrete slab" served as the foundation for the grandstand, and

ing . . . covering about 420,000 square feet."[45] He also estimated the total cost of its materials—including translucent, light-diffusing plastic; steel and aluminum cables; reinforced concrete; and seat cushions—at $15.4 million.[46]

Despite Wright's optimism that "someday New York may have a race track pavilion up to modern times," his innovative project was never built.[47] However, in 1963, when the existing 1905 Belmont Park racecourse was "closed for reasons of public safety," the architect's "avant garde design" was once again considered, but not selected, for the redesign for the new facility.[48]

LEFT: Wright directs construction on the Guggenheim Museum. Cohen, Short, and contract superintendent Charles W. Spero surround him, 1957.

FACING: Wright and Sweeney converse at the architect's Sixty Years of Living Architecture exhibit. A model of the Price Tower, which was rising in Oklahoma at the time, stands between them, 1953.

kinds of weather, watching, supervising, advising, correcting, and feeling, no doubt, a deep sense of satisfaction along with the anguish and frustration of it all," said Pfeiffer. As the structure took shape, New York friends and colleagues often wrote their impressions to its architect: "What a pleasure to walk up Fifth Avenue about once a week to see the grand form of the Museum emerging!" noted architect Hugh Ferriss. Conductor Leopold Stokowski, who passed the museum daily, said: "I am thrilled by its beauty and originality. . . . I feel it is going to begin an entirely new era in New York architecture."[49]

In characteristic fashion, Wright described the edifice-in-process in relation to nature: "[It's] the only concern along Fifth Avenue that sees the park. We've cooperated with it." But several features Wright had planned to further incorporate nature into the design and to provide view to the park, including a roof garden and a tea garden, were eliminated in earlier rounds of cost-cutting changes. In the end, he justified the inward focus of the structure by uncharacteristically citing precedent: "It has been firmly established that people go to a museum to look *in* and not *out*."[50]

Over the years, the plans underwent many more revisions made to satisfy code requirements, improve its design, or trim costs. In addition to size reductions, elements that were eradicated included a colorful marble exterior, a series of artist studios around the top ring of galleries, glass tubing in the elevator shafts and dome, and an observatory with a revolving dome and telescope. A curator's apartment and an "ocular chamber" for experimental sound and light projections planned for the adjacent four-story administrative tower, as well as a two-story "historical gallery" (intended to become an income-producing fifteen-story apartment building) would also go unrealized. As the spiral began to take shape, serious philosophical differences between architect and director regarding the disposition of interior spaces and exhibit methods for the art collection would produce even more alterations as the two reached a standoff.[51]

THE IMPASSE

Sweeney, an experienced and respected museum curator, had strong views about many aspects of museum design and the exhibition of art that he attempted to impose on Wright. But the architect dismissed the director as "a standard museum man with established ideas and friends," and he was not pleased with

Sweeney's modification demands, many of which came very late in the process. The most serious point of contention between the two men—one that would consume them and the museum's board for the remainder of Wright's life—was the question of the appropriate display and illumination of the paintings.[52]

Wright, who believed the ramp of his building was uniquely "suited to the display of pictures," sought to "free the paintings from all the clichés" of conventional museums by resting them, unencumbered by glass or frames, in thirty soft ivory-colored alcoves along the ramp's walls. Slanted at about fifteen degrees, the walls would allow the paintings to be viewed as they might be seen on an artist's easel—their "natural" position. "The grand sweep of the new edifice makes the yielding tilt of the picture itself . . . more normal to the line of vision . . . more as the painter saw it himself in changing light," Wright said. Objecting to the harsh artificial light under which art was typically displayed, the architect planned for continuous wall skylights with adjustable louvers to provide illumination from above with supplementary incandescent light employed as necessary.[53]

MoMA veteran Sweeney held firm that his job was to "show off a magnificent collection to its fullest" in the museum's "architecturally spectacular" interior. To him, this meant displaying art in a rigidly modernist fashion—paintings hung in strict upright, not tilted, positions against stark white walls, bathed in florescent light. At the Guggenheim, he would accomplish this "verticality" by affixing the paintings to the ends of horizontal bars extending from the building's angled walls.[54]

In the months preceding his death, Wright worked actively to see his own display plan, which he considered integral to the design of the building, accomplished, imploring Sweeney to take a chance on his pioneering vision: "...The Guggenheim memorial is intended by its design to liberalize this 'static' folly" (of showing paintings in a typical "rectilinear frame of reference")....This new museum...is not yet fully comprehended by the professionals.... Divided we would waste a great opportunity in the world of Art and Architecture—the world where the arts will stand or fall together."[55]

Wright's battles with Sweeney became more acrimonious as the director's demands multiplied and costs escalated. In March 1956, Wright accused Sweeney of trying "to belie the significance and beauty of the whole concept by making an unsuitable warehouse of the museum." If the director prevailed, Wright promised to remove his name from the architectural plans, adding, "I will be ashamed to see the name Guggenheim go up on the building."[56]

Some influential members of the art community sympathized with Sweeney's concerns. In 1956, twenty-one artists, including Willem de Kooning, Franz Kline, and Robert Motherwell, penned a vehement protest about the museum's design to the director and the trustees. Based on published accounts that revealed the sloping walls and spiraling floor, they concluded that the Guggenheim's interior was "not suitable for a sympathetic display of painting and sculpture . . . [indicating] callous disregard for the fundamental rectilinear frame of reference necessary for the adequate visual contemplation of works of art." The group strongly urged the museum to reconsider Wright's plan. Suggesting the architect was more interested in expressing his own personality than in "providing proper quarters for pictures," one signer added, "we shall be compelled to paint to suit Mr. Wright's architecture," with several artists pointing out the architect's negative published opinions about modern art to substantiate their complaints.[57]

Guggenheim replied to the artists' letter publicly, terming their criticisms unwarranted. He pointed out that the ramp's grade was only three percent, just one percent over the city's grade specifications for sidewalks, a difference that would be "unnoticeable" to pedestrians. Wright wrote a more heated reply to his "fellow artists," negating their "rectilinear frame of reference" as "callous disregard of nature": ". . . you all, curator included, know too little of the nature of the mother art: architecture," he said. At the same time, Wright continued to insist that his goal was "not to subjugate painting to the building . . . on the contrary it was to make the building and the painting an uninterrupted, beautiful symphony such as never existed in the World of Art before."[58]

By 1958, neither Sweeney nor Wright had budged in stance. Guggenheim attempted to break the gridlock by invoking process and reminding Wright of the limits of his responsibilities. "The architectural integrity of your building will be preserved," he wrote, but "the technique of exhibiting the art of the museum is the function of the Director of the Museum . . . you argue to invade [his] duties and rights." He also stated that his own job was to "satisfy the Trustees," who required a functional building in which to display art. Naming no names, he sought—above all—a "mutually satisfactory solution to the remaining simple problems that only prima donnas, with their petty vanities, would haggle over too long." Guggenheim went on to advise Wright, however, that he was welcome to physically demonstrate his display concept for all to see and judge. Late that year, the architect replied: "It is humiliating to me at this time in my life to be subjected to the comparative experiment as though on a race track." Perhaps believing that his words alone should be enough to convince his client, it was not until January 1959 that Wright requested paintings from Sweeney for a demonstration of his plan, which would never take place. In the end, resolution occurred when the architect died and Sweeney persuaded the board to accept his white walls.[59]

Wright's 1956 "Middle of the Road" illustration demonstrates his plan for leaning paintings against the curved walls of the museum as well as showcasing them on moveable partitions that allowed for display variation. Wright proposed that cushioned hassocks be placed along the ramp to encourage contemplation of featured art.

A TOUR WITH ALINE SAARINEN . . . AND A FIRST GLIMPSE FOR THE PUBLIC

In September 1957, *New York Times* critic Aline Saarinen, a longtime supporter of Wright's work, joined the architect for a construction tour of the rising museum, which she called Wright's "first imprint on [our] cityscape . . . the most daring and revolutionary in New York." The nattily dressed ninety-year-old architect greeted Saarinen at the site and explained to her his "snail-like structure," emphasizing that it would "bring Central Park across the street" via foliage along its front. Commenting on the artists whose work would be housed there, he commended Piet Mondrian and Vasily Kandinsky for "seeking spiritual relationships," but added "many painters today have taken art from the region of the soul and turned it over to the nervous system."[60]

As they strolled the building, Wright described its key aspects to Saarinen, including a "grand gallery" at the top of the entrance ramp for permanently exhibited paintings, and the multiple alcoves in which artworks could be grouped in a variety of ways. The dome above the building's atrium, he observed,

Guggenheim Museum under
construction, 1957.

ensured one would "never lose the sense of the sky," and that visitors would feel a sense of integration—
of "continuous space" within the structure's curved walls. This building was designed specifically for the
art it houses, implied the architect: "Here, you will see twentieth-century arts and architecture in their
true relation." Wright predicted the building would be finished late spring 1958 at a cost of $3.5 million,
$1.5 million over its construction bequest nearly ten years earlier, and would accommodate nine hundred
to one thousand visitors.[61]

As Wright and Saarinen left the rising spiral, the architect expounded on the building's natural synergy:
"When it is finished and you go into it, you will *feel* the building. You will feel it as a curving wave that
never breaks. You will feel its quiet and consistency. . . . *You* put a capital 'G' on God. All my life I've been
putting a capital 'N' on Nature. I know in my heart that it is all the body of God we're ever going to
see." The two got into a taxi, and, when the driver expressed enthusiasm for his celebrated passenger,
Wright said to Saarinen: "That's notoriety, but it isn't fame. Do I have fame, I wonder?"[62]

While Wright's projected completion date for his new museum would once again prove premature, its
notoriety—and fame—would begin to swell the following August when its scaffolding came down and
the public got its first full view of the controversial structure.[63] Reactions ranged from "scorn" to "admiration" for Wright's "culture dome." Querying a crowd of onlookers as the building reached completion,
a *Times* reporter pronounced that a majority of passersby were either "puzzled or displeased" by the
museum, eliciting comments from "brilliant" to "unusual to say the least" to "ahead of its time." An architect remarked, "A building like this needs a large site. It might have worked in Central Park, but not
here." "All it needs is a cherry on top," added a passing nurse. But a nearby doorman saw it differently:
"That building is solid as hell . . . another eighth wonder of the world."[64]

Several artists visiting from Illinois predicted the Guggenheim would contain "a whole museumful of pictures that people will want to straighten"—"It's obvious that Wright didn't have us in mind—his building is all that counts." Yet one echoed the architect's own words: "the building itself is your easel . . . now the walls become the frame," making each artwork important—"certainly more than if it were one of twenty pictures lined up in a row in a room."[65]

Fourteen more months would pass before anyone would be able to judge the final structure or its interior eccentricities firsthand—work on the building would not conclude until fall 1959. While the press, the public, and the city's power players would turn out in droves for the museum's October opening, the man responsible for their object of fascination—the spiral on Fifth Avenue—would not be among them; three months after his last trip to New York that January, Frank Lloyd Wright was gone.[66]

When its scaffolding came down, curious onlookers pondered the unusual form of the nearly completed museum, 1958.

AFTER WRIGHT
A NEW YORK LEGACY

[
If I had another fifteen years to work,
I could rebuild this entire country.
I could change the nation.

Frank Lloyd Wright, *The Mike Wallace Interview*, September 1, 1957
]

The Wrights left their Plaza suite for the last time on January 27, 1959. Six weeks later, on April 9, America's greatest architect died following emergency surgery for an intestinal obstruction, just six months before the long-awaited opening of the Guggenheim. On April 17, Olgivanna Wright telegrammed the Plaza's manager: "This will authorize John DeKoven [*sic*] Hill to make an inventory of our property in Suite 223 . . . please also send bill to date to me at Taliesin West." Six days later, she informed the hotel that William Short would transact "all business related to liquidating our Plaza apartment." Short packed the suite's furnishings, which were loaded on a truck bound for Taliesin.[1]

Following Wright's death, memorial tributes from across the country and around the world poured in to Taliesin. President Eisenhower wrote to Mrs. Wright, praising her husband's "imaginative talents [that] contributed much to our country . . . his buildings will long stand as a fitting tribute to him." Major newspapers, magazines, and architectural journals ran countless features on the man the *New York Times* called the "radical of architecture," regarded by many as "the greatest architect of the twentieth century." Many of the features suggested that Wright was so far ahead of his time that it would take years to fully comprehend and appreciate his work. MoMA, the museum Wright had berated so often, termed him the individual that "transformed the concept of architecture," and featured a memorial exhibit of photographs of his work. Wright historian and one-time MoMA associate Henry-Russell Hitchcock, who had once called Wright "the Michelangelo of the twentieth century," lamented: "In some sense, we have lost our brashest youthful genius as well as our one Old Master."[2]

Frank Lloyd Wright,
1867–1959.

Friends, foes, and peers alike also paid personal homage to Wright. Philip Johnson called him "the type of genius that comes only once every three or four hundred years." Eero Saarinen effused, "When history sifts down to its short list of lasting names of this century, Frank Lloyd Wright will be on [it]." Mies van der Rohe reflected, "In his undiminishing power, he resembles a giant tree in a wide landscape which year after year attains a more noble crown." Elizabeth Gordon, who described him as "'The Lone Ranger' in American architecture . . . as much a crusading social thinker as . . . a designer," dedicated the entire October 1959 issue of *House Beautiful* to his creative legacy: "Your Heritage from Frank Lloyd Wright."[3]

Always looking toward the future, Wright once said, "I have never wanted to be finished. I have never wanted to feel that what I have done was the best I could do." The astounding $30 million of commissions he left behind were directly assumed by his successor firm, Taliesin Associated Architects.[4] While the architect would never return to New York, his presence in the city would, in one very vital way, only now make itself known, for Wright's Manhattan masterwork—the longest and most contentious project of his career—was about to debut.

Olgivanna Wright, center, stands to the right of Mayor Wagner during the Guggenheim Museum's ribbon-cutting ceremony. Guggenheim stands to Wagner's left.

THE GUGGENHEIM OPENS AT LAST

On October 21, 1959, the $3 million structure that Wright once promised would make the Metropolitan Museum "look like a Protestant barn" finally opened its doors, revealing its long-considered eccentricities to New Yorkers and tourists alike. That morning, architect and friend Edward Durell Stone and his wife, Maria, met Olgivanna and her daughter, Iovanna, Wes Peters, and Eugene Masselink (Frank Lloyd Wright's secretary) at the Plaza Hotel and accompanied them to the museum.[5]

Three hundred devotees and detractors filled the Guggenheim's downstairs auditorium for noontime ceremonies. The serene circular space played host to a series of speeches by distinguished persons, including Secretary of Health, Education, and Welfare Arthur S. Flemming; Mayor of New York City Robert F. Wagner; United States Ambassador to the United Nations Henry Cabot Lodge; Solomon R. Guggenheim's daughter, Countess Castle Stewart; and Harry Guggenheim. Mrs. Wright and Sweeney, who held well-publicized, polemical views about the museum, were not invited to speak for fear their conflicting comments might make the institution a subject of ridicule. The controversial director emeritus, Hilla Rebay, was at home in Connecticut, far from all of the festivities.[6]

While the speakers' comments largely focused on the art promotion and education ideals of the Guggenheim Foundation, they also remarked on the new building, praising its architect. Flemming delivered the keynote, relaying President Eisenhower's description of Wright as "a symbol of our free society which welcomes new expressions of the creative spirit of man." Calling the building a "unique addition in concrete to our skyline," Lodge believed it to be a "refreshing" new edifice for Fifth Avenue and a welcome contrast to New York's sea of glass structures. Commending Wright, he also reminded an audience enmeshed in the Cold War that the controversy the architect provoked could flourish only in a free country. Recalling his Uncle Solomon's vision, Guggenheim predicted that the museum would "live long among the architectural treasures of man." He described his architect's building as "a complete break from the traditional museums of the past . . . not only an evolution but a revolution."[7] Of all the speakers, however, Robert Moses was the most colorful.

For many years, the infamous parks commissioner had been consistently critical of the design of the Guggenheim and the art it would house. On this day, with the architect's widow close by, Moses' words were more amiable: "With all his pretended extravagant contempt for New York, Cousin Frank was convinced in his heart that the Big City could not survive without at least one major building designed by him, and we are now conferring the ultimate honors on the maestro in absentia." Expressing support for "the exploitation of art which I cannot understand," he solicitously added that the building was "evidence that Mr. Wright's youthful and creative spirit will always live."[8]

Following a ribbon-cutting ceremony presided over by Wagner, the public had its first encounter with the building. Over fifteen hundred people were ushered into the soaring atrium Johnson described as "one of the greatest rooms created in the twentieth century." All afternoon, the line to enter the museum stretched a block long. In total, nearly three thousand visitors, far more curious about the eccentric new museum than the art within it, visited the Guggenheim on opening day.[9]

A SWIRL OF CONTROVERSY

That day, as the public jammed the space, the floodgates of critical opinion opened as well, unleashing reactions "rang[ing] from shocked disapproval to awed admiration," according to Stone.[10] Was the building a monument or a museum . . . about architecture or art? What about the inclined ramp and the unusual way the art was displayed? These questions and more weighed on the minds of all those who passed judgment on the coiled structure, including the press, architectural historians, museum directors, architects, artists, and the public itself.

New York's professional community had its first glimpse of the museum on October 19. That afternoon, a preview was held for the press and art critics, followed by an evening reception for artists and architects. Pursuant to these events and the opening, a barrage of diverging opinions began to appear in the media. *Time* magazine, one of Wright's favorite publications, called his inverted ziggurat "a mighty tower and babel of discord," describing controversy its architect would likely have enjoyed. During a construction site visit, Wright once commented to his colleague Short: "Bill, they will still try to figure this one

out a thousand years from now!" A colleague reflected, "Wright . . . would no doubt have welcomed this brouhaha as one means of making architecture a subject of public concern."[12]

Compared with the contained severity of the International Style, the Guggenheim made a fresh, if showy, statement. One writer termed it designed by "an architectural genius who, although he hated abstract art, has paradoxically created the most abstract building of our age." *Newsday* extolled the new museum in glowing terms: "the world's supreme showcase for modern art . . . lauded by many as the architecture of tomorrow" and Wright as "an architect whom many considered to be a century ahead of his time. . . . Like it or not, the Guggenheim Museum has brought controversy back into a field that seemed doomed to musty decay," the newspaper summarized.[13]

While the *New York Herald Tribune* called the edifice "the most beautiful building in America," the *New York Daily Mirror* critiqued "a building that should be put in a museum to show how mad the twentieth century is." The *Times* covered the structure and its opening three times on its front page within a week, with lines clearly drawn between art and architecture. On its pages, Ada Louise Huxtable extolled the "luminous, soaring, unified space," but reasoned, "This is less a museum than a monument to Frank Lloyd Wright. . . . A man of extraordinary genius, he and his work would take second place to nothing. . . . It is inescapable, whether one likes it or not."[14]

The museum was described by the *AIA Journal* as "distinctly out of place" in relation to the staid apartment buildings and townhouses surrounding it. Huxtable reported that Wright champions had admonished those who objected to the building as it rose: "[T]he first baroque building in Rome looked just as startling in the city streets," they said. Lewis Mumford, one of the building's sharpest critics, took Wright to task for turning his back on the park's open landscape as well as to "the varied natural light that were his for the asking" through the creation of a closed spiral form, calling the decision the "bitterest pill" of the resulting structure.[15]

THE "CHAMBERED NAUTILUS"[16]

If the exterior of the museum and its relationship to the city provoked polarized critical comment, its remarkable interior did not—the museum's great central atrium received nearly universal praise. Passing through a low entry, visitors stepped into a vast space that soared six stories high before them. Recalling the great entrance halls of the world's famous Beaux-Art museums, the Guggenheim's atrium was something very new. Turning its back on the cacophony of the city, the space delivered a tranquil yet awe-inspiring experience. "In that room," Johnson said, "museum fatigue is abolished, circulation obvious, simple, direct. It is . . . exciting . . . to be in." Mumford complimented its "exalted proportions." Sweeney observed: "[It is] the heart of the building and gives it the spectacular individuality . . . Wright sought in his avoidance of the conventional concept of an art museum."[17]

Complementing the magnificent space, the building's ramp provided the important element of human scale. Yet, critics disparaged its disconcerting slant as challenging for viewing paintings and people alike, as well as for creating an inflexible path for visitors. One writer noted that while the paintings appeared "askew," the unique experience of seeing works of art at a distance across the atrium and anticipating a close-up viewing when the incline delivered the visitor to them was quite alluring. But Mumford bluntly labeled the ramp an "error that no ingenuity can overcome" despite the museum's best efforts to "neutralize Wright's blunders," referring to Sweeney's method of hanging works of art away from the curved walls.[18]

The director's opening exhibit featured one hundred and thirty-four selected pieces from seventy-five painters and sculptors represented in the Guggenheim Collection. His display plan for exhibiting the paintings would prove to be the most controversial aspect of the new museum, and critical responses to it varied. *Newsday* predictably termed Sweeney's "horizontal bar device" an "outstanding feature of the museum . . . the virtually shadowless lighting [that] has the effect of bathing each painting in a diffused glow rather than a glare." *Times* writer John Canaday acknowledged

Guggenheim admires the museum's vast atrium on opening day.

that while the director's approach compromised "architectural harmony . . . no better compromise could be found," declaring Wright the "Pyrrhic victor." Peter Blake, editor of *Architectural Forum,* a publication that historically supported Wright and his work, praised Sweeney's method as "close to pure genius . . . removed from the powerful architecture . . . [the art works are] given a chance to speak clearly for themselves." But *Art News* disparaged the paintings as "marshmallows stuck to the ends of twigs," dubbing the intense light behind them "glare to shave by," a sentiment seconded by architectural historian Vincent Scully. Huxtable summed up the entire effect as "stunning, if not quite what Wright intended."[19]

Olgivanna disagreed with any and all praise for Sweeney's display plan. She felt it and other contraventions against her husband's aesthetic intentions to be quite serious, telling a reporter that it was likely Wright would not have been present at the opening. "He was too great an artist to forgive the slightest transgression in a creative work," she said. "The white paint is too glaring. . . . And, the paintings, they should have been hung directly on the walls. . . . But we who are not so highly developed can overlook the changes they made in his design. . . . I myself think the place is beautiful, and what changes they did make are not really effective enough to destroy the effect that my husband wanted to produce."[20]

A far less contentious aspect of the building, one Sweeney described as "Wright's most original museum note," was its social quality. The distinctive interactions between humans and art—and among humans themselves—proved to be one of the institution's most exceptional features. Visitors vicariously became an artistic element in the space, setting up a voyeuristic dynamic one writer called "a secondary frieze, a living mosaic." Mumford termed the overall effect "a new kind of mobile sculpture, whose dynamic flow is accentuated by the silhouettes of the spectators." "There is sociability in participation evident on all sides among the spectators," Sweeney concurred. "The play of light and color from one side of the building to the other and the mobile rhythms of the ramp parapets awaken a liveliness in the visitor."[21]

The contemplative museum experience originally envisioned by Rebay and Wright was swept away by the passage of time and evolving circumstances. A new audience for the avant-garde began developing during World War II. By 1959, the business of culture was burgeoning, museums were enjoying record attendances, and modern art was playing a major role. The Guggenheim would grow to become a public forum for a broad dialogue between art and New York City—dramatically demonstrated by the record-breaking response of the museum's most avid constituents.[22]

A PUBLIC SWARM

From the moment it opened, the public clamored to see Wright's monumental masterwork. Many described their initial visit as "much too heady an experience to be assimilated easily," expressing a desire to return. And return they did—in droves. The Sunday following the museum's debut, a crowd of ten thousand waited in a line stretching from Fifth Avenue across Eighty-Ninth Street to Madison Avenue. Despite the bribing of guards, a third of them were turned away. "The public, of course, is completely in the late old rascal's thrall," one writer reflected, crediting the museum with reaching the masses that may never have sought out modern art but came to see the building.[23]

In its first year of operation, one million visitors flocked to the Guggenheim, continuing at an annual rate of seven hundred and fifty thousand for the next few years. A number of international notables were counted among them, including Italian architect Gio Ponti, India's Prime Minister Jawaharlal Nehru, Swedish Princesses Birgitta and Désirée, Empress Farah of Iran, and even a group of Soviet government administrators shocked at seeing the type of radical modern works banned in their own controlled country.[24]

Visitor responses to the museum proved to be perceptive, insightful, and varied: ". . . the building overshadows the art only temporarily, because of its precocious and exciting aspects, and because it too is a work of art," one wrote to the *Times*. "The 'fiery debate' over Frank Lloyd Wright's museum is again the eternal battle of the farsighted genius versus the nearsighted public," penned another. "If a museum is to be a mediocrity in design, then please let's not have a genius such as Wright design one or at least let us urge the genius to restrain his creative capacities."[25]

On opening day, crowds waited for hours to enter the museum in a line that circled the block.

Guggenheim believed that while the throngs of visitors may have been initially attracted to the museum by the controversy surrounding it and because of an awareness of Wright's work, they returned because "they are inspired and delighted with what they see. We believe that the building is both beautiful and functional, [employing] a revolutionary method of interest and value for viewing art. Its overwhelming acceptance indicates that the public agrees with us." For Wright, who often expressed his preference for fame over notoriety, the response would have been immensely gratifying.[26]

Sweeney's display method at the museum, counter to Wright's own, featured paintings hung away from white walls, illuminated by bright florescent light.

"DIFFERING IDEALS"[27]

When the Guggenheim opened, Sweeney referred to it as a "stimulating challenge [that has] the distinction of being unique." Nine months later, he resigned from his post. The *Times* reported "differing ideals" between Sweeney and the Guggenheim Foundation as the cause, but neither would reveal what these were. Reflecting a growing trend toward museum-as-educator and the foundation's own goals, Guggenheim expressed desire to establish new educational programs for the museum's rapidly expanding audience. Huxtable astutely mused that the real reason for the director's departure was that Wright simply "fought Sweeney to a draw from the grave, and Sweeney resigned in apoplectic frustration."[28]

INSPIRED BY THE SPIRAL

The cultural reverberations generated by the Guggenheim Museum were immediate and immutable. From the moment it opened, the "walk-in work of art" inspired creative communities of prominent designers, artists, and architects alike. Perhaps most significantly, however, it launched the trend toward "museum as art," which, while palpable in the decades after the Guggenheim's opening, swelled to an international movement by the dawn of the twenty-first century.[29]

In the years immediately following its debut, the museum's design created an architectural sensation: "All across the country, round buildings are springing up like so many round pegs in a land where rectangular or square-shaped structures have so long been dominant," the *Times* reported. Paying apparent homage to the "see-and-be-seen" dynamic of the Guggenheim, former Wright nemesis Philip Johnson designed a lobby with stacked balconies for his 1964 New York State Theater at Lincoln Center, and his unrealized 1965–66 immigrant memorial for Ellis Island utilized the spiral in its design.[30]

As the 1970s approached and museum attendance continued to soar, the Wright-designed Guggenheim's influence was evident in another way. Renowned architects were being increasingly commissioned to design museums for world-class art collections: Marcel Breuer's Whitney Museum of American Art debuted in New York in 1966, and Mies' Neue Nationalgalerie (New National Gallery) bowed in Berlin in 1968. A decade later, I.M. Pei's East Wing for the National Gallery of Art opened in Washington, D.C. These seminal structures and others like them further heightened the profiles of their internationally prominent locations. "The new museums skim the top talent of the twentieth century and are obviously meant to stand as [masterpieces] for the ages," Huxtable reflected as the buildings swelled in number, observing that there was a "good chance" the structures themselves would "end up as the whole show."[31]

Gehry's expressionistic Guggenheim Museum Bilbao demonstrates the same startling contrast with its urban context that Wright's Guggenheim evidenced on New York's Fifth Avenue nearly forty years earlier.

Today, the worldwide trend toward museums designed by celebrated architects—termed "museum mania" by architecture critic Martin Filler—has generated buildings that have in themselves become "the whole show." The expressionistic Guggenheim Bilbao, designed by Frank Gehry, launched the trend when it burst onto Spain's cultural scene in 1997.[32] Like Wright's Guggenheim before it, the undulating edifice proved highly influential, initiating a fresh era for "museum as art" and paving the way for notable structures to come, including Santiago Calatrava's 2001 Quadracci Pavilion at the Milwaukee Art Museum, and Zaha Hadid's 2003 Contemporary Arts Center in Cincinnati.

Six years after Wright's museum opened, Director Thomas M. Messer described it as ". . . a landmark sought out by travelers from every corner of the earth who come to enjoy it for its own sake and for its contents."[33] Inspired by the pioneering spiral on Fifth Avenue, the same can be said for a host of museums today.

The director's successor was Thomas M. Messer, a Czech-born art historian who, to some extent, reversed Sweeney's alterations to the museum's interior—its display walls were frequently painted a light ivory buff, and paintings were hung closer to them on cushioned brackets that allowed for leveling—gestures that probably still would not have satisfied its exacting creator.[34]

A MUSEUM OBSERVED

Like its architect, the Solomon R. Guggenheim Museum was commanding, controversial, and undeniably magnetic. Just as Harry Guggenheim predicted, Wright's building instantly revolutionized the concept of what a museum "was". . . and might be thereafter. Describing the building as ". . . an extraordinarily personal statement in the midst of a conformist city," Blake prophetically reflected, "If Wright had built nothing else, this space would assure him a special place in the history of architecture. . . . And it will be a constant admonition to all those who see it . . . that creation is, among other things, a constant process of challenging and questioning accepted notions, everywhere."[35]

"The most controversial [building] . . . ever to rise in New York . . . a subject of conjecture and debate for millions," according to the *Times,* was Frank Lloyd Wright's greatest gift to and most tangible achievement in the city. According to Jed Perl, the museum assumed "immediate iconographic power," becoming a world-renowned symbol of the nation's largest metropolis. In 1960, Johnson said, "Civilizations are sometimes remembered only by their buildings," implying that the Guggenheim would be one of those defining structures for America. Huxtable credited the museum with far-reaching influence, inspiring some of the fluid, expressionistic forms we see from today's leading architects: "[The museum represented Wright's] search for a plastic, sculptural architecture . . . where mass and space were one—a concept that would become architecture's leading edge by the end of the twentieth century."[36]

Just inside the Guggenheim's entrance, a memorial plaque designed by Wright features the inscription: "'Let Each Man Exercise the Art He Knows' —Aristophanes." At the museum's opening, Moses said about his "cousin," "After some ninety years, his body wore out, but his mind . . . was undiminished to the end, and his youthful crusading spirit will surely live, for no man of talent was ever less awed by his enemies or more certain of artistic resurrection."[37] For much of his life, New York was such an antagonist for Wright. Although he remained a critic of the metropolis to the end, during his last five years, he also called Manhattan home. There, by practicing the art he knew, he created an enduring legacy for the city and the world.

Frank Lloyd Wright's "temple in a park on the Avenue," 1965.

I consider myself a success only insofar as my life is useful, revealing, and rewarding to my kind. Who knows who is a success until long after the circumstances? Success is measured not in ordinary terms, but what will transpire fifty years later. So fifty years from now, you will know whether or not I am a successful person.

Frank Lloyd Wright, 1957[38]

Wright in New York, 1953.

ACKNOWLEDGEMENTS

The genesis of this book was a twenty-minute session paper delivered at the Frank Lloyd Wright Building Conservancy's 2002 conference in White Plains, New York. It soon became a collaborative project that same year between two writers—a New Yorker living in Virginia and a Virginian living in New York. The authors had much in common, including admiration for the architecture of Frank Lloyd Wright, a love of New York, fond memories of the Plaza Hotel, and a desire to recount the story of the convergence of architect, city, and hotel during one remarkable five-year period in the 1950s.

Many individuals took an interest in the project and helped in varied but invaluable ways as it developed. We appreciate the contributions of each, but would like to mention those without whom this book would not have been realized.

Our research began at the Frank Lloyd Wright Archives at Taliesin West in Scottsdale, Arizona. We are deeply indebted to the following persons there for their warm reception and ongoing support: Director Bruce Brooks Pfeiffer for his encyclopedic knowledge about Wright's work and for his extraordinary patience in answering the endless questions we posed; Margo Stipe, registrar and art collections administrator, for her educated and efficient responses to our research requests and for bringing much additional information of importance to our attention; Oskar Munoz, assistant director, for sharing the archive's wealth of visual images and for his willingness to dig ever deeper into the vaults to find just the photograph we hoped might exist; Indira Berndtson, historic studies administrator, for suggesting and providing transcripts from the archive's extensive oral history collection that shed additional light on our subject.

Special thanks are extended to Bruce, Margo, and Indira, as well as to Hilary Ballon and David G. De Long for their invaluable insights and suggestions provided as readers of our manuscript.

We are extremely grateful to Mike Wallace of CBS, who was an ongoing supporter of this project from its inception. We appreciate him allowing us the unexpected privilege of a personal interview and for his contribution of the book's foreword. Mike's assistant, Jay-Me Brown, was a valued communications conduit and source of assistance.

Gratitude is expressed to the following individuals who generously shared their unique knowledge of Wright, as well as his visits to New York and the Plaza in the 1950s: John Amarantides, Virginia T. Boyd, Cornelia Brierly, Anna and Perla Delson, R. Joseph Fabris, Pedro E. Guerrero, Mary Jane Hamilton, Jack Holzhueter, Neil Levine, Susan Jacobs Lockhart, Patrick J. Meehan, Loren Pope, Tony Puttnam, John Rattenbury, Roland and Ronny Reisley, Dr. Joe Rorke, Arnold Roy, Edgar Tafel, Tom Waddell, and Eric Lloyd Wright.

Others who provided specific information, access, help, or support include Morin Bishop, Barbara Chilenskas, Lorraine Diehl, Paul Doherty, Curtis Gathje, Steve Gilford, Dennis Hart, Martin Hart, Jamie Kimber, Peter Lawson-Johnston, Suzette Lucas, Karl Ludvigsen, Kathy Mayer, Kathy McGilvery, Francis Morrone, Keiran Murphy, George Nichols, Susan Olsen, Kristen Richards, Frank Sanchis, Mary Seyfried, Eric Shapiro, Tom Tisch, and Doug Volker.

We extend our gratitude to the following organizations and institutions and their staff members, as well: ABCNews VideoSource: Tony Brackett; ABC Television Archives: Coral Petretti; American Institute of Architects: Nancy Hadley; Architectural League of New York Archives, Smithsonian Institution: Judy Throm; Archives of American Art, Smithsonian Institution: Wendy Hurlock Baker; The Art Archive: Jamie Vuignier and Veronique Colaprete; Art Institute of Chicago, Department of Textiles: Christa Thurman and Chi Nguyen; AP/Wide World Photos: Kevin O'Sullivan; Avery Architectural and Fine Arts Library, Columbia University: Janet Parks, Julie Tozer, Chris Sala, and Gerald Beasley; BBC Worldwide Americas, Inc. (CBS Television Archives): Lisa Oberhofer and Pearl Lieberman; Balthazar Korab, Ltd.: Carl Kalitta; Bancroft Library, University of California–Berkeley: David Kessler; Canadian Centre for Architecture: Julie Noel, Sophie Deschamps, and Nathalie Roy; the *Capital Times,* Madison, Wisconsin: Dennis McCormick; the *Chicago Tribune:* Yedida Soloff; Cooper-Hewitt, National Design Museum, Smithsonian Institution: Elizabeth Broman; Corbis: Jonathan Chodosh; Culver Pictures: Allen Reuben; Elad Properties: Shannon Lynch; ESTO: Erica Stoller and Christine Cordazzo; Everett Collection, Inc.: Glenn Bradie; F. Schumacher & Company: Avodica Ash, Corinne Kevorkian, and Laura Silvers; FremantleMedia; Getty Images: Rona Tuccillo, Karrie McCarthy, Matthew Perrone, and Elliot Markman; Heritage Furniture Industries, Inc.: Boyd Rufty and Jeff Spencer; *House Beautiful:* Jonathan Chernes; IPN Stock: Margot Bennett and Adam Staffa; Library of American Broadcasting, University of Maryland: Karen King and Michael Henry; Mercedes-Benz USA: Pat Molina, Maryalice Ritzmann, and Valentine O'Connor; Museum of Broadcast Communications: Daniel Berger; Museum of the City of New York: Faye Haun and Eileen Morales; Museum of Modern Art: Kathleen Tunney, MacKenzie Bennett, and Christian Larsen; Museum of Television and Radio: Jane Klain; NBC Television: Yuien Chin, Meg Nakahara, Blythe Boyston, and Erica Schwartz; New York Historical Society: Sarah Osborne; the *New York Times:* Lisa English and Michael Massmann (Redux Pictures); New York Public Library: S. K. Saks; *Newsday* and LAT Reprints: Sharon Minix and Trisha Van Horsen; Pedro E. Guerrero Photography: Pedro E. Guerrero and Dixie Legler; Photofest: Jill Goodwin and Ron Mandelbaum; Plaza Hotel: Tom Cibitano, Michelle Goldstein, and Marisa Intile; Price Tower Arts Center: Kay Johnson; The Sherwin-Williams Company: Donna Watter and Vivien Tsang; The Solomon R. Guggenheim Museum: Kimberly Bush and Francine Snyder; Steinway & Sons: Loretta Russo; Time & Life Pictures: Jeff Burak; United Press International: Charlyne Y. Dunbar; Waldorf Astoria Hotel: Jim Blauvelt and Karen Krugel; Wisconsin Historical Society: Joe Kapler and Harry Miller; Wrightian Architectural Archives Japan: Karen Severns; and Zuma Press: Gretchen Murray.

Special thanks to Stephany Evans of Imprint Agency, Inc., and to Suzanne Gibbs Taylor, Hollie Keith, Laura Ayrey, Carrie Westover, Kurt Wahlner, Melissa Dymock, and Renee Wald at Gibbs Smith, Publisher, for making the publication of this book possible.

The process of researching and writing a book demands much of an author and her family and friends.
We would like to extend the following dedications and personal appreciations.

JANE KING HESSION

I dedicate this book to my parents, my sons, and my husband.

I thank:

My coauthor, Debra, for being the first person to understand the promise of this collaborative project and for having the passion, dedication, and vision to see it through to the very end.

My friends, especially in Minnesota, who always remembered to ask, "How's the book coming?" Your interest gave me the boost I often needed. To Tim Quigley for giving me the opportunity to become involved in the "Wright world" and for generously sharing his prodigious knowledge of Wright's work with me.

My fellow Conservancy board members, current and former, Taliesin insiders, Wright scholars, homeowners, and aficionados who offered valuable information, helpful suggestions, and interesting tidbits along the way.

My friends in Virginia, especially my colleagues at Woodlawn Plantation and the Pope-Leighey House who cheered me on in many ways. Special thanks to Susan and David Stafford for understanding that a good meal, a glass of wine, and the company of friends can quickly smooth a writer's furrowed brow.

Above all, I acknowledge my family, especially my parents, with whom I first experienced the wonder of New York City and the magic of the Plaza Hotel. I will be forever grateful to my wise and loving mother for encouraging me to take pleasure in the simple moments and little things in life, which have a powerful magic of their own. My cousin Barbara Moore helped me keep my sense of humor by giving freely of hers. My "sister" Bettina Blakeney bore the Hudson mantle of responsibility with grace and sent boxes of "cookie love" at exactly the right moments. My sons, Brendan and Connor, taught me most of what matters in life. I thank them for reminding me when I forgot their valuable lessons. No matter where you are, boys, you will always be with me.

Finally, my deep appreciation goes to my husband, Bill Olexy, who traveled with me each and every day on the road to manuscript completion. No matter how rough the journey, he always offered love, encouragement, and a safe haven. You are my compass, Bill.

DEBRA PICKREL

I dedicate this book to my parents.

I thank:

My coauthor, Jane, whose Frank Lloyd Wright Building Conservancy conference session paper, "Frank Lloyd Wright at the Plaza: Two New York Views," was the wellspring of this initiative. Her intelligent and insightful partnership fostered the fulfillment of my long-held dream of becoming a book author.

My family: my mother, Barbara, who provided exceptionally loving, patient, and interminable support throughout this process; my brother, Doug and sister-in-law, Tracie, who provided refreshing levity; my aunt, Phyllis, who has been an inspiration to me; and my cousin, Kathy, who really is more like a sister. In loving memory of my father, Waughford ("Buddy"), a kindred spirit whose love of learning, passion for history, and enthusiasm for accomplishment brought me so much joy and made such a deep impression on my life.

My friends close to home who read my text, gave me honest feedback, and offered unceasing encouragement: Carol, Debra, Henry, Jennifer, Jim, Laura, Laurinda, Lisa, Liz, Lexi and Henry, Liza, Michael and Stephen, and Tina and Ted.

My friends from Virginia who are like family and have always been there for me: Ginger, Gray (and Suzanne and my goddaughter Annabel), Sally, and Todd. I also appreciate Lois and Jane.

My North Carolina sorority sisters with whom I have shared some of the most special times of my life . . . and still do: Becky, Betsy, Claire, Danita, Glenda, Karen, Laura, Maggie, May, Melanie, Monica, Rhonda, Robin, Sandy, Stephanie, Susan, and many more.

My graduate school classmates who always found time in the midst of busy academic schedules to cheer me on: Gina, Mike, Richard, Sarah, Shanon, Rob, Trent, and, especially, Kate, Kim, and Mary. I also extend appreciation to several faculty members for their words of support and inspiration: Bernd (and Enell), Dale, Mel, Pat, Richard, and Stuart.

My friends and associates on the Frank Lloyd Wright Building Conservancy board of directors and in the Wright community—our common interest inspired me toward this project, especially Donna, Jack, Jerry, John, John and Edith, Kyle and Carol, Lynda, and Paul and Phyllis.

And Erik Larson, whose superb scholarship and writing acumen I can only aspire to, but whose encouragement at the beginning of this endeavor meant so much to me.

NOTES

In citing works in the notes, short titles have generally been used. Sources and individuals frequently cited have been identified by the following abbreviations:

BBP	Bruce Brooks Pfeiffer
EG	Elizabeth Gordon
FLW	Frank Lloyd Wright
FLWA	The Frank Lloyd Wright Archives, Taliesin West, Scottsdale, Arizona
FLWF	The Frank Lloyd Wright Foundation, Taliesin West, Scottsdale, Arizona
FLWP/SRGA	The Frank Lloyd Wright Papers, A0006, The Solomon R. Guggenheim Archives, New York, New York
HFG	Harry F. Guggenheim
JdH	John deKoven Hill
MH	Maximilian Hoffman
MoMA	Museum of Modern Art, New York, New York
OLW	Olgivanna Lloyd Wright
RC	René Carrillo
WZ	William Zeckendorf

Frank Lloyd Wright's correspondence, drawings, photographs, and other archival materials are preserved at the Frank Lloyd Wright Archives, Taliesin West, Scottsdale, Arizona.

The correspondence in the Frank Lloyd Wright Archives is indexed in Anthony Alofsin, ed., *Frank Lloyd Wright: An Index to the Taliesin Correspondence,* 5 vols., New York and London: Garland, 1988.

Dates for Frank Lloyd Wright projects are from "List of Projects by Assigned Number," compiled by Bruce Brooks Pfeiffer. "Volume 1: The Frank Lloyd Wright Project, Accession #860202," The Getty Research Institute, Los Angeles.

INTRODUCTION

1. "Greediest mouth," quote from FLW, *Autobiography,* 330; "Rat trap" quote from Illson, "Wright Gives List of What's Amiss."

2. Eleven years had passed since Wright received a handwritten note from Baroness Hilla Rebay, curator of the Solomon R. Guggenheim Foundation, asking, "Could you ever come to New York and discuss with me a building for our collection of non-objective art." (Rebay, letter to FLW, June 1, 1943, FLWA.)

3. Literally, *Taliesin* is the Welsh word for "shining brow." In his autobiography, Wright, who was born in Wisconsin of Welsh descent, wrote of Taliesin as "a Welsh poet, a druid-bard who sang to Wales the glories of fine art. Many legends cling to that beloved reverend name in Wales" (FLW, *Autobiography,* 167).

4. Olgivanna, (née Olga Lazovich) Hinzenberg (1898–1985), who was Montenegrin by birth, became Wright's third wife in 1928.

5. Built and unbuilt project numbers as of 1954 provided by Bruce Brooks Pfeiffer (BBP, letter to author Hession, September 29, 2006).

6. The unrealized project was St. Mark's-in-the-Bouwerie (1929).

7. Stern, et al., *New York 1960,* 14.

8. Ibid., 1205.

9. Ibid., 29.

10. Ennis, "'57 Set a Record for New Office Space."

11. Stern, et al., *New York 1960,* 14, 19, 29, and generally.

12. Charles Luckman as quoted in Stern, et al., *New York: 1960,* 61.

13. New York began to lose its dominance of the television industry during the mid-1950s as some programming moved from New York to Hollywood (Boddy, *Fifties Television,* 1).

14. The "Golden Age" of television, approximately 1949 to 1960, generally refers to the "proliferation of original and classic dramas produced for live television during America's postwar years" ("'Golden Age' of Television Drama").

15. Perl, *New Art City,* 10, 20.

16. Ibid., 63.

17. "A Conversation with Jed Perl."

18. Riis, "How the Other Half Lives," 119.

19. White, *Here is New York,* 25–27.

20. Ibid.

21. Ibid., 19.

22. French and Company on East Fifty-Seventh Street and Ralph M. Chait on East Fifty-Eighth Street were among Wright's favorites. Art gallery and Noguchi information from Meech, *Art of Japan,* 255. Also, BBP, e-mail message to author Pickrel, July 29, 2003. Pfeiffer said Wright was "an avid theater-goer."

23. Muschamp, *Man About Town,* 15.

24. Cooke, "Memories of Frank Lloyd Wright," 42–44.

25. BBP and Wojtowicz, eds., *Wright and Mumford,* 222.

26. "Nautilus's Prune," 20–21. On occasion, Wright also stayed in other New York hotels, including Brevoort House at Fifth Avenue and Eighth Street.

27. Gathje, *At the Plaza,* 23.

28. Alofsin, *The Lost Years,* 30. Cheney and her husband, Edwin, were clients of Wright's in Oak Park.

29. Sadly, this was not to be. In August 1914, Cheney, her two children, and four others were murdered at Taliesin by a deranged servant who also set fire to the house (Twombly, *Frank Lloyd Wright,* 167).

30. Mumford, *Sketches from Life,* 432.

31. The relationship between the two men was pursued primarily through correspondence. Their disagreement over America's involvement in World War II led to a rift. In 1952, after a long period of estrangement, they met for lunch, once again, at the Plaza to repair their damaged friendship. (BBP and Wojtowicz, *Wright and Mumford,* generally.)

32. OLW, *Our House,* 171. Prior to his occupancy, a portion of Guggenheim's private quarters known as the "State Suite" was reserved for visiting dignitaries (Stern, et al., *New York 1960,* 1123). Guggenheim, who died in 1949 before Wright took up residence, is credited by some sources with helping the architect foster a relationship with the Plaza staff. According to Brendan Gill, Wright later stayed at the hotel "apparently" at the expense of Harry F. Guggenheim, Solomon's nephew (Gill, *Many Masks,* 461).

33. Barney, *God-Almighty Joneses,* 10.

34. FLW, note to JdH, 1954. (John deKoven Hill Papers, FLWA.) Wright's identification of Hardenbergh as "master of German Renaissance," is probably in reference to his treatment of certain interior spaces at the Plaza, notably the Oak Room, Wright's favorite public space (Gathje, *At the Plaza,* 32).

35. Meech, *Art of Japan,* 19.

CHAPTER ONE

"Taliesin East":
At Home and At Work in New York

1. BBP, *Guggenheim Correspondence,* 195.

2. Ibid.

3. The Waldorf and Astoria were adjoining hotels. Both were demolished in 1929 to make way for the Empire State Building. Today, the Waldorf-Astoria Hotel stands at 301 Park Avenue, between Forty-Ninth and Fiftieth streets. (Stern, et al., *New York 1930,* 612.)

4. Gathje, *At the Plaza,* 20.

5. Plaza Hotel promotional piece, as seen in Gathje, *At the Plaza,* 18. This "new" Plaza Hotel was the second to stand on its site. The first Plaza was originally designed by Carl Pfeiffer. A mortgage foreclosure during construction resulted in the hiring of "McKim, Mead and White to transform the structure into a luxury hotel in the Classical Style." That building was razed in 1905. (Stern, et al., *New York 1900,* 61.)

6. Reynolds, *Architecture of the City of New York,* 186, 197.

7. Reynolds, *Architecture of the City of New York,* 187. In his will, New York newspaper magnate Joseph Pulitzer bequeathed $50,000 to the city of New York to build the Pulitzer Fountain "like those in the Place de la Concorde, Paris, France." Saint-Gaudens originally cast the statue of Sherman for the Paris Exposition of 1900.

8. Foreman and Stimson, *Vanderbilts,* 69.

9. Gathje, *At the Plaza,* x.

10. Ibid., 23.

11. Ibid., 42.

12. Ibid., generally.

13. Ibid.

14. Roland Reisley (Wright client), e-mail to author Pickrel, February 2, 2003.

15. "The Wright Word."

16. "Outside the Profession," 26–27. The Palm Court wreckage to which Wright refers was the removal of the domed glass ceiling in 1944. This happened for a number of reasons, among them to accommodate air-conditioning units. (Gathje, *At the Plaza,* 26.) In 2004, Elad Properties purchased the Plaza Hotel. Following a major restoration/renovation, the hotel will reopen in October 2007, the hotel's one-hundredth anniversary. In addition to restoring the glass ceiling of the Palm Court, the redesign will produce 182 private residences and 282 hotel rooms. ("Private Residences at the Plaza," 232.)

17. Gathje, telephone interview with author Hession, April 10, 2003. Gathje said the largest suites in the house all faced Fifth Avenue, which was the "desired view" when the hotel was built. He added, "Because fire fighting [at the time] was not as progressive as it is today," lower floors were considered safer and were therefore in greater demand by people of means, while upper floors were reserved for the less well-to-do.

18. BBP, telephone interview with author Hession, September 9, 2002.

19. Gathje, *At the Plaza,* 69, 73. The three other celebrity suites were named for English author Somerset Maugham, American interior designer Lady Mendl (Elsie de Wolfe), and English photographer Cecil Beaton.

20. Hilton purchased the hotel in 1943 for $7.4 million and sold it in 1953 to Park Fifty-ninth Street Corporation for $15 million (Gathje, *At the Plaza,* 163).

21. JdH, interview with Maggie Valentine, FLWA.

22. Ibid.

23. FLW, note to JdH, 1954, FLWA.

24. Wright designed the original house in 1889 and added the studio in 1897. Wright married Catherine Lee Tobin in 1889; they divorced in 1922.

25. Stoller and Levine, *Taliesin West,* 4.

26. Wright lived apart from his primary residences for extended periods of time on at least two other occasions. When he lived in Europe between October 1909 and October 1910, Wright drew up preliminary plans for a "combined house and studio" for a site in Fiesole, Italy, that was not built. (Levine, *Architecture,* 69; also Alofsin, *Lost Years,* 51–53.) Between February and October 1923, Wright lived and worked in rented studio spaces in Los Angeles (De Long, *Designs for an American Landscape,* 186–88). According to Pfeiffer, Wright did not establish a home and studio in Los Angeles "comparable to either the Plaza or Imperial [Hotel] where he lived for extended periods." (Margo Stipe [curator and registrar of collections], FLWA, quoting BBP in an e-mail to author Hession, June 28, 2006.)

27. The original annex to the old Imperial Hotel, the building Wright's new hotel replaced, burned in 1919. That year, Wright designed a new annex with "charming quarters," comprising private living spaces and "a commodious studio-bedroom built as a penthouse above the roof." He lived there with Miriam Noel, who became his second wife in 1923; they divorced in 1927. (FLW, *Autobiography,* 203.)

28. Ibid.

29. Karen Severns (Wrightian Architectural Archives Japan), e-mail to author Hession, March 14, 2006. Also, Meech, *Art of Japan,* 153.

30. Ibid., 157, quoted from Miriam Noel Wright, "The Romance of Miriam Wright," 1932, 2.

31. Ibid.

32. Documentation suggests the renovation of the suite took place between June and December 1954. The living room, initially used as the office, was renovated by July, and the bedroom, later used as the studio/bedroom, was refurbished in November. Several sources contend Wright began to rent suite 223–225 sometime in 1953. Plaza Hotel bills show Wright was charged on a monthly basis for rooms at the Plaza beginning in August 1953. However, the bills do not identify the rooms in question. As Wright had a forty-year history of staying in various rooms at the Plaza, the date he first rented suite 223–225 cannot be determined. However, by August 1, 1954, he was renting the suite exclusively (generally FLW correspondence, FLWA). There are "no definitive records of Wright's stays" in the [Plaza] hotel's archive. (Gathje, interview with author Pickrel, July 10, 2003.)

33. OLW, *Shining Brow,* 173.

34. FLW, letter to John Steinway, November 1, 1954, FLWA.

35. BBP, *Guggenheim Correspondence,* 192.

36. Annotations on the original plan indicate Wright considered bronze velvet for the drapes (Plaza drawing #5532.007, FLWA). Apprentices refurbished the long-neglected shutters (JdH, interview with Valentine, FLWA).

37. Several suite visitors, including client Loren Pope and broadcast journalist Andy Rooney (now of *60 Minutes*), recalled large oriental rugs in the suite, suggesting redecoration over time (Meehan, *Wright Remembered,* 74; Tafel, *About Wright,* 202).

38. Heritage-Henredon chair information from Margo Stipe, interview with author Hession at Taliesin West, Scottsdale, Arizona, March 10, 2006; also Tom Waddell, Wisconsin Collection Manager, FLWF.

39. Annotation Plaza drawing #5532.007, FLWA.

40. R. Joseph Fabris, interview with author Hession at Taliesin, Spring Green, August 19, 2003.

41. Annotation Plaza drawing #5532.007, FLWA.

42. John Rattenbury, "Recollection, 2002," FLWA.

43. OLW, *Our House,* 287.

44. For Wright, Asian art was more than an avocation. "Wright's career as a dealer at one time rivaled that as an architect in terms of both the attention he devoted to it and the financial gain." (Meech, *Art of Japan,* 14.)

45. Ibid., 254–55. After Wright's death, Olgivanna

sold many of the pieces from the suite and from his larger collection (ibid., 258–60). Inventory and descriptions of Asian artifacts in this paragraph and the next from Meech; also Stipe, interview with author Hession, March 10, 2006.

46. Barney, *Almighty Joneses,* 10.

47. Over time, it is probable that Wright had more than one piano in the suite. There was a misunderstanding between Wright and Steinway & Sons over at least one piano. In November 1954, Wright requested a "concert grand" from "the noble house of Steinway." He appealed for "largess" and provided the foundation's tax-exempt "charter." Wright received the piano, but a dispute ensued over the definition of "largess." In July, the company wrote to Wright explaining that in absence of receipt of cash for the unpaid bill, the piano would be confiscated. According to Steinway & Sons records, Wright never owned the piano in question. (FLW, letter to John Steinway, November 1, 1954; Steinway, letter to FLW, July 15, 1955, FLWA; also, Loretta Russo [Steinway & Sons], e-mail message to author Hession, May 26, 2006.)

48. *Library of American Art: Georgia O'Keeffe,* 137.

49. The lotus screen and the Heritage-Henredon vase are still owned by the FLWF. Stipe, interview with author Hession, March 10, 2006; also Joseph M. Seo (Oriental Art Gallery) receipt, October 5, 1953, FLWA.

50. OLW, "Our House."

51. JdH, interview with Valentine, FLWA. Beginning in December 1956, Wright arranged to rent room 229 at the Plaza, in which Hill periodically stayed (Eugene Voit [Plaza Hotel], letter to FLW, November 27, 1956, FLWA).

52. JdH, interview with Valentine, FLWA.

53. OLW, *Our House,* 288.

54. Ibid.

55. Meehan, *Wright Remembered,* 74.

56. Ibid.

57. Ibid.

58. "Wright Revisited," 26–27.

59. "Legendary" quote and author information from Johnston, obituary: "Ben Raeburn"; also Ben Raeburn, video interview with Indira Berndtson and Greg Williams, FLWA.

60. Both "Rebhuhn" and "Raeburn" were changed from the original "Rebhun." In the 1930s, Raeburn worked as office manager for his uncle, Ben Rebhuhn, publisher of the Falstaff Press. In 1939, Raeburn was sentenced to two years in prison for "sending what were then considered obscene material through the mails" for the press. Rebhuhn also served time. In 1940, Wright wrote a letter to the Parole Board in Washington, D.C., asking for "mercy in this matter of parole" for both men. Sentencing information: Johnston, obituary: "Ben Raeburn"; also Ronald Rebhuhn, interview with George M. Goodwin, July 10, 1994, and FLW letter to Walter K. Urich, August 19, 1940, FLWA.

61. Details and quotes of meeting from Raeburn, interview with Berndtson and Williams.

62. Ibid.

63. Caedmon Records was formed in 1952 by two young Hunter College graduates: Barbara Cohen (Holdridge) and Marianne Roney (Mantell). Wright was one of a series of twentieth-century luminaries, including Dylan Thomas, Colette, e.e. cummings, and Tennessee Williams, to record for the label that strove to "produce talking records that would not talk down to their audience." ("Closing the Poetry Gap.")

64. Raeburn, interview with Berndtson and Williams.

65. Longmans, Green originally published *An Autobiography* in 1932. Duell, Sloan and Pearce published an expanded version in 1943. Horizon also published four books by Olgivanna and, after Wright's death, published additional anthologies of his works and writings.

66. Fleischer, "Letter From New York."

67. The suite was also known to some as "Taliesin the Third," a reference to its chronological rank among Wright's residences (OLW, *Our House,* 287).

68. BBP, e-mail to author Pickrel, July 29, 2003.

69. Ibid.

70. To lighten his load, Hill had Wright's Mercedes-Benz, which was garaged downstairs, at his disposal. Automobile dealer Maximilian Hoffman, a client of Wright's, provided the car for the architect's use (see chapter 3). (JdH, interview with Valentine, FLWA.)

71. Tafel, *Apprentice to Genius,* 208.

72. The Guerrero photographs were shot in one session in January 1959. Wright, who died four months later on April 9, never saw them (Pedro Guerrero, telephone interview with author Hession, September 13, 2002). Guerrero photographed the suite in color, but the photographs have been published most often in black and white, including in Guerrero's 1994 book *Picturing Wright* (Dixie Legler, e-mail to author Hession, July 12, 2006).

73. OLW, *Our House,* 287.

74. Ibid., 287–88.

75. BBP, *Crowning Decade,* 188. Schneider, who later married apprentice John Rattenbury, served as Olgivanna's general secretary at the time.

76. Ibid.

77. OLW, *Our House,* 288.

78. Ibid.

79. BBP, *Crowning Decade,* 188.

80. Generally, FLW's Plaza Hotel bills, FLWA.

81. S. B. Lee, letter to FLW, March 30, 1954, FLWA; letters to S.B. Lee, April 5, 1954 and August 22, 1957, FLWA.

82. BBP, telephone interview with author Hession, September 9, 2002.

83. BBP, e-mail to author Pickrel, July 29, 2003.

84. Room description by Gathje, *At the Plaza,* 30. According to Olgivanna, her husband pointed out "the beauty of the painted ceiling" whenever he was in the room (OLW, *Shining Brow,* 173).

85. Barney, *God-Almighty Joneses,* 10.

86. Ibid.

87. Gathje, *At the Plaza,* 32.

88. Ibid.

89. Everett Shinn (1876–1953) was an American painter and member of the Ashcan School, a group of "American artists who attacked social injustice in the early 20th century" (Frazier, *Dictionary of Art History,* 36, 631). Date of the murals from Gathje, *At the Plaza,* 76. Elad Properties plans to restore the Shinn murals as part of their refurbishment of the hotel ("Private Residences at the Plaza").

90. Wright refers to the Masieri Memorial (1953, unbuilt). Quote from "Outside the Profession," 26–27. Air-conditioning quote from "Nautilus's Prune," 20–21.

91. Gill, *Many Masks,* 490.

92. Ibid.

93. Marty, *Taliesin Fellowship,* 63.

94. Ibid.

CHAPTER TWO

**Battling the "Glass Box Boys":
The Skyscraper and the City**

1. "Golden age," construction reports, and midtown as epicenter from Stern, et al., *New York 1960,* 51, 61–62. "Architectural symbols" from Levine, *Architecture,* 366.

2. Hitchcock information from Kentgens-Craig, "Search for Modernity," 306–7; and Hitchcock, *Modern Architecture,* 162. Hitchcock termed the style's practitioners the "New Pioneers." Origin of International Style from Gelernter, *History of American Architecture,* 237–238. "It utilized" from Bender, "Review: Scully's Way."

3. Bauhaus description from Gelernter, *History of American Architecture,* 37, 238. International Style

description adapted from Hitchcock and Johnson, *International Style,* 20. Modernism in America from Gelernter, *History of American Architecture,* 241–55. Le Corbusier was the proponent of highly functional "machines for living in" and described proper office buildings as "adequate machines for business for swarms of people—human beehives" (Brock, "Le Corbusier Scans Gotham's Towers"). Wright called him "the mechanist" (Breit, "Talk with Frank Lloyd Wright").

4. Advantages of International Style structures from Peter, *Oral History,* 42.

5. Curtain wall technology and sheathing from Condit, *Chicago School of Architecture,* 80–81, 83, and from Gelernter, *History of American Architecture,* 204–6. Prior to the development of curtain wall technology, a building's height was determined by the limitations of its load-bearing masonry wall construction, "the thickness of [which] grows in proportion to the height of the building." In a curtain wall building, the steel frame is the structure. The curtain wall itself, or sheathing of the building, is non-load bearing and therefore can be constructed of a variety of materials. (Trachtenberg and Hyman, *Architecture from Prehistory to Postmodernity,* 473–80.)

6. "Brick and terracotta," ibid. Mies's aesthetic from Gelernter, *History of American Architecture,* 266–67. "Prototypes" from Ennis, "Building is Designer's Testament."

7. Wright as quoted in Burns and Novick, *Frank Lloyd Wright.*

8. Description of Park Avenue from Stern, et al., *New York 1960,* 330. UN design committee and final scheme from Stoller and Loeffler, *United Nations,* 1, 7. Secretariat Building details from ibid.,7, 9, and "The Story of the United Nations Headquarters." Wright described the structure as a "tombstone" . . . "a super-crate, to ship a fiasco to hell." (Astragal cable reply, *The Architects' Journal*: 183; and "Published Comment on the United Nations Headquarters," 158–59.) The complex's other two primary buildings, the General Assembly and the Conference Building, were completed in 1952 (ibid.). Following the war, Park Avenue's rent-controlled apartments, with rates based on 1943 post-Depression levels, were unprofitable, and rezoning led to the area's dramatic conversion from what was largely a chic residential district into a bustling commercial center (Stern, et al., *New York 1960,* 330).

9. "Twenty-one story" from ibid., 338. "Earlier imaginings" from Krinsky, *Gordon Bunshaft,* 18–20. Plaza description from Louchheim, "Newest Building in the Newest Style." Seagram Building from Stern, et al., *New York 1960,* 342, 346. SOM's Bunshaft also worked briefly for Edward Durrell Stone. The basic organization of Lever House was

presaged by George Howe and William Lescaze's 1932 PSFS Building in Philadelphia, the first American skyscraper to fully reflect the principles of European modernism. (Gelernter, *History of American Architecture,* 252.) Wright called SOM "three blind Mies" and "Skiddings, Own-more, and Sterile" (Stern, et al., *New York 1960,* 50, 340; and Gill, *Many Masks,* 444). Le Corbusier was cut from the final list of architects under consideration for the Seagram Building commission because he lived in Paris. Johnson was a notable critic, curator, and author-turned-architect who organized Mies's (as well as Le Corbusier's) first visits to America. Mies asked him to partner on the Seagram design based on his long-term support. Johnson commissioned Mies to design his New York apartment. (Schulze, *Philip Johnson,* 243–44; and "About Philip Johnson.") For more information about Johnson, see endnote 50.

10. "Architecture has" from Astragal cable reply, *The Architects' Journal,* 183. Wright's rejection from Schulze, *Philip Johnson,* 243. Other prominent architects were also rejected for the UN committee: Alvar Aalto because Finland did not belong to the UN, and Mies and Gropius because their German birth and careers made them "unpalatable" (Stern, et al., *New York 1960,* 609). In 1953, Mumford expounded: ". . . for [Wright], cooperation is a kind of self-betrayal" (Mumford, "The Sky Line," 109).

11. "Mountain range" from Louchheim, "Development of the Skyscraper." Aline B. Louchheim married architect Eero Saarinen in 1953. The two were good friends with the Wrights. "Lack spiritual" from McAndrew, "Our Architecture is Our Portrait." "Dramatic revolution" from Stern, et al., *New York 1960,* 332. "Stark glass" from Huxtable, "Park Avenue School of Architecture."

12. Gill, *Many Masks,* 483.

13. Wright quoted in Meehan, *Master Architect,* 75.

14. Wright's background from Smith, *America's Master Architect,* 8. "Nature was" from Levine, *Architecture,* xvii. The Transcendentalists saw God in nature's beauty.

15. "Free architecture" from BBP, *Collected Writings,* 60. "Architecture of nature" from Meehan, *Master Architect,* 75. "Specious" from FLW, *American Architecture,* 80. Qualities of organic architecture from Rattenbury, "Living with Frank Lloyd Wright."

16. Wright's thoughts on "individuality" from FLW, *Frank Lloyd Wright on Architecture,* 33–34. "Democratic freedom" from FLW, *American Architecture,* 76. "Principle" from FLW, *Story of the Tower,* 11. "Richardson, Sullivan, and Wright are always regarded as the great triumvirate of American architecture," says architectural historian Condit in *Chicago School of Architecture,* 44. Sullivan was a principal of the Chicago firm Adler and Sullivan. The German descriptor *Lieber Meister* translates as

"beloved (or "dear") master."

17. "From the inside" from Peter, *Oral History,* 123. "The total absence" from Wright, *Future of Architecture,* 95. In March 1901, Wright delivered a seminal speech, "The Art and Craft of the Machine," at the Chicago Arts and Crafts Society at Hull House, addressing the machine's capabilities to enhance modern life.

18. Continuity explanation from FLW, *Natural House,* 20. "I have" from Peter, *Oral History,* 25. "Architecture . . . would just" from Meehan, *Master Architect,* 313.

19. Wright quoted in BBP, *His Living Voice,* 49.

20. "Artistic form" from Saarinen, "Pioneer of Modern Architecture." (The exterior walls of previous skyscrapers were articulated in "layers.") Nineteen twenties and new commissions from Ballon, "Vertical Dimension," 5–9. Wright's first two unexecuted tower commissions were the Luxfer Prism Office Building for Chicago in 1895 and the Press Building for San Francisco in 1912.

21. This is a representational list of New York's "glass box" buildings constructed between 1954 and 1959. Some have changed ownership since construction. (Stern, et al., *New York 1960,* 301, 335, 337, 356, 377; and White and Willensky, *AIA Guide to New York City.* 232, 278, 282, 284, 297.)

22. National Life Commission from ibid., 7. Sheathing from Levine, *Architecture,* 175. "Work of art" and "never constructed" from BBP, *Treasures,* 30. "First sheltered-glass" from BBP, *Collected Writings,* 154. Wright dedicated this building to Sullivan.

23. Date of letter from BBP, e-mail to author Pickrel, October 23, 2006. The St. Mark's-in-the-Bouwerie project is dated 1929. Design description from Ballon, "Plan for St. Mark's-in-the-Bowery"; and Ballon, "From New York to Bartlesville," 104. Wright employed the modern materials and prefabricated construction that the au courant European modernists favored, with distinctive results. The idea of elevating the towers from the ground—in this case, on pedestals—and placing them in a park-like setting was borrowed from Le Corbusier (ibid.). Guthrie met Wright in 1900, commissioning a house from him in 1908 (unconstructed) and was also the client for the architect's 1927 Steel Cathedral project (non-site specific). "Bowery" is an adaptation of the Dutch word *bouwerie,* meaning "farm." (Ballon, "Plan for St. Mark's-in-the-Bowery"; and Hoffman, *Frank Lloyd Wright,* 63.)

24. "Modern" from "What Architects are Talking About," 53–54. "Some of the most" from "Frank Lloyd Wright, Architect: St. Mark's Tower," 1–4.

25. "Odd-type" from "Odd-Type Buildings." Taproot plan as model from Ballon, "Plan for St. Mark's-in-the-Bowery"; and Levine, *Architecture,*

n69, 472.

26. Building date from Louchheim, "Wright Analyzes Architect's Needs." Building description from Gill, *Many Masks*, 373. Mumford viewed the Johnson Wax Research Tower as Wright's "answer" to the International Style: "an outplaying of Mies . . . at his own game" (Mumford, "The Sky Line," 115).

27. Building details from Ennis, "Skyscraper Rises in Rural Setting"; Louchheim, "Wright Analyzes Architect's Needs"; and Ballon, "Frank Lloyd Wright and the Vertical Dimension," 11. Price Tower was constructed from 1952 to 1956.

28. Social implications of the skyscraper from Ballon, "From New York to Bartlesville," 104. "The skyscraper is" from BBP, *Collected Writings*, 154. Wright believed that the urban skyscraper had "unintentionally, hastened the process of decentralization" (ibid.). Seriously interested in city planning, Wright developed a "Skyscraper Regulation" plan in 1926 in an attempt to mitigate city congestion. The scheme set guidelines for the height and direction of tall structures to minimize caverns and shadows, and incorporated strategic traffic systems, balcony sidewalks, garden plantings, and restaurant and recreation areas to humanize the arrangement. (BBP, *Treasures*, 37.)

29. Suggestion from sons from Ramírez-Montagut, "The Tower Rises," frontispiece. "Every side" from Ballon, "From New York to Bartlesville," 111. "The central steel" from FLW, *Story of the Tower*, 16. "The building," ibid., 17. Bruce Goff, a noted Oklahoma architect and Wright admirer, recommended Wright to Price's sons (Ramírez-Montagut, "The Tower Rises," frontispiece). Load transference to the building's inner core meant individual floors could be thinner at their edges and thicker at their centers (Alofsin, "Pinwheel on the Prairie," 30). Harold Price Sr. was also Wright's client for the 1954 Price (or "Grandma") House in Paradise Valley, Arizona.

30. Generally, ibid., 36. "Mellow" from FLW, *Story of the Tower*, 19.

31. Alofsin, "Pinwheel on the Prairie," 32.

32. Peter, "The Clichés Are His Own." *The Disappearing City* reference from Levine, *Architecture*, 218. Wright believed the automobile, telephone, and telegraph eliminated the need for urban concentration (Ballon, "From New York to Bartlesville," 108).

33. Community description, generally, Levine, *Architecture*, 220–22. "Out in the country" from "metropolitan misery" from FLW, *Future of Architecture*, 151, 153. "Bring the country" from Meehan, *Master Architect*, 130. Wright said overcrowding in New York was compounded by its "gridiron" plan, which clogged traffic and fed congestion (FLW, *Future of Architecture*, 156).

34. Details of community from Levine, *Architecture*, 220–21; and "Architect Models New Type of City," 16–17. The fundamental unit of Broadacre City was the single-family house. The architect termed the least elaborate of these "Usonian" (Levine, *Architecture*, 222); for more information, see chapter three, Usonian Exhibition House reference. Benefits of country tower siting from FLW, *The Living City*, 52–62. St. Mark's inclusion and model date from Levine, *Architecture*, 220–21. The model represented four square miles ("Architect Models New Type of City," 16–17). Edgar Kaufmann, Wright's Fallingwater client, partially funded its construction (Levine, *Architecture*, 470, n37). Construction and Rockefeller Center display (April 15 to May 15, 1935) from De Long, "Evolution of the Living City," 28. The model was also shown in Madison, Wisconsin; Pittsburgh; Washington, D.C.; and the Iowa County Fair in Wisconsin and in Marquette, Michigan (ibid.). Wright cautioned that the model was not to be considered an actual design (ibid., 31).

35. Ibid., BBP, *Crowning Decade*, 20. "Road Machine" description from Legler, ed., "Frank Lloyd Wright's Automobiles," 10. Foreseeing escalating highway congestion, Wright supported the use of smaller cars to mediate these circumstances and also the waste of natural resources. Predicting the eventual downfall of passenger trains, Wright envisioned high-speed monorail trains for his "living city" (De Long, "Evolution of the Living City," 25–26, 31, 36, 38).

36. "Advancing suburbanization" from Abbott, *Urban America*, 36, 42. "Whether the" from Peter, "The Clichés are His Own." Peter Blake, former editor of *Architectural Forum*, reflected on Broadacre: "If Corbu [Le Corbusier] and Mies supplied the basic functional and structural framework for tomorrow's city, Wright suggested something even more important: a way to give life to the city" (Blake, *Master Builders*, 418). Urban studies scholar Michael Quinn Dudley credits the Broadacre project with presaging the defense dispersal movement of the Cold War years (Dudley, "Sprawl As Strategy: City Planners Face the Bomb," 52–63).

37. "Flexibility" from FLW, *Story of the Tower*, 17. "Three offices" and descriptions of spaces from Alofsin, "Pinwheel on the Prairie," 35; and Ramírez-Montagut, "Exhibition Catalog," 132, 145.

38. Ibid., 35.

39. Ibid., 41. "Here is" from "Frank Lloyd Wright's Concrete and Copper Skyscraper," 101. When plans were released for the building, *Time* predicted: "When the Price Tower is completed, in about a year, at an estimated cost of $1,500,000, it may well be the costliest building, foot for foot, ever erected in the U.S." ("Real Estate: Prairie Skyscraper," 94). Bruce Goff was one of the build-

ing's sole residential tenants from 1956 to 1963. Sizeable rents and constricted space hindered demand for the apartments (Kirkham and Perkins, "Interiors, Furniture, and Furnishings," 96–97).

40. "Tree that escaped" from Ennis, "Skyscraper Rises in Rural Setting." "Witness the release" from BBP, *Collected Writings*, 154. The Price Tower was featured in a 1953 skyscraper exhibit at New York's Architectural League (Louchheim, "Development of the Skyscraper").

41. "Neither international" from Wright, "Frank Lloyd Wright Speaks Up," 87. FLW, interview by Mitzman, "The Changing Face of Park Avenue."

42. "America first" from Mumford, "The Sky Line," 110. "Old totalitarian cult" from FLW, "Frank Lloyd Wright Speaks Up," 88. "Nuremberg" from Cooke, "Memories of Frank Lloyd Wright," 43. "Communistic shadow" from FLW, "Frank Lloyd Wright Speaks Up," 87. "Simplicity and abstraction" from Gelernter, *History of American Architecture*, 220.

43. Kentgens-Craig, *The Bauhaus*, xix–xx.

44. Gropius comment from Peter, *Oral History*, 179. Mies's comment from Kentgens-Craig, *The Bauhaus*, xx, sourced from William H. Jordy, "The Aftermath of the Bauhaus in America," 489. In a 1955 interview, Mies relayed that he had "learned a lot from Wright. . . . You know, the way he puts a building in the landscape and the free way he uses space and so on" (Peter, *Oral History*, 159).

45. "Holland was" from "Nautilus's Prune," 21. "A style which" from Woolf, "Pioneer in Architecture Surveys It," 15. Pfeiffer comment from BBP, *Collected Writings*, 45, 49–50.

46. First retrospective from Brock, "A Pioneer in Architecture"; and Stipe, registrar and arts collections administrator, FLWA, e-mail to author Pickrel, April 10, 2006. Description of MoMA from Stern, et al., *New York 1960*, 1205.

47. Smith, "The Show to End All Shows," 24–28.

48. Promulgation of term from Kentgens-Craig, "Search for Modernity," 305. Details of exhibition from Kentgens-Craig, *The Bauhaus*, xi–xiii, 305–6. "Heavily influenced" from Bender, "Review: Scully's Way." Johnson joined MoMA in 1930, becoming the first director of its Department of Architecture in 1932. In 1941, he enrolled in Harvard's Graduate School of Design to study architecture. In 1946, following wartime service, Johnson returned to MoMA, writing and curating while building an architectural career. He left MoMA in 1954 to focus on the practice of architecture, following comments from Wright that he "practiced when he felt like it" and the rest of the time remained in a "protected position from which you criticize all of us." Johnson's most recognized work is likely his own residence, "The Glass House" (1949) in New

Canaan, Connecticut, which Wright abhorred. "First director" from "Art in Review"; Wright's comments and generally, from Schulze, *Philip Johnson,* 82–86, 186–90, 223, 225; Goldberger, "Philip Johnson Dead at 98"; and Stern, et al., *New York 1960,* 1205.

49. "Conceived to showcase" and participants from Smith, "The Show to End All Shows," 24; "the work of the Europeans" from Kentgens-Craig, *The Bauhaus,* xi-xiii. The exhibit traveled after its New York showing. Its first stop was the Sears Roebuck Building in Chicago, Wright's home turf, where it opened on June 8, 1932 (ibid., n54, 61). Wright called the European modernists "Philip's foreign legion" (Schulze, *Philip Johnson,* 223).

50. "The greatest architect": Johnson formally delivered this comment during his 1954 "Seven Crutches" lecture, but said that he had passed the thought—which was "conceived in a retaliatory frame of mind"—around his New York circle of friends as early as 1932 or 1933. He later apologized for the statement (Schulze, *Philip Johnson,* 222; and Johnson, *Writings,* 192–93). Description of Wright's inclusion from Smith, "The Show to End All Shows," 24.

51. Comments from Brock, "Architecture Styled 'International.'" Hitchcock (whose stance was softer than Johnson's) credited Wright with "the revision and replacement of traditional concepts which alone could bring a new architecture generally into being." Mumford convinced Johnson to include Wright in the exhibit, then secured Wright's reluctant agreement to participate. Later, when Wright threatened to withdraw, Mumford coerced him to change his mind by expressing concern about the architect's "own place" and what his absence might imply. (Smith, "The Show to End All Shows," 24–28.) Years later, Johnson reflected: "[In the end, Wright] sent a beautiful model . . . all the time, he really wanted to get shown." (Burns and Novick, *Frank Lloyd Wright.*)

52. "When [Wright] began," ibid. These seminal buildings were designed and constructed following the 1932 formation of the Taliesin Fellowship, a group of men and women who would be known as Wright's "apprentices" (Levine, *Architecture,* 218).

53. "Rebuffing" from Tafel, *Apprentice to Genius,* 65–66. "Mended fences" from Smith, "The Show to End All Shows," 32; and Meehan, *Wright Remembered,* 45. "Considering Mies" from Tafel, *Apprentice to Genius,* 70. Mies's stay at Taliesin, ibid., 69–70. End of friendship from Meehan, *Wright Remembered,* 53. Johnson meeting from Smith, "The Show to End All Shows," 23–28. Swatting flies at Taliesin, Wright was known to exclaim, "That's Gropius!" or "That's Corbusier!," striking down his modernist adversaries one by one (Tafel, *About Wright,* 57). In 1937, both Gropius and Mies immigrated to America on the heels of the Nazis' rise to

power and their subsequent instigation of the closing of the Bauhaus in July 1933. Gropius was the design school's founding director, and Mies was its last. Gropius practiced architecture with Maxwell Fry in London from 1934 to 1937 before coming to the United States. Gropius and Mies became American citizens in 1944. Their appointments to highly visible academic positions resulted in the overturning of the country's pervasive Beaux-Arts curriculum in favor of the Bauhaus aesthetic, shaping the future of the nation's built complexion. Mies was director of the Department of Architecture at Chicago's Armour Institute (now Illinois Institute of Technology, or IIT) from 1938 to 1958. Gropius, who shared an architecture practice with Marcel Breuer from 1938 to 1941, was appointed chair of the department of architecture at Harvard's Graduate School of Design in 1938, a position he held until 1952. He was awarded the AIA Gold Medal in 1959, and Mies received it in 1960. (Generally, Droste, *Bauhaus: 1919–1933,* 236, 245, 249; Kentgens-Craig, *The Bauhaus,* 35, 176; Gelernter, *History of American Architecture,* 255; and Lupfer and Sigel, *Walter Gropius,* 93.)

54. "I defy" from Gill, *Many Masks,* 486. "He claims" from Lescaze, "Architect's History." Other European "glass box boys" practicing in America: Austrian Rudolph Schindler, an early practitioner of modernism, worked for Wright in Chicago before establishing his own practice in Los Angeles in 1921. He collaborated with fellow countryman and émigré Richard Neutra beginning in 1925. ("Rudolph M. Schindler.") New York architect William Lescaze emigrated from Switzerland in the 1920s. (Lanmon, *William Lescaze,* 20, 28.)

55. Unbuilt details from Ballon, "Vertical Dimension," 5. "Still shut out" from Ballon, "Plan for St. Mark's-in-the-Bowery." In addition to the projects mentioned in this chapter, these Wright tower designs also remain unconstructed: Crystal Heights (1939, Washington, D.C.), Rogers Lacy Hotel (1946, Dallas), and the Golden Beacon (1956, Chicago).

56. Wright as quoted in Buck, "Sky City Plan."

57. Building details from Ballon, "Vertical Dimension," 12. "I detest" from Buck, "Sky City Plan." "Cloudscraper" from "Frank Lloyd Wright Day," 21. "A mouse" from "Wright Plans a Mile-High Building Here."

58. "100,000," "tetrahedron," and "steel-in-tension" from BBP, *Treasures,* 138; "to a point" from Buck, "Sky City Plan No Idle Dream, Says Wright"; "the future," "large green," and "sweep New York" from Meehan, *Master Architect,* 237; and "rehouse" from "Frank Lloyd Wright Day," 106.

59. Wright's cost estimate and "no one can" from BBP, *Treasures,* 138, 140. "Like a great" from Hoppen, *Seven Ages,* 167.

60. "Pretentious shells" from BBP, *Collected Writings,* 45, 49–50. "I'm only" from Peter, *Oral History,* 132.

61. "Violent therapy" from Saarinen, "Pioneer of Modern Architecture," 44, 47. "New Formalists" and rise of Expressionism from Gelernter, *History of American Architecture,* 269–70, 273–79.

CHAPTER THREE

Courting the New Consumer:
Foreign Automobiles and Domestic Designs

1. Stern, et al., *New York 1960,* 8. (Ibid.) The term "Megalopolis" was coined by French urban geographer Jean Gottmann in 1961.

2. Cohen, *Consumers' Republic,* 251, 293; "happy-go-spending," 194 (*Redbook* magazine's 1957 promotional film *In the Suburbs* coined this term).

3. Ibid., 292–93; Hine, *Populuxe,* 3–5; and Bryson, "The Greatest Good," 114. WZ quote, and generally, from Stern, et al., *New York 1960,* 14, 19, 29.

4. "The most important" from FLW Statement to the Press, undated, FLWP/SRGA. Comment about luxuries and "kept the butcher" from FLW, *Autobiography,* 118; and BBP, "Frank Lloyd Wright in Manhattan," 7–8.

5. Wright's extant retail spaces include the V. C. Morris Gift Shop (1948, San Francisco), now Xanadu Gallery, purveying "folk art international"; the Anderton Court Shops (1950, Beverly Hills, California); and the Hoffman Showroom, now owned by Mercedes-Benz North America.

6. FLW, *Autobiography,* 322–23.

7. Legler, "Architecture and the Automobile," 5–7. Wright's Gordon Strong Automobile Objective and Planetarium project was a recreational facility encircled by a spiraling roadway. In the 1930s, "automobility" figured prominently in Wright's Broadacre plan (see chapter two: "The Tall Tower in the City Reimagined"). He also developed a concept for standardized gas stations. In the 1940s, his automotive projects included a drive-up laundry and concepts for drive-in banking, a showroom for a Packard dealer, and a Self-Service Garage (1949, Pittsburgh) for Edgar J. Kaufmann. (BBP, *Treasures,* 71, 88, 104.)

8. Luo, "New in the Showroom." Wright designed a mirrored floor and ceiling for the display area, but they were not realized in initial construction. A mirrored ceiling in the design of the Mercedes-Benz logo was installed over the turntable in 1981.

9. BBP, *Treasures,* 34, 104; and Storrer, *Frank Lloyd Wright Companion,* 323, 408. The spiral defined the shape of the Strong Objective, created the traffic flow in the Self-Service Garage, and led shoppers

from the first to second floors of the Morris Gift Shop.

10. Stern, et al., *New York 1960,* 574, 590; Wanamaker quote from Leach, *Land of Desire,* 39; and, generally, 40, 63.

11. Stern, et al., *New York 1960,* 593. The clean lines of the International Style inspired two of the city's well-designed showrooms—Walter Dorwin Teague's 1938 Ford showroom at 1710 Broadway, and the Chrysler Building's 1938 Chrysler Automobile Salon by Reinhard & Hofmeister (405 Lexington Avenue). The Ford showroom was a chic multi-floor affair, but the dramatic Chrysler Salon was perhaps more alluring because of its exclusive East Side location in one of the city's signature buildings. (Ibid., 303–5.)

12. Storrer, *Frank Lloyd Wright Companion,* 408; and Ludvigsen, "Baron of Park Avenue," 154–56. Hoffman was born on November 12, 1904.

13. BBP and Futagawa, eds., *Wright Monograph,* 329; Ludvigsen, "Baron of Park Avenue," 156–57; and Storrer, *Frank Lloyd Wright Companion,* 408.

14. "Lacking funding" and location of first showroom and Jaguar showroom from Ludvigsen, "Baron of Park Avenue," 156–58. "Automotive row" from Stern, et al., *New York 1960,* 593.

15. Johnson's recommendation of Wright and "got along very well" from Ludvigsen, "Baron of Park Avenue," 165. Hoffman worked with foreign manufacturers not only to sell their models but also to help them select and design cars for the U.S. market (ibid., 153).

16. MH, letter to FLW, December 30, 1953, FLWA.

17. Facade description from Cooper, "Offices Will Rise." The building was designed by Emery Roth & Sons.

18. Legler, "Architecture and the Automobile," 5.

19. "Strategies and forms" from Peatross, "Symbol and Catalyst," 170; carport and car design from Legler, ed., "Frank Lloyd Wright's Automobiles," 10. Wright designed the "Automobile with Cantilevered Top" in the 1920s, followed by the "Road Machine" in 1955. The porte cochere, defined as a "carriage porch . . . a doorway large enough to let a vehicle pass from street to parking area," was the carport's historical predecessor. (Harris, *Illustrated Dictionary,* 430.)

20. Legler, ed., "Frank Lloyd Wright's Automobiles," 9–11. Wright was a notorious speedster who insisted on owning the latest automobile models. His first car, a 1910 Stoddard-Dayton sport roadster, was one of only three vehicles in Oak Park at the time it was delivered. Over the course of his lifetime, he would acquire a Knox roadster, a Cadillac Phaeton, a Packard, a Cord, a Lincoln

Zephyr, two Lincoln Continentals, a Bentley, a Riley, a Mercedes sedan, a fleet of Crosleys for his apprentices, a Hillman, an Acedes roadster, a Jaguar coupe, and two Dodges. The architect requested that virtually all of his vehicles be painted his signature Cherokee Red, and many of them featured custom design elements.

21. FLW, letter to MH, July 14, 1952, FLWA. In 1953, Wright, perhaps aware of the affect that his comments about automobiles might have on Hoffman's business, told *The New Yorker* that the Jaguar was his favorite car, "capable of reaching ninety without a tremor" ("Outside the Profession," 26). Four years later, after Hoffman had lost the franchise, Wright told the magazine, "I drive a Mercedes." ("Wright Revisited," 26.)

22. *Times* announcement from "Automobile Agency Leases on Park Avenue." FLW and MH, letters between them, March 4, March 30, June 11 and 29, 1954, FLWA. Wright's announcement that he was opening a New York office from "Wright Says Problems are Solved."

23. Projected January 1955 opening dates (the 2nd, then the 27th), then an April 27th date, are mentioned in FLW and MH, letters between them, December 21, 1954; January 1 and April 14, 1955, FLWA. Hoffman invited Wright to the showroom's May 5 opening (MH, telegram to FLW, April 21, 1955, FLWA). Wright replied he would be in New York on that date (FLW, handwritten reply, April 22, 1955, on copy of MH's April 21 telegram, FLWA), but the authors could find no documentation that he attended. Jaguar buy-back and models featured in the showroom from Ludvigsen, "Baron of Park Avenue," 161, 165. After the buy-back, Hoffman immediately invested further in Mercedes-Benz (BBP and Futagawa, eds., *Wright Monograph,* 329).

24. *Architectural Forum* described by Boyd, "The House Beautiful," 21; showroom description from "Frank Lloyd Wright Designs," 132–33. Contemporary critical comments about the space include "squeezed . . . lack[ing] a strong presence" (Stern, et al., *New York 1960,* 593); a ramp that had "the scandalous architectural defect of leading nowhere" (Gill, *Many Masks,* 475); a design that meant that "sitting or standing customers [could] inspect the merchandise from all angles as it, not they, circulate" (Twombly, *Frank Lloyd Wright,* 358).

25. MH, letter to FLW, November 10, 1952, FLWA.

26. Purchase information from MH, letter to FLW, October 13, 1954, FLWA. "2.2 acre" and "three bedroom" from Tisch, *Max Hoffman House* brochure, 1–2. "Several visits" from BBP, *Treasures,* 122. Plans sent from MH, letter to FLW, December 27, 1954, FLWA. "Seaside cottage" from Storrer, *Frank Lloyd Wright Companion,* 418. Scheme details from Tisch, *Max Hoffman House,* 1. "Just too big!"

from BBP, *Treasures,* 122. Second and third designs information from Tisch, *Max Hoffman House,* 1–2; and BBP and Futagawa, eds., *Wright Monograph,* 172.

27. "Warm and domestic" from MH, letter to FLW, October 13, 1955, FLWA. "Finest materials" from Tisch, *Max Hoffman House,* 1–2. "Inferior desecrator" and "who knows the nature" from FLW, letter to MH, February 25, 1957, FLWA. "Hoffman complied" from Storrer, *Frank Lloyd Wright Companion,* 418.

28. Karl E. Ludvigsen, "The Baron of Park Avenue," 165. "Took several years" implied by FLW and MH, letters between them, July 16, 1955; January 18, 1956; January 23, 1957; November 19, 1957; FLWA.

29. Wright's comments from FLW, letter to MH, October 13, 1955, FLWA; "third of the architect's designs" from Storrer, *Frank Lloyd Wright Companion,* 418.

30. Cohen, *Consumers' Republic,* 195, 251, 292–93. By 1920, more than eight million automobiles were registered in the United States—one car for every thirteen people. By 1930, this number increased to one car for every five people. By the 1950s, massive automobile ownership and federally funded highways were actively feeding suburban growth—there was a population boom of 43 percent in these areas between 1947 and 1953 alone. (Raymond Mohl, *New City,* 35; and Carl Abbott, *Urban America,* 37.)

31. "Modern emancipator" from FLW, *Future of Architecture,* 82. The Dutch firm was the Leerdam Glass Company. The architect also designed furniture produced in volume for his commercial buildings, but the pieces were not sold on the open market (Hanks, *Decorative Designs,* 185).

32. *Ladies' Home Journal* was one of these publications, promoting Wright's plans for a prairie house and a suburban house in 1901 (Boyd, "Designing an American Way of Living," 12).

33. Ibid. "First concerted effort" from "Taliesin to the Trade," 132.

34. Iovine, "Elizabeth Gordon, 94, Dies." Gordon was from Indiana. Married to Carl Hafey Norcross, a writer who was an expert on aviation and planned communities, the single-minded editor used her maiden name throughout her career.

35. Jackson, *Encyclopedia of New York,* 536, 713. Hearst Corporation (of which Hearst Magazines is a division) was founded by newspaper mogul William Randolph Hearst.

36. Popularity of "shelter" magazines, ibid., 713. "Ripe for Wright" from Pickrel, "Encore," 116.

37. "Focus of creativity" quote from Filler, "Surveying a Century," 117; "Victorian excess" from Maddex, House Beautiful, 21; "furthered the good life" from Gropp, "Salute to Genius," 5. Other com-

ments informed by Gropp, foreword, in Maddex, House Beautiful, 14; Maddex, House Beautiful, 20–22; and Boyd, "House Beautiful," 20.

38. "Taste goes" and European Modernism references from Pittel, "What Style Reveals," 32; also, Boyd, "House Beautiful," n39, 51; and Maddex, House Beautiful, 30.

39. "Neither barrenly" from Boyd, "House Beautiful," 7. The term "American Modern" was introduced in the magazine's September 1938 issue.

40. "A propaganda and teaching tool" and, generally, from Iovine, "Elizabeth Gordon, 94, Dies." "Ideological founder" from EG's introductory text to FLW's "Frank Lloyd Wright Speaks Up," 87. And, generally, Maddex, House Beautiful, 33. House & Garden, for example, did not cover Wright's work between 1910 and 1948, and not again until 1984, with the exception of one 1951 feature on Usonia, a community in Pleasantville, New York.

41. Iovine, "Elizabeth Gordon, 94, Dies"; "The Most Influential" from Gropp in Maddex, House Beautiful, 14; ". . . the greatest architect alive" and "perhaps the closest" from ibid., 33, 21. While covering traditional settings and furniture, the magazine was primarily focused on contemporary trends and products (JdH, interview with Margolies, FLWA). Gordon said a unique aspect of House Beautiful was that nearly a quarter of its editorial was staff-created. She employed architectural draftsmen and also "farmed out" design work, creating completely original end products, the construction of which was paid for by outside individuals or institutions (EG, letter to Indira Berndtson, administrator, historic studies, FLWA, September 17, 1996, cover page, FLWA). Gordon more than quadrupled House Beautiful's circulation during her tenure, from 200,000 to 900,000 (Boyd, "The House Beautiful," n39, 52). The magazine employed some of the finest photographers of the day, including Ezra Stoller and Maynard Parker.

42. Office location from Hill interview with Margolies interview also, EG, "Next America," 126–30, 251. Gordon's remarks were made at a time when Wright's Guggenheim design was embroiled in building permit issues that might have precluded its construction, perhaps exacerbating his ire against the popular International Style. (Secrest, Frank Lloyd Wright, 552.)

43. According to Hill, resigning staff members left not because they thought the editor's perspective was regressive or that it flew in the face of the times, but because she had criticized a vital design source for the future (JdH interview with Margolies).

44. Tugendhat House and Villa Savoye locations from Pittel, "What Style Reveals," 43; dates from Hitchcock and Johnson, The International Style, 187,

119; Gordon's quotes from EG, "Threat to the Next America," 126–30, 251; "communism" from Iovine, "Elizabeth Gordon, 94, Dies"; "better living" from JdH interview with Margolies.

45. Pepis, "Home Design."

46. "The architect who could combine" from RC, interview with Berndtson, July 18, 1996, FLWA.

47. Wright's quotes from Maddex, House Beautiful, 34; and Margolies, "Remembering Mr. Wright," 13.

48. "Big Market" from FLW, letter to EG, March 27, 1953, FLWA. "Beth" and "Mr. Wright" name references from Maddex, House Beautiful, 34. The magazine's cramped editorial offices were headquartered in the former Essex Hotel and were not air-conditioned. Wright did not spend time there. (JdH interview with Margolies, FLWA) Gordon's quotes on Wright from Margolies, "Meeting Mr. Wright," 136; also, Margolies, "Remembering Mr. Wright," 14.

49. EG, telegram to FLW (asking him about a suitable replacement for Fitch), May 20, 1953, FLWA. Generally, JdH interview with Margolies; and Maddex, House Beautiful, 36. In addition to Hill and Robert Mosher, apprentices Curtis Besinger and Kenneth Lockhart also served on Gordon's editorial team.

50. House Beautiful feature and statement dates from Maddex, House Beautiful, 35. According to architectural historian David De Long, the term "Usonia" was "[Wright's] acronym for the United States of North America." (De Long, "Evolution of the Living City," 26.) Wright developed budget-minded housing concepts throughout his career and began constructing Usonian houses in the 1930s.

51. Maddex, House Beautiful, 35, 37. Hill recalled possible sourcing of Usonian Exhibition House accessories from America House, a New York shop run by Wright's daughter Frances that specialized in pottery, silver, metalwork, and woodwork items sourced nationwide (JdH interview with Margolies, FLWA). Wright designed most of the furniture for the house himself (Boyd, "Designing an American Way of Living," 15). "It wasn't like" from Margolies, "Remembering Mr. Wright," 13; "Leadership Recognized" advertisement from NYT, October 27, 1955; "Your valiant spirit" from FLW, telegram to EG, illegible date, 1955, FLWA.

52. Boyd, "House Beautiful," 31. Minic Accessories description from Hanks, Decorative Designs, 194. Editorial quotes from "And Now, Frank Lloyd Wright Designs!" 336. Heritage-Henredon was a merchandising and advertising partnership between Henredon Furniture Industries, Inc., of Morganton, North Carolina, and Heritage of High Point, North Carolina. Heritage manufactured

occasional tables and upholstered sofas and chairs. Henredon manufactured bedroom and dining room pieces. (Hanks, Decorative Designs, 205–6.)

53. Editorial quotes from "And Now, Frank Lloyd Wright Designs!" 336. Hill reported Wright was "enthusiastic" about the partnerships and had cordial relationships with the senior executives at each of the licensee firms (JdH interview with Margolies, FLWA).

54. Boyd, "House Beautiful," 38. Editorial quotes from "And Now, Frank Lloyd Wright Designs!" 282, 336–37.

55. Ibid., 338.

56. "Colors selected by" from Boyd, "Designing an American Way of Living," 20. Hill said Olgivanna had an "amazing color sense" and fueled her husband's "second career" (JdH interview with Margolies, FLWA). Product availability from "And Now, Frank Lloyd Wright Designs!," 282. Also, generally, Maddex, House Beautiful, 150. By the time the Taliesin Ensemble came to market, there were many architect- and designer-created home products available. Designer Russel Wright (no relation), worked with his wife, Mary, to produce informal dishes, fabrics, and furniture "in harmony with nature" that Wright deemed "good design." (Generally and quotes from Easel, Russel Wright, cover notes, 40; FLW, letter to Russel Wright, October 26, 1954, FLWA.) Dorothy Draper, an interior design pioneer Wright termed "the greatest inferior desecrator of all," began a product partnership with Schumacher in the 1940s, masterminding an exuberant "Espana" signature collection of fabrics, wallpaper, and carpets, as well as Heritage-Henredon furniture, that debuted the same year as the Frank Lloyd Wright lines (Albrecht, High Style, 23, 25). The Taliesin Ensemble was unique because it was designed by an architect and promoted through one of America's most powerful shelter magazines in a singularly dedicated issue.

57. Carrillo's title from Thurman, "'Make Designs,'" 154; "show him some" from RC interview with Berndtson. "Dance performance costumes" from Thurman, "'Make Designs,'" 153.

58. At the time, there was little fabric or wallpaper on the market that could be used by architects or designers in contemporary interiors. Carrillo viewed a Wright partnership as a way to fill this void. (Ibid., 156.)

59. "Never heard of," ibid., 154. Thurman also says, "First, Gordon went alone to see Wright," but the authors could not confirm this among available sources. Previous orders from "Our Company/History"; and Slavin, Opulent Textiles, 9, 169.

60. Generally, RC interview by Berndtson; "Gordon approached" from Flanagan, "Reproducing

Wright," 28. At the age of ninety, Gordon stated in a letter to Berndtson: "I was told that it was Mrs. Wright's idea to have a line of home furnishings designed to promote the 'Taliesin' name. I thought this was wishful thinking on her part, but I gave it a big boost with a big 'do' dinner evening at the Waldorf-Astoria [Hotel]." Olgivanna played a part in the selection of the Martin-Senour paint colors, but no other evidence could be found regarding any role she may have played in the initiation of the licensed lines. Gordon's strong editorial support for Wright and his products seems to contradict her "wishful thinking" comment. (EG, letter to Berndtson, September 17, 1996, 5, FLWA.)

61. "Our Company/History"; and Slavin, *Opulent Textiles,* 9, 169.

62. Boyd, "House Beautiful," 33, 42; and n120, 53; Boyd, "Designing an American Way of Living," 19; RC telephone interview by Berndtson; and Hanks, *Decorative Designs,* 195. The fabrics cost $3.40 to $13.50 a yard, and the wallpapers, $5.95 to $7.95 a roll. Textile expert Christa Thurman notes several design sources for the Schumacher "Taliesin Line": "selected elements taken from [Wright's] existing architectural designs," apprentice Ling Po and other apprentices who colored the designs "under Wright's direction," and Schumacher's own designers. (Thurman, "'Make Designs to Your Heart's Content,'" 158, 161.)

63. Boyd, "House Beautiful," 36; and Hanks, *Decorative Designs,* 189, 191, 193.

64. "Advanced word" from Lyon, "Tower Ticker"; "biggest furor" from Douglas, "Furniture on Display"; also Douglas, "Furniture on View." Hourly tours of the exhibit were available to the general public beginning March 15, 1956.

65. Review and Wright's comment from Pepis, "Conventional Furniture."

66. Display vignette information from RC interview by Berndtson; "completely unrelated" and generally, Pepis, "Conventional Furniture."

67. RC interview by Berndtson, FLWA; also, FLW, letter to RC, September 5, 1955, FLWA.

68. Ibid. (letter), and ibid. (interview). Following their reconciliation, Carrillo invited Wright to speak to the American Institute of Decorators at the Waldorf-Astoria Hotel. Insulting the entire profession and decorators by name, Wright was booed off the stage, and Carrillo found himself in embarrassing disfavor with the city's decorating community. "Wonderful if exhausting" from "New Era for Wright at 86," 20.

69. Pepis, "Conventional Furniture."

70. "Signed masterpieces" from Abraham & Straus Fulton Street at Hoyt store (Brooklyn) display ad, *NYT,* November 17, 1955.

71. B. Altman & Co. Fifth Avenue store display ad, *NYT,* November 14, 1955; and Bloomingdale's Lexington Avenue at Fifty-Ninth Street store display ads, *NYT,* October 9 and November 13, 1955, 35 and 71, respectively. Comparative research on selected items reveals that Wright's accessory table prices were in line with the national average, while the upholstered pieces carried a premium (Derks, *Value of a Dollar,* 337).

72. "And Now, Frank Lloyd Wright Designs!," 336; and William Stuart, letter to FLW, June 24, 1955, FLWA. When Martin-Senour renovated its Chicago offices in 1956, Wright colors were used on the walls, and public tours were held ("Paint Company to Hold Tour of New Office").

73. Hanks, *Decorative Designs,* 191.

74. JdH interview with Margolies, FLWA; "richness" from "And Now, Frank Lloyd Wright Designs!," 337; and FLW, note to T. Henry Wilson at Heritage-Henredon, May 18, 1956, FLWA. Wright designed a house for Wilson, but it was not constructed.

75. Boyd, "House Beautiful," 41; "Wright's . . . furniture was ahead of its time" from Boyd, "Designing an American Way of Living," 18. Wright wrote to Heritage-Henredon executive Ralph Edwards expressing a lack of surprise at the "dwindle" of the line, noting that, among other concerns, his "unit-system of various pieces fitting together into larger and finally quite complete systems of house furnishings" had gone largely unrealized. He suggested that the company write the line off "as a zizz-boom-ahh h h —fizzle . . . and try again some other day some other way." (FLW, letter to Edwards, November 24, 1956, FLWA.)

76. RC interview by Berndtson, FLWA. Carrillo last saw Wright during a visit to the Rayward House (1955, New Canaan, Connecticut) with Gordon, MoMA's Alfred Barr, and Johnson. The Wright product lines were not specifically intended for interiors the architect designed. (Thurman, "'Make Designs,'" 159.)

77. H. L. Rose, letter to "The Frank Lloyd Wright Taliesin Line" dealers, undated, 1956, FLWA.

78. Boyd, "House Beautiful, " 23–24, 30. "The war was over" from Flanagan, "Reproducing Wright," 28.

79. Boyd, "House Beautiful," 23–24. "Often, his clients" quote from Wright, *My Father, Frank Lloyd Wright,* 118. In his early years, the architect even designed dresses for his wife Catherine and the wives of some of his clients so that the mistress of the house might better contribute to his vision for the domestic whole (Hanks, *Decorative Designs,* 24–26).

80. "Prefabricated Housing"; Moe and D'Alessio, *Uncommon Sense,* 74–75.

81. Sales statistics from Ennis, "Prefabrication." Erdman, Wright's program partner, became involved in the production of quality prefabs in the 1950s (Moe and D'Alessio, *Uncommon Sense,* 58–61, 71, 75–76, 81–87). Name from Engels, "Wrong Than Wright." Nine of the constructed houses were from Wright's L-shaped "Prefab 1" plan, and two were from the square "Prefab 2" scheme (Storrer, *Frank Lloyd Wright Companion,* 436–45). First in eastern United States from Kellogg, "First Frank Lloyd Wright House."

82. Profession and place of residence from Hall, "Landmark 1959 Home." The Cass's son Peter was ill with a rare nerve disease, and even though her husband felt moving would be beneficial for the family, Catherine Cass did not (Engels, "Wrong Than Wright"; and Martin, "Home Sweet Landmark"). Watching Wallace, "decided to write," and "crazy," ibid. William Cass, letter to FLW, October 7, 1957, FLWA. Suggestion to contact Erdman from "Prefabricated House Bears Unmistakable Stamp" and Moe and D'Alessio, *Uncommon Sense,* 80–91.

83. "Wright's first attempt," ibid., 81–84. Erdman described the program as ". . . the biggest thing that ever happened" to his company ("Today's Prefabs," 119). *House & Home* magazine, a monthly industry publication, featured a cover story about the program, enthusing that the prefabrication business would now realize "the prestige associated with the greatest name in contemporary architecture" (ibid., 117). Wright's "Usonian" designs, created for individual clients, represented his most successful attempt at affordable housing. His prefabricated housing concepts also included the American Ready-Cuts (1911–1918), the 1938 "All Steel" and "Quadruple" (Sun Top) houses, the Usonian "Automatics," and even a fantastical 1957 "Air House" for U.S. Rubber Corporation. (Generally, BBP and Futagawa, eds., *Wright Monograph,* 275.) "Grace, proportion" from Fowler, "Wright Designs Pre-Fab Houses." "Distinctively Wright" and Madison model from Kellogg, "Mass-Produced House." "Three designs" from Storrer, *Frank Lloyd Wright Companion,* 436–45.

84. Screening process and "shipped" from Kellogg, "First Frank Lloyd Wright House in City." The Wright Foundation carried on the task of homebuyer approval following the architect's death. "Erected" and Delson from "Prefabricated House Bears Unmistakable Stamp." "Catherine objected" from Engels, "Wrong Than Wright." "All-American dollar" from Hall, "Landmark 1959 Home." Pricing of 1950s prefabs from "Today's Prefabs," 123–29. Final cost from "Prefabricated House Bears Unmistakable Stamp." Erdman's dealer price list quoted standard Wright three- or four-bedroom prefabs (2,130 to 2,830 square feet) at $16,400 to

$19,100. Wright's architectural fee for each house was $750. (Moe and D'Alessio, *Uncommon Sense,* 85–86.) The Cass lot cost $7,500. Charges for local contractors, unaccustomed to assembling prefabs, totaled $35,000. ("Prefabricated House Bears Unmistakable Stamp" and Kellogg, "First Frank Lloyd Wright House in City.")

85. Size, roof, and interior finishings from "Prefabricated House Bears Unmistakable Stamp." Walls and battens from Kahn, "One Wright Dream." Doors and windows from Storrer, *Frank Lloyd Wright Companion,* 436.

86. Rooms and spaces from Kellogg, "First Frank Lloyd Wright House in City" and "Prefabricated House Bears Unmistakable Stamp." Heating system from Storrer, *Frank Lloyd Wright Companion,* 436. (This system was unusual for its time and for most Wright homes.) Use of texture and room arrangement from "Prefabricated House Bears Unmistakable Stamp." Macy's from Engels, "Wrong Than Wright." Move-in date from Kellogg, "First Frank Lloyd Wright House in City." Wright planned to visit the Cass House on April 5, 1959 while it was still under construction, but illness (and his subsequent death) precluded his plan (Martin, "Home Sweet Landmark").

87. "Casting bread" from Fowler, "Wright Designs Pre-Fab Houses."

88. FLW, Taliesin Fellowship Lecture (March 7, 1954), 6, FLWA.

89. Boyd, "House Beautiful": 33. Interest in reaching people from Huxtable, *Frank Lloyd Wright,* 88. The Frank Lloyd Wright Foundation continues to license designs from the Frank Lloyd Wright Archives for product production today.

CHAPTER FOUR

In the Spotlight:
A Celebrity among Celebrities

1. "Fighting the Box."

2. Sweeney, *Annotated Bibliography,* xxxix.

3. Levine, *Architecture,* 366.

4. Maria Stone, as quoted in Tafel, *About Wright,* 60.

5. Brendan Gill likened Wright to Twain (*Book Beat*). Arthur Miller said Wright "tended to deliver resonant declarations in a tone reminiscent of W. C. Field's nasal drawl" (Miller, *Timebends,* 468).

6. Miller, letter to Tafel, March 7, 1986, as published in Tafel, *About Wright,* 83.

7. Secrest, *Frank Lloyd Wright,* 428.

8. *Book Beat.*

9. Miller, *Timebends,* 46.

10. In his autobiography, Wright claims to be 5' 8 $^{1}/_{2}$" tall. Generally, most sources place his height between 5' 6" and 5' 8" tall. Gill cited Miller's height as 6' 2" (*Book Beat*).

11. Miller, *Timebends,* 467. Although Wright and the Millers never corresponded in writing, one source maintains that Morton A. Miller, a cousin of Arthur Miller, made a written overture to Wright on June 26, 1957, at the Millers' behest. (Unidentified sender, to "Orme," July 11, 1959, FLWA.)

12. Miller, *Timebends,* 467.

13. Ibid.

14. Ibid.

15. BBP, *Treasures,* 143.

16. Ibid.

17. "Clubhouse . . . Marilyn's Bunker," 146, FLWA.

18. BBP, *Crowning Decade,* 176.

19. Ibid., 118.

20. Ibid.

21. Wright was disappointed as well. The Millers left without inviting him to dinner. (Ibid., 119.)

22. *Frank Lloyd Wright: The Mike Wallace Interviews.*

23. Ibid.

24. "Marilyn's New Life," 110.

25. Miller, letter to Tafel, March 7, 1986, in Tafel, *About Wright,* 82.

26. Miller, *Timebends,* 468.

27. Miller, letter to Tafel, March 7, 1986, in Tafel, *About Wright,* 82.

28. Miller, *Timebends,* 468.

29. Ibid.

30. Notation on drawing #5719.005, FLWA.

31. Miller, *Timebends,* 468.

32. Ibid., and generally. Miller was guessing at the dimensions; they do not appear on the plans.

33. Ibid., 468.

34. There were other problems. The Millers never paid Wright for his architectural services, claiming, through their lawyer, that "no contract was entered into," discussions with Wright had been merely "personal," and that the design for the house was "far out of agreed price range and not usable." (Paul Weiss, telegram to OLW, July 31, 1959, FLWA.)

35. The couple divorced in 1961, and Monroe died of an apparent drug overdose in 1962.

36. However, nearly four decades later in 1994, the design was revived and revised once more, this time by Taliesin Architects as the Grand Waikapu Country Club on the island of Maui, Hawaii. Leading the project team was John Rattenbury, the apprentice who so many years ago did not meet Marilyn Monroe at the Plaza.

37. General information about the meeting, from Meehan, *Master Architect,* 243–45.

38. Ibid., 245.

39. All quotes this paragraph from "Meeting of the Titans," as seen in Meehan, *Master Architect,* 243–53.

40. All quotes this paragraph, ibid.

41. "Mike Todd Party."

42. Ibid. Cronkite, who claimed he was "shanghaied" into covering the event, remembered the evening not only as "low TV," but also an "essay on empty extravagance."

43. The technology of Todd-AO, a collaborative effort between Todd and the American Optical Company, was based on Todd's experimentations with Cinerama, an earlier widescreen technology he developed.

44. Quote and general information, Todd, *A Valuable Property,* 350.

45. Ibid. According to Mike Todd Jr., his father read about Fuller's dome in a *Time* magazine article on Kaiser. The drawings for the original Kaiser Aluminum Dome, prepared by Kaiser Engineers, were based on an "exclusive license" that Kaiser held on one of Fuller's patented geodesic dome designs. ("Kaiser Aluminum Dome.")

46. Todd, *A Valuable Property,* 350.

47. Ibid. Although Todd would not live long enough to "revolutionize the theater business," he struck upon an idea that would forever change how and where Americans went to the movies. Todd was only one among many who saw the potential of the aluminum dome. In fact, Kaiser Aluminum aggressively marketed the dome as suitable for athletic facilities, supermarkets, civic auditoriums, factories, and churches. ("Kaiser Aluminum Dome.")

48. Weaver is the father of actress Sigourney Weaver.

49. Press Release, November 5, 1957, Sylvester Weaver Papers.

50. "Theatre of the future (?) . . ."

51. "Wright to Design Dome Theater," 61.

52. Todd, *A Valuable Property,* 350.

53. Ibid. Wright had prior personal or professional contact with each of these men. He and Todd were friends as early as 1946 when they met in Todd's office in New York. Todd and his new bride, actress Joan Blondell, visited the Wrights in 1947. In

1955, Wright contributed the first in a series of articles on applications of light metals in the new American home to *Alumination Magazine,* a publication of Kaiser Aluminum. Wright appeared at least three times on the Weaver-created *Today* show in the mid-1950s, and in 1955, Weaver asked Wright, "as a leader in world thought," to appear on *1976,* a show planned to forecast the state of America on its bicentennial. "Bucky" Fuller, who was a friend of Wright's, visited Taliesin several times over the years beginning in the 1930s. (Peters, interview with Berndtson; and, generally, correspondence, FLWA.)

54. BBP, *Treasures,* 156.

55. "Memorandum of Understanding."

56. "Brains, Money and Imagination."

57. Todd, *A Valuable Property,* 351.

58. Ibid., and "Memorandum of Understanding." Peters also confirmed that Wright and Kaiser "didn't get along too well" (Peters, interview with Berndtson).

59. "4 to Make Theatres of Aluminum Domes." Location of first theater from "Memorandum of Understanding."

60. Specifications from "Memorandum of Understanding"; details of the concrete shells, from BBP, *Treasures,* 156.

61. Curvature quote, ibid., 156.

62. FLW annotation on drawing #5819.001, FLWA.

63. Ibid.

64. Ibid.

65. He was the only one to do so. Press releases and correspondence generically refer to the structure as a multipurpose aluminum dome auditorium or theater. The group recognized the need for a "more electrifying" name, perhaps using the word "rama." "Kaiserama" and "Domorama" were under consideration. (Generally, FLWA and Sylvester Weaver Papers.)

66. FLW, telegram to Mike Todd, March 7, 1958, FLWA.

67. BBP, *Treasures,* 156.

68. When an inventory of Wright's drawings was conducted in 1969, it was discovered that the original drawings for the theater project were missing. Olgivanna wrote to Kaiser Aluminum to see if they might have them. Although many at Kaiser remembered Wright's involvement, no one recalled "ever seeing any drawings made for the project." Their whereabouts remain a mystery. (OLW, letter to F. A. Loebach of Kaiser Aluminum, November 22, 1969; Loebach, letter to OLW, December 2, 1969, FLWA.)

69. Illness prevented Elizabeth Taylor from accompanying her husband to New York. Todd's

plane crashed in Grants, New Mexico, on March 22. (Cohn, *Mike Todd,* 341–42.)

70. Todd Jr. said his father lost interest in the project sometime earlier when he and Taylor were Kaiser's "guests" at a premier of *Around the World in 80 Days* in the Kaiser Dome at the industrialist's Hawaiian Village Hotel. When Todd was presented with a "full tab for everything except the complimentary basket of fruit, he decided Kaiser was not a kindred spirit. [He] forgot about owning twenty geodesic domes." (Todd, *A Valuable Property,* 351.)

71. Generally, "Wright's Plans."

72. "Wright, 88."

73. BBP, *Treasures,* 148.

74. BBP, *Collected Writings,* 229.

75. "Wright Going to Iraq."

76. "Wright's Plans."

77. Ibid.

78. "Iraq Halts Work."

79. Cannell, *I. M. Pei,* 89.

80. Herbert I. Silverson quoted in Amon, "Legacy."

81. Ibid.

82. WZ, *Autobiography,* 69. At the time, Zeckendorf (Webb and Knapp) had an option on the seventeen-acre parcel (ibid., 65).

83. Other key players in the complex ninety-six-hour negotiations were William O'Dwyer, mayor of New York City; Nelson Rockefeller, who first approached his father John D. Rockefeller, Jr. about the financing; Robert Moses, who "for every snag that arose . . . had a knife"; and architect Wallace K. Harrison (Caro, *Power Broker,* 771–75). In an interesting personal footnote, Zeckendorf's son, William Jr., later married Guri Lie, the daughter of Trygve Lie, Secretary General of the United Nations, at the time of the deal ("The United Nations at 50").

84. WZ, *Autobiography,* 242.

85. Ibid. Despite—or perhaps because of—the conviviality, Wright fell and gashed his head while negotiating the wine cellar stairs. Later in the emergency room, Zeckendorf remembered "this fierce old man" insisted that an intern suture his wound without the use of any anesthetic.

86. OLW, *The Shining Brow,* 27.

87. FLW, "Shape of the City."

88. FLW lecture April 24, 1957, University of California–Berkeley, in Meehan, *The Master Architect,* 224–27.

89. FLW, letter to WZ, undated, FLWA.

90. WZ, letter to FLW, July 8, 1958, FLWA.

91. There is no documentation in the FLWA that identifies the specific location of the site.

92. FLW, letter to WZ, November 28, 1957, FLWA. In an interview published in 1958, Wright also mentioned a restaurant he planned to design for Zeckendorf "in New York on the North Side," claiming the realtor wanted it to be "the finest restaurant in the world. We will call it The Zeckendorf." There is no correspondence or documentation related to the project in the FLWA. ("Frank Lloyd Wright on Restaurant Architecture," 106.)

93. Gill, *Many Masks,* 494.

94. "Wright Building Saved." Although the *Times* reported Zeckendorf's intention was to give the house to the National Trust, he wrote to Wright reporting that he had "instructed immediate implementation of the deeding of the Robie House to your Foundation." Wright's death precluded this arrangement. In 1963, Zeckendorf gave the house to the University of Chicago. (WZ, letter to FLW, October 13, 1958, FLWA.)

95. FLW, telegram to WZ, December 20, 1957; and WZ, telegram to FLW, undated, FLWA.

96. Generally, FLW/WZ correspondence, FLWA. The plaque was never realized.

CHAPTER FIVE

**Master of the Medium:
In America's Living Rooms**

1. Wallace interview with authors Hession and Pickrel.

2. Ibid.

3. Okrent, *Great Fortune,* generally. Before the complex was officially named "Rockefeller Center," it was informally known as "Radio City" (Okrent, 178).

4. Trager, *New York Chronology,* 460.

5. Boddy, *Fifties Television,* 29, and generally.

6. The April 30 event also marked the beginning of regular American television broadcasts (Gelernter, *Lost World,* 167–68).

7. Steinberg, *TV Facts,* 85–86.

8. Details of the broadcast from Meehan, *Master Architect,* 59–64.

9. NBC Collection, Library of Congress, also, Meehan, *Master Architect,* 273; Meehan, *Truth Against the World,* 3. Olgivanna also appeared twice on *The Tex and Jinx Show,* 1956 ("On Radio").

10. Although Wright's correspondence indicates both appearances were scheduled, no documentation exists to confirm that the November 21 or 28, 1953, *Lecture Hall* or the October 7, 1956, *Monitor*

appearances occurred. *NBC Lecture Hall* quote and invitation to appear from Gioia Marconi, telegram to FLW, October 1953, FLWA; *Monitor* information from Weaver with Coffey, *Best Seat in the House,* 267.

11. FLW, letter to "General" David Sarnoff, October 22, 1954, FLWA.

12. Ibid.

13. Wright never received the requested equipment (BBP, conversation with author Hession, March 8, 2006, at Taliesin West).

14. At the invitation of the Sulgrave Manor Board, Wright traveled to London in 1939 to deliver a series of lectures. (Wright, *Autobiography,* 534–35.)

15. Although correspondence and published reports suggest Wright appeared on approximately two dozen television shows between 1953 and 1958, few of these shows are viewable today. For most of the 1950s (prior to commercial application of the videotape), the only method of recording live television shows for rebroadcast (in other time zones) was the kinescope, or the filming of a tele-vised screen image as a show aired. Many kinescopes were later discarded, and some shows were never recorded at all. According to one source, "Many of the shows from the '50s are just missing" (Erica Schwartz [NBC Universal], e-mail to author Pickrel, November 30, 2005).

16. *Conversations with Elder Wise Men* aired on NBC from 1952 to 1956. The name of the series eventually changed to *Conversations with Distinguished Persons,* to accommodate female sub-jects and because a few guests objected to being called elders. In 1957, some of the programs, includ-ing Wright's, were rebroadcast, and new segments were produced for the *Wisdom* series, which aired on NBC from 1957 to 1965. (Generally, The *Wisdom* Collection.) Further clouding the issue, the first airing of Wright's episode was promoted as *Conversations with Elder Statesman.* ("News of TV and Radio.")

17. Weaver with Coffey, *Best Seat in the House,* 239.

18. Ibid.

19. The *Wisdom* Collection.

20. Nelson, *Wisdom,* ix.

21. Ben Park (NBC), letter and contract, to FLW, November 14, 1952, FLWA.

22. Walter Gropius appeared five years later, in 1958 (Nelson, *Wisdom,* 193, 253).

23. *Wisdom: A Conversation with Frank Lloyd Wright;* and Meehan, *Master Architect,* 56.

24. Ibid.

25. Ibid.

26. Ibid.

27. Secrest, *Frank Lloyd Wright,* generally.

28. Ibid., 21.

29. Ibid., 22.

30. "Bureaucrat" quote from FLW, *Autobiography,* 479; "Pittsburgh" quote from "Atomic Mr. Wright," 98; "AIA" quote from "Appreciation of Frank Lloyd Wright," 4.

31. "After Hours: Himself," 87.

32. Sweeney, *Frank Lloyd Wright,* xv.

33. Ibid.

34. "Chronological Lists of U.S. Newspapers."

35. *Wisdom: A Conversation with Frank Lloyd Wright;* and Meehan, *Master Architect,* 56.

36. *The Wright Stuff.*

37. Ibid.

38. Gould, "Television in Review," 39.

39. Ibid.

40. According to the NBC News Archives and published *NYT* television listings, Wright appeared two other times on the *Today* show with Garroway; only silent footage remains of his November 17, 1954, show, and footage from November 30, 1955, is missing.

41. Weaver with Coffey, *Best Seat in the House,* 233–35, and generally.

42. *Today* show.

43. Crist, "Grass in the Streets." Crist interviewed Wright in his Plaza suite.

44. Ibid.

45. Equally perceptively, Garroway responded, "that will be next year," hinting at future technolo-gies. He was correct. In 1954, RCA introduced the first televisions capable of receiving color images. (Trager, *New York Chronology,* 598.)

46. All quotes in this paragraph from *Today* show.

47. Ibid.

48. *What's My Line?*

49. Ibid.

50. All quotes in this paragraph, ibid.

51. The first segment aired live on September 1. The second part was recorded that same night but was broadcast on September 28.

52. Wallace, interview with authors Hession and Pickrel.

53. Ibid.

54. Ibid.

55. *Frank Lloyd Wright: The Mike Wallace Interviews.*

56. Wallace and Gates, *Close Encounters,* 61.

57. Wallace, interview with authors Hession and Pickrel.

58. Ibid.

59. Ibid.

60. Ibid.

61. *Frank Lloyd Wright: The Mike Wallace Interviews.*

62. *The Wright Stuff.* Today, from his perspective as a sixty-year veteran of television journalism, Wallace remembers Wright as one of the most fascinating people he ever encountered: "Very smart, very sure of himself, arrogant to a point, and brooked no crit-icism." Looking back, he recalled interviewing only one other person who matched Wright in supreme confidence and self-assurance: the Ayatollah Khomeini. "Fascinating people" quote from Wallace and Gates, *Close Encounters,* 61; Khomeini quote from *The Wright Stuff.*

63. Lawrence Spivak, letter to FLW, January 29, 1959, FLWA.

64. Spivak was not alone in the error, but the fault may have been Wright's. Architecture critic Ada Louise Huxtable suggests that Wright shaved two years off his published birth date at some point in his career. "It made a case for precocious talent . . . and it kept him shy of the dreaded 90-mark during his brilliant late work of the 1950s." (Huxtable, *Frank Lloyd Wright,* 1.)

65. FLW, letter to Spivak, February 28, 1959, FLWA.

66. FLW, "Mass Media."

67. Ibid.

68. Ibid.

69. Ibid.

70. Ibid.

71. Hilary Ballon, note to author Hession, October 15, 2006.

72. *The Wright Stuff.*

73. Ibid.

74. Ibid.

CHAPTER SIX

The Guggenheim Rising:
The Spiral on Fifth Avenue

1. "Opening an office": Wright was referring to his Plaza suite. "Wright Says Problems are Solved for the New Guggenheim Museum." "Temple of spirit" from Hilla Rebay, letter to FLW, June, 1, 1943, in Pfeiffer, selected and with commentary by *Frank Lloyd Wright: The Guggenheim Correspondence,* 4.

2. Wright coined the word "archeseum," defining

it as "a building in which to see the highest" (Knox, "Museum Designed by Wright to Rise"). "Unmercifully hard" from BBP, *Guggenheim Correspondence*, 234. Plans from BBP "Exploring Wright Sites in the East," 11. The six sets of plans comprised 749 individual drawings.

3. "Could you ever" from Rebay, letter to FLW, June 1, 1943, FLWA.

4. Foundation mission from Lukach, *Rebay*, 98.

5. Ibid., 144. The Guggenheims' collection was not solely limited to non-objective art. Rebay's description of non-objective art from ibid.

6. Rebay created a plush, monochromatic, contemplative space with paintings mounted "like precious stones" in silver frames, complemented by piped-in classical music. Prior to the move to Fifty-Fourth Street, Rebay and Guggenheim considered several museum options, including a freestanding institution associated with the Rockefeller Center complex and a pavilion (designed by Rebay) at the 1939 New York World's Fair in Flushing Meadows. (Lukach, *Rebay*, ibid., 134–41, and generally.)

7. Desire for permanent quarters from ibid., 182.

8. Wright as candidate from ibid., 183. "I need" from Rebay letter to FLW, June 1, 1943, in BBP, *Guggenheim Correspondence*, 4. "Of course, I" from FLW, letter to Rebay, June 10, 1943, ibid., 6. Agreement terms from Solomon Guggenheim, letter to FLW, July 29, 1943, in ibid., 8–9.

9. Moses details from Caro, *Power Broker*, generally. "He can do" from FLW, letter to Rebay, March 1, 1945, in BBP, *Guggenheim Correspondence*, 58–59. Moses held positions of power in New York City from 1924 to 1968. The museum sites he suggested included a plot in Riverdale overlooking the Hudson River, a lot on Fifty-Fourth Street near MoMA, a location on Park Avenue between Sixty-Ninth and Seventieth streets, and another next to the Morgan Library on Madison Avenue and Thirty-Seventh Street. (FLW, letter to SRG, July 14, 1943, from BBP, *Guggenheim Correspondence*, 9–12 generally. Morgan Library site, Levine, *Architecture*, 317.)

10. Museum location from Levine, *Architecture*, 317. "Light, fresh air" from FLW, letter to Rebay, March 13, 1944, in BBP, *Guggenheim Correspondence*, 45. *NYT* announcement from "Ultra-Modern Museum." Today, the length of Fifth Avenue stretching from the Metropolitan Museum of Art at Eighty-Second Street to the Museum of the City of New York at One Hundred Third Street is known as "Museum Mile," comprising nine museums including the Guggenheim.

11. By creating a perpendicular design, he wrote Rebay, "we can go where we please" (FLW, letter to Rebay, December 30, 1943, in BBP, *Guggenheim Correspondence*, 25).

12. Assyrian ziggurat from "Art: Optimistic Ziggurat," 74. Wright stated that his unusual plan represented "the first . . . true logarithmic spiral . . . worked out as a complete building" ("Museum Building to Rise as Spiral"). Gordon Strong project from BBP, *Guggenheim Correspondence*, 27; BBP, *Treasures*, 34. Museum exterior and ramp from Twombly, *Frank Lloyd Wright*, 316. For an in-depth discussion of the history of the design development of the Guggenheim Museum, as well as Wright's "inversion" of the traditional ziggurat form, see Levine, *Architecture*, 298–363. Re: Gordon Strong: The unique project, which was not built, was designed for Sugarloaf Mountain in Maryland. Envisioned as a destination for motorists, the spiraling ramped structure was to provide shops, restaurants, a planetarium, and spectacular views (BBP, *Guggenheim Correspondence*, 27; BBP, *Treasures*, 34). In 1928–29, Le Corbusier designed an unbuilt spiral museum (the Musée Mondial, or Museum of World Culture) for the outskirts of Geneva. Wright was determined to prove his prescience in the use of the form, citing the Strong project as the example. (De Long, *Designs for an American Landscape*, 98; and Levine, *Architecture*, 302.)

13. Model reveal, "undemocratic," "pure optimism," and "the thing" from "Art: Optimistic Ziggurat," 74. Construction announcement from "Museum Building to Rise as Spiral." In spring 1946, the temporary galleries of the Guggenheim Collection at 24 East Fifty-Fourth Street showcased photographs of the model in a public exhibition ("Working Display Opens at Gallery"). Rebay echoed Wright's sentiments, expressing her wish for "one impressive quite high roofed hall, a sanctum . . . to rest the greatest of all paintings permanently" (Rebay, letter to FLW, April 5, 1944, in Lukach, *Rebay*, 190).

14. Bidding challenges from BBP, *Guggenheim Correspondence*, 74. Cost and other construction deterrents from "The Guggenheim Museum," 8.

15. Mansion site from Lukach, *Rebay*, 207. "Fright" and "someday" from "Typical Plans," 137. As a cost-saving alternative to renovation of the mansion, Wright unsuccessfully proposed an annex of his own design that would not only serve as temporary museum quarters, but would later function as office space and a residence for the curator (BBP, *Guggenheim Correspondence*, 96–97). After the demolition of the mansion on the site and during construction of the Wright-designed building, the collection was housed at its third temporary quarters at Seven East Seventy-Second Street (Solomon R. Guggenheim Foundation Press Release).

16. Endowment figure from Saarinen, "Lively Gallery." Lack of reference to Wright in will from Levine, *Architecture*, 337. In June 1949, Wright assured Guggenheim "the original museum as now replanned" could be built for $2 million (FLW letter to Rebay, June 23, 1949, in BBP, *Guggenheim Correspondence*, 123). "As stated in his will, upon Guggenheim's death, his daughter Eleanor's husband, Earl Castle Stewart, became president of the board of trustees and Harry F. Guggenheim became chairman. However, because Castle Stewart lived in the United Kingdom, Guggenheim assumed de facto leadership responsibilities in 1952. Upon Stewart's 1957 resignation, Guggenheim became president. (Solomon R. Guggenheim Press Release.)

17. Louchheim's comments from Louchheim, "Museum in Query." Rebay's resignation and appointment as "Director Emeritus" from Saarinen, "Lively Gallery." According to Lukach, the board requested Rebay's resignation as artistic director (Lukach, *Rebay*, 293). Louchheim went so far as to suggest that the Foundation place the Wright building, Guggenheim collections and monies under the jurisdiction of the MoMA or the Whitney, who, in her opinion, better served "the interests of the public, artists, and modern art" (Louchheim, "Museum in Query").

18. Sweeney held the MoMA position from 1945 to 1946 (Huxtable, *Frank Lloyd Wright*, 233; and "New Director Appointed by Guggenheim Museum").

19. Opening date from "Throngs Inspect Wright's Exhibit," 34. Visitor count from Saarinen, "Lively Gallery." The exhibition was supported by a $10,000 grant from the Solomon R. Guggenheim Foundation. Guggenheim advised Wright that any budget overages incurred in mounting the exhibit that were not offset by the grant plus admission fees would be up to the architect, not the Museum, to pay. Guggenheim also offered to extend the length of the exhibition to help Wright in this respect as needed. (HFG, letter to FLW, November 19, 1953, FLWP/SRGA.) Estimated by Wright at $30,000–35,000 (*The Usonian House*), the final cost of the Usonian Exhibition House, despite hands-on help from students and Wright's apprentices, was $46,000. Former Wright apprentice David Henken was the builder of the Usonian Exhibition House. (Goldberger, "Wright House is Found.")

20. "Largest exhibition" on Wright from BBP, "Frank Lloyd Wright in Manhattan," 8. "Devoted to one man" from "Exhibitions at Home and Abroad," 11. Wright wrote to Guggenheim director Sweeney that he had "refused" MoMA the exhibit (FLW, letter to Sweeney, May 5, 1953, FLWA). However, Rebay wrote to Wright the following month that MoMA had "apparently refused the exhibition, even though I saw you waiting for Mr. Johnson in that Museum's entrance; a man you did not wish to have in Taliesin a short while ago . . ." (Rebay, letter to FLW, June 29, 1953, FLWP/SRGA.)

21. Kaufmann relationship from BBP, *Frank Lloyd Wright: Letters to Architects,* 174; and Goodwin, "Wright's Beth Sholom Synagogue." Several accounts have been written regarding the conception of the exhibit. The most recent scholarship on the subject, referenced here, is from Ainsworth, "Modernism Contested," 63–178. Other comments generally informed by BBP, "Frank Lloyd Wright in Manhattan," 8; "Exhibitions at Home and Abroad," 11, 12; and Levine, *Architecture,* 374.

22. "Outside the Profession," 27.

23. "After Hours: Himself," 88.

24. Other exhibitions included rooms at *House Beautiful*'s The Art of Daily Living with the Los Angeles County Fair Association, 1954, which were dedicated to Wright and organized by Hill, as well as a prefabricated exhibition house (June 1959) for the "Parade of Homes" in Madison, Wisconsin. Unlike the New York house, which was dismantled along with the exhibit pavilion, the Madison house was sold after the exhibition. (Boyd, "Designing An American Way of Living," 12–15.)

25. Pfeiffer notes that Wright contributed some of his priceless Asian artworks to the New York house's "suburban" décor. (E-mail from BBP to author Pickrel, November 9, 2006).

26. *The Usonian House.*

27. "The old colonial" from "House of Wright is Previewed Here," 35. *House Beautiful* coverage from Boyd, "Designing An American Way of Living," 15.

28. Purchase of property, Wright's revisions, and 1952 plan from Levine, *Architecture,* 338. Number of violations from ibid., 341. "Working out" from FLW, letter to HFG, December 8, 1953, in BBP, *Guggenheim Correspondence,* 191. Real estate mogul William Zeckendorf, who would become a client and friend of Wright (see chapter four), sold the lot to the Guggenheim Foundation. A thirteen-story apartment building that stood on the lot would eventually be demolished. ("Guggenheim Fund to Build Museum.")

29. Unger, *The Guggenheims,* 271–73.

30. "Daughter of" and "Daily News" from Keeler, *Newsday,* 4. "Strength, his energy" from OLW, "Our House." Relationship with the Wrights from BBP, *Guggenheim Correspondence,* 143.

31. Solomon R. Guggenheim Press Release.

32. "Lieber Harry," generally, FLW, letters to HFG, FLWA. *Carido* does not have a literal Spanish translation. Possibly, the term is a variant of the Spanish *Querido Francisco* (Dear Frank), which Guggenheim, a former ambassador to Cuba, alternately used to address his friend. (HFG, letter to FLW, March 9, 1956, FLWP/SRGA.) Guggenheim could also be direct with the relentless architect: "Please lay off for all time this 'Archeseum' stuff,"

he wrote, referring to Wright's insistence that the museum be so named (HFG, letter to FLW, July 2, 1956, FLWP/SRGA).

33. "Let me assure you" from FLW, letter to Rebay, June 2, 1945, BBP, *Guggenheim Correspondence,* 61. In a letter to Moses, Wright quoted a remark by Moses' wife, Mary: "Frank, Bob will never use you on a job—he hates modern architecture so" (FLW, letter to Robert Moses, October 6, 1955, FLWA).

34. "Shortening" from FLW, letter to Moses, October 6, 1955, FLWA. "To help some" from Moses, letter to HFG, October 20, 1955, FLWA. "Many thanks" from HFG, letter to Moses, October 21, 1955, FLWA.

35. "Damn it" from Secrest, *Frank Lloyd Wright,* 551. Permit date, Levine, *Architecture,* 347. "Long heralded" from *NYT* editors' reactions and quotes from "The Hot Cross Bun." "Come to learn" from Tafel, *Apprentice to Genius,* 209–10. Short details from BBP, *Guggenheim Correspondence,* 16–17. Construction would begin following the demolition of the temporary museum and apartment building on the site.

36. Groundbreaking and "a magnificent" from BBP, *Guggenheim Correspondence,* 216.

37. Unger, *The Guggenheims,* 240, 244.

38. Keeler, *Newsday,* 230. Keeler added that the idea was to "provide stiffer competition to the gleaming new tracks in New Jersey."

39. BBP, *Treasures,* 130.

40. FLW, letter to HFG, June 11, 1957, FLWA.

41. FLW, *A Testament,* 214–15; and project drawings, FLWA.

42. Carter, *Alistair Cooke,* 322.

43. BBP, *Treasures,* 130.

44. FLW, *A Testament,* 214–15; and project drawings, FLWA.

45. J. J. Povlika, letter to FLW, February 26, 1957, FLWA.

46. Ibid.

47. FLW, letter to HFG, June 25, 1956, FLWA.

48. Nichols, "Belmont Park Shut."

49. "In all kinds" from BBP, *Guggenheim Correspondence,* 234. "What a pleasure" from Hugh Ferriss, letter to FLW, March 26, 1958, FLWA. "I am thrilled" from Leopold Stokowski, letter to FLW, 1957, in BBP, *Guggenheim Correspondence,* 246. In 1952, Ferriss requested Wright's permission to create a drawing of the Guggenheim. He sent Wright a sketch that suggested the museum's "striking contrast with the distant Metropolitan." (Ferriss, letter to FLW, May 1, 1952, FLWA.) Wright forwarded

Stokowski's note to Guggenheim, saying it was "appreciation from a high source." (FLW, letter to HFG, in BBP, *Guggenheim Correspondence,* 241.)

50. "The only concern" from Saarinen, "Tour with Mr. Wright." "It has been" from FLW, letter to HFG, October 2, 1957, in BBP, *Guggenheim Correspondence,* 241.

51. Building changes from Levine, *Architecture,* generally, 323–41. The top of the museum was designed to project twenty-four feet beyond its building line, making it "self-cleaning"—all moisture would drip free of the building section below it. Wright also conceived an air-conditioning system that would draw dust from visitors' feet and clothes as they entered the building, making it safe for the museum's paintings to be exposed and unframed. ("Museum Building to Rise as Spiral.")

52. Sweeney background and change requests from DeVree, "Modern Movement." "A standard museum man" from FLW, letter to Alicia Patterson (Guggenheim), December 12, 1953, in BBP, *Guggenheim Correspondence,* 192. The *Times* said the exhibit demonstrated a "broadening of the aims of the institution and an admirable sense of displaying the collection" that also reflected a fresh standard of quality (DeVree, "Modern Movement").

53. "Suited to" from "Museum Building to Rise As Spiral"; also Levine, *Architecture,* 327. "Free the paintings" from BBP, *Guggenheim Correspondence,* 38. Number of alcoves from Wood, "At Guggenheim Museum." Color of alcoves from BBP, *Guggenheim Correspondence,* 284. "Art will be seen as if through an open window, and of all places, in New York! It astounds me!" Wright said. ("Art: Museum à la Wright.") Slant of walls from "First View of the Guggenheim," 46. "The grand sweep" from BBP, *Guggenheim Correspondence,* 295–96. "Objecting to" from Canaday, "Wright Vs. Painting." Wright's lighting plan from Secrest, *Frank Lloyd Wright,* 58; and Genauer, "Guggenheim Museum is Ready for Public."

54. "Show off" from "Last Monument." Sweeney's display principles from Genauer, "Guggenheim Museum." Resulting display method from Wood, "At Guggenheim Museum."

55. BBP, *Guggenheim Correspondence,* 284, 295–96. As early as 1953, Harry Guggenheim reiterated to Wright: "The plans for the interior of the Museum . . . were developed many years ago. We have an entirely different approach and very different plan for the present and future operation of the Museum. I have no doubt that if you had a conference with Sweeney this would be made very clear." (HFG, letter to FLW, August 18, 1953, FLWP/SRGA.)

56. "To belie" and "I will" from FLW, letter to Sweeney, March 9, 1956, in BBP, *Guggenheim Correspondence,* 224.

57. "Not suitable," and, generally, BBP, *Guggenheim Correspondence,* 242 (Pfeiffer incorrectly dates this letter to 1957). "Providing proper" and "we shall" from "21 Artists Assail Museum Interior." (When the *Times* reporter asked one participant why the group didn't protest during the museum's planning stages, he replied that every artist he knew disapproved of the plan, "but we just didn't get together on it.") Rebay had expressed concern some years earlier that the building itself might dominate the paintings displayed within. (Levine, *Architecture,* 326.)

58. Guggenheim's reply from "Guggenheim Chides Critics of Museum." Wright's reply from BBP, *Guggenheim Correspondence,* 243. Wright's goal from BBP, "Frank Lloyd Wright in Manhattan," 9.

59. "The architectural integrity," "satisfy," and "mutually satisfactory" from HFG, letter to FLW, March 31, 1958, FLWP/SRGA. Demonstration invitation from HFG, letter to FLW, May 8, 1958, FLWP/SRGA. "It is humiliating" from FLW, letter to HFG, November 26, 1958, FLWA. Paintings request from BBP, *Guggenheim Correspondence,* 285. Fruitlessly, Wright also wrote to Albert Thiele, Guggenheim Foundation board member and chairman of the building committee, to solicit support, referencing his original client: ". . . I know of what he wanted and what I am now trying to preserve" (HFG, letter to FLW, July 28, 1958, FLWP/SRGA). At an October 19 dinner at his home, Guggenheim announced in Olgivanna's presence: "In some details of the interior I had to follow Museum Director Sweeney's suggestions. I felt that to be his right since he is the director. But when trustees change, when the directors change, the interior can be restored at any time to Mr. Wright's exact design." (OLW, *Shining Brow,* 181.)

60. "First imprint" and Wright's comments from Saarinen, "Tour with Mr. Wright." The piece incorrectly cites the architect's age as eighty-eight. When conversation turned to Wright's personal artistic preferences, he mentioned *Guernica* by Picasso (a "great artist without reverence or respect for humanity") as a favorite painting, but expressed a strong preference for works by Giotto and Rembrandt.

61. Wright's comments from ibid. Building completion and cost from ibid., and "Wright Retreats on Museum Plans."

62. Wright's comments from Saarinen, "Tour with Mr. Wright." The issue of fame was clearly on Wright's mind in his last years.

63. Date of scaffolding dismantlement from "Guggenheim Museum Progresses."

64. "Scorn," "admiration," and "culture dome" from Preston, "Museum Review." Crowd comments from Mitgang, "Sidewalk Views." Wes Peters later stated that Wright "talked once about putting the building in Central Park" (Tafel, *About Wright,* 169). Mumford reported that the public likened Lever House to "the eighth wonder of the world" when it opened (Tyrnaeur, "Forever Modern," 320).

65. Mitgang, "Sidewalk Views."

66. "The Guggenheim Museum," 9.

CHAPTER SEVEN

After Wright:
A New York Legacy

1. Date of last visit from OLW, *Shining Brow,* 174. Cause and date of death and "laid to rest" (below) from Huxtable, *Frank Lloyd Wright,* 245. Wright was laid to rest in the Lloyd-Jones graveyard just outside Unity Chapel, a shingle-style structure commissioned by his Uncle Jenkin in 1885 and designed by J. Lyman Silsbee. Eighteen-year-old Wright assisted in its construction. Chapel details from Secrest, *Frank Lloyd Wright,* 6–7. OLW, telegrams to the manager of the Plaza Hotel, April 17 and 23, 1959, FLWA. William Short (clerk of the works on the Guggenheim site) packed furnishings from OLW, *Shining Brow,* 174.

2. Dwight D. Eisenhower, letter to OLW, April 22, 1959, FLWA. "Radical of architecture" from Stern, "Dramatic Buildings." "Greatest architect" from "Frank Lloyd Wright Dies." "Transformed" from "Museum Opens Tribute to the Architect Today." Hitchcock wrote *In the Nature of Materials: The Buildings of Frank Lloyd Wright 1887–1941* (New York: Duell, Sloan & Pearce, 1942), a monograph of Wright's work to 1941. "Michelangelo" from Levine, *The Architecture of Frank Lloyd Wright,* 423. "In some sense" from Hitchcock, "Editorial," 25.

3. "Type of genius" from "Philip Johnson on Frank Lloyd Wright," 47. "When history" and "in his undiminishing" from "Frank Lloyd Wright: 1869–1959," 113–14. "'The Lone Ranger'" from Pickrel, "Encore," 116.

4. "I have never wanted" from BBP, *His Living Voice,* 66. "$30,000,000 of work" from Farr, "Frank Lloyd Wright: Defiant Genius," 83. Taliesin Associated Architects, under the architectural direction of Wes Peters, would work to complete all of Wright's works in progress and would receive fifty new commissions of its own in the four years following the architect's death ("Frank Lloyd Wright's Work Is Carried On," 8).

5. Opening date from Knox, "New Art Museum Opens on 5th Ave." $3,000,000 cost and "Protestant barn" from "Last Monument," 67. Met by the Stones from OLW, *Shining Brow,* 177, 186. Invited by Guggenheim, Olgivanna and Iovanna flew to New York several days before the opening to attend a series of celebratory events.

6. Number of guests from "Unwrap New Museum." Audience composition and speaker list from Knox, "New Art Museum is Dedicated Here," 1. Ceremony time from BBP, *Guggenheim Correspondence,* 303. Ceremony location from "600 an Hour." Mrs. Wright and Sweeney "not invited to speak" from Unger, *The Guggenheims,* 383. Guggenheim invited the two to separate celebratory dinners as well (ibid., 559). Rebay's absence from the Solomon R. Guggenheim Museum, The New York City Landmarks Preservation Commission Designation, 10. There are varying accounts of why Rebay was absent. One states she was not invited because of estrangement from the Guggenheim heirs (Patterson, *Fifth Avenue,* 212). Another says "she disapproved of the inaugural exhibition for including too many representational paintings and came to none of the ceremonies" (Unger, *The Guggenheims,* 383). Mrs. Wright described the auditorium as "permeated with Mr. Wright's presence" that day (OLW, *Shining Brow,* 187). The *New York Herald Tribune* described the space as having "the grace and nobility of a small eighteenth century theater" (Genauer, "Guggenheim Museum is Ready for Public").

7. "Speakers' comments," Flemming information, "unique addition," and "free country" from Knox, "New Art Museum is Dedicated Here." "Refreshing" and contrast to glass buildings from OLW, *Shining Brow,* 182. "This kind of museum, therefore, is only possible in a democracy," Lodge said, emphasizing that an artist could not flourish in a totalitarian autocracy. (All of Lodge's comments from Ambassador Lodge Text, 1–2.) "Live long" and "complete break" from Speech of Harry F. Guggenheim, 1–2. Guggenheim also lauded director Sweeney's exhibition as "devised in unusual and forceful form" (Knox, "New Art Museum is Dedicated Here").

8. During a speech at the Municipal Art Society five months earlier, Moses made egregious comments for which Olgivanna could not forgive him: "I venture to predict that long after the public has wearied of Frank Lloyd Wright's inverted oatmeal dish and silo with their awkward cantilevering, their jaundiced skin and the ingenious spiral ramp leading down past the abstractions which mirror the tortured maladjustments of our time, the Metropolitan will still wear well" (OLW, *Shining Brow,* 183; and Knox, "Moses Gets Prize"). "Big city could not survive" from "600 an Hour." "The exploitation of art" from Knox, "New Art Museum is Dedicated Here." "Evidence that" from "Unwrap New Museum."

9. Wagner's role from OLW, *Shining Brow,* 187. "Over fifteen hundred" from "Unwrap New Museum." Wright informed the chairman of New York City's Board of Standards and Appeals that no more than 350 people would be in the museum at any one time (also that the paintings would be dis-

played without frames), which incensed Guggenheim, who perceived the move as the architect's attempt to control every aspect of the public's experience within the space (HFG, letter to FLW, January 9, 1956, FLWP/SRGA). "One of the greatest" from Alden, "Art Experts." "The line" from Knox, "New Art Museum is Dedicated Here." Closed on Mondays, admission to the museum was fifty cents (ibid.).

10. Stone, "Hero, Prophet, Adventurer," 15.

11. Wright's descriptors, respectively: "Nautilus's Prune," *The New Yorker,* July 12, 1952: 20; "Frank Lloyd Wright's Masterwork," *Architectural Forum,* April 1952, 17; ibid. Other descriptors, respectively: Alden, "Art Experts Laud Wright's Design;" "Art: Optimistic Ziggurat," 74; Mitgang, "Sidewalk Views of That Museum;" Opening day news footage, CBS Archives; Preston, "Museum Review;" Balch, "Wright's 'Fantasy' Sparks Controversy;" Mitgang, ibid; Opening day news footage, ibid., Mitgang, ibid.; Huxtable, "That Museum: Wright or Wrong?;" Mitgang, ibid.; "Letters to the Times," May 12, 1956; Mitgang, ibid.; Opening day news footage, ibid.; Alden, ibid.; Haverstick, "To Be or Not to Be," 13; Mitgang, ibid.; "21 Artists Assail Museum Interior;" "N.Y. Opens Museum Built Like Corkscrew;" "Letters," October 27, 1957; Mitgang, ibid.

12. "One of Wright's favorite publications" from *Frank Lloyd Wright: The Mike Wallace Interviews.* "A mighty tower" from "Last Monument." "Figure this one" from Moholy-Nagy, "Aging of Modern Architecture," 136. "Wright . . . would no doubt" from Stone, "Hero, Prophet, Adventurer," 15.

13. "An architectural genius" from James, "Wright on Fifth Avenue," 65. "The world's supreme showcase" and "an architect whom" from Wood, "At Guggenheim Museum." "Like it or not" from "The New Museum."

14. "The most beautiful" from Genauer, "Guggenheim Museum," cover. "A building that" from "Last Monument," 67. *Times* coverage from Perl, "Art at Mid-Century." Huxtable's comments from Huxtable, "That Museum?"

15. Watterson, "The Editor's Page," 124. Historian Vincent Scully described the museum as "ballooning outward among its starched neighbors, like the pulsing sanctuary of a primitive cult drumming on Fifth Avenue" (Scully Jr., *Masters of Architecture,* 30). "The first baroque" from Huxtable, "That Museum?" "The varied natural" from Mumford, "Critical Opinion," 16. One writer expressed desire to see the museum "in isolation—ideally in an open space where a natural background would enhance its organic, spiral shape and where its circular plan could be savoured in the round" (James, "Wright on Fifth Avenue," 63). The museum's main floor featured several floor-to-ceiling windows providing park views.

16. Wright as quoted in "Frank Lloyd Wright's Masterwork," 17.

17. "Museum fatigue" from Johnson, "Letter to the Museum Director," 25. "Exalted proportions" from Mumford, "Critical Opinion," 16. "[It is] the heart" from Sweeney, "Chambered Nautilus," 14–15.

18. Ramp disparagement from Canaday, "Wright Vs. Painting." "Askew" from McAucliffe, "The Guggenheim," 66. "Error" from Mumford, "Critical Opinion," 16. When queried about the low height of the atrium wall, Sweeney said he didn't "get vertigo" (Knox, "New Art Museum is Dedicated Here"). Some of the ramp's drama and function was lost when "the top of the spiral was shut for storage (at some point), amputating its ascent, hiding the domed skylight that was the climax of the design"; this was later corrected (Huxtable, *Frank Lloyd Wright,* 234).

19. Opening exhibit from "N.Y. Opens Museum." "Bar device" from Wood, "At Guggenheim Museum"; and Canaday, "Wright Vs. Painting." *Architectural Forum* support from Secrest, *Frank Lloyd Wright,* 552. (The magazine featured Wright's work in singularly dedicated issues in January 1938, January 1948, and June 1959.) "Close to pure" from Blake, "Critical Opinion," 20. "Glare" from "First View of the Guggenheim," 67. Vincent Scully termed the lighting effect "a department store harshness of glare." (Scully, *Masters of Architecture,* 31.) "Stunning" from Huxtable, "That Museum?" On opening day, Guggenheim issued a press statement declaring that while Wright's display plan "was not acceptable to the trustees . . . the architect's aim . . . that the paintings would appear to be floating in space . . . happily has been achieved" (Statement by Mr. Guggenheim, 1). Wright's actual words were that each painting should be "freely floated in a sympathetic atmosphere of architecture"—"not hung 'square' but gracefully yield[ing] to movement as set up by these slightly curving massive walls . . . as jade or a jewel set as a signet in a ring" (an excerpt from FLW, *A Testament,* in Statement by Mr. Guggenheim, 2–3).

20. All comments from "600 an Hour." Asked to identify "they," Mrs. Wright replied, "It's really difficult to tell . . . but the Guggenheim Foundation could have prevented [the modifications], certainly" (ibid.).

21. Sweeney's comments from Sweeney, "Chambered Nautilus," 15. "A secondary frieze" from McAucliffe, "The Guggenheim," 69. "A new kind" from Mumford, "Critical Opinion," 16.

22. Art audience growth from Perl, *New Art City,* 391. According to Perl, visiting soldiers flocked to MoMA during World War II, a destination he called "the center of the evolving visual-arts scene of the 1950s." By 1960, the museum had become "a civic necessity," according to Philip Johnson, who equated the institutions to public shrines as significant as churches or city halls. (Huxtable, "What Should a Museum Be?")

23. "Much too heady" from "600 an Hour." "Old rascal" from "Frank Lloyd Wright's Sole Legacy," 89.

24. "One million" from Knox, "Guggenheim Picks Museum Director," 21. Ponti from Benjamin, "City Wins Bravos." Nehru from "Guggenheim Art." Princesses Birgitta and Désirée from Petersen, "Museums Visited by Royal Sisters." Empress Farah from Saxon, "Empress Visits 2 Museums Here." Soviet administrators from Shabad, "Russians Lecture N.Y.U."

25. "The building overshadows" from Lawrence, "Letters to the *Times.*" "If a museum is" from LaRusso, "Letters to the *Times.*"

26. Guggenheim's comments from Huxtable, "What Should a Museum Be?" "Preferred fame to notoriety" from "A Visit with Frank Lloyd Wright," 28.

27. Knox, "Guggenheim Museum Director Resigns."

28. "Stimulating challenge" from Huxtable, "That Museum?"; the date of resignation was July 20, 1960 (ibid.). "Differing ideals" from Knox, "Guggenheim Museum Director Resigns." "Fought Sweeney" from Huxtable, *Frank Lloyd Wright,* 235. "Officially he resigned, but it was clear that he was actually fired" (Unger, *The Guggenheims,* 383). Sweeney was a proponent of the "dictionary" definition of a museum, allowing the visitor to observe art on his or her own terms—not as a venue for popular programming, art-play, or social events ("A Museum Director Resigns"; and Canaday, "Easy Does It"). Sweeney was a highbrow elitist, while Guggenheim was a businessman concerned about revenues (Unger, *The Guggenheims,* 384). He subsequently became director of the Museum of Fine Arts of Houston ("Sweeney to Head Houston Museum"). There, he worked with Mies (who had been commissioned to create a master plan for MFAH in 1953) on a substantial structural addition ("Caroline Wiess Law Building").

29. "Walk-in" from Canaday, "Two Torch Bearers." Huxtable said "a museum is also art" (Huxtable, "Architecture"). Custom milliners designed hats that resembled the Guggenheim's profile and named them for the new museum ("Mr. Arnold: Buildings and Botany"; "Sally Victor Hats"). Pop artists painted on suddenly popular shaped canvases, used the structure's ziggurat form as a subject for their work, and created installations specifically for its expressive space (Levine quoted in Frankel, *Frank Lloyd Wright's Guggenheim Museum,* 69; and Lucie-Smith, "Pragmatists," 314).

30. "All across" from Dugan, "Circular Layout." Johnson's works from Perl, *New Art City,* 377; and Stern, et al., *New York 1960,* 1136. Johnson's design

for his New York State Pavilion for the 1964 World's Fair was also described as "an extravaganza of echoing circles" (Perl, *New Art City,* 384).

31. Huxtable, "Architecture."

32. "Museum mania" from Filler, "Museums and the Maecenas Touch," 99. In 1998, Gehry also designed a second Guggenheim Museum for New York City. Conceived for lower Manhattan, the design remains unrealized ("Frank Gehry: Architect").

33. Messer, "Editorial," 25.

34. Reexamining the directorship function in the wake of Sweeney's departure, Guggenheim divided the position's responsibilities—an administrator would handle business matters, and the director would oversee "art" alone. Messer was originally hired as "director," but the two areas of responsibility were later re-merged under his auspices. (Unger, *The Guggenheims,* 384–85.) "To some extent" from the Solomon R. Guggenheim Museum, The New York City Landmarks Preservation Commission Designation, 12. "Display walls" and "paintings were hung" from "Evolution of a Museum," 30. In 1962, Lawrence Alloway, a British art critic and lecturer, was appointed as the museum's curator, reporting to Messer ("The Guggenheim Names Curator," 5). Alloway is credited with coining, or being one of the coiners of, the term "pop art" (Esterow, "Curator Resigns").

35. Guggenheim's comment from "First View of the Guggenheim," 68. Blake quote from "Critical Opinion," 20. "Perhaps the idea of a museum will now be thought about again, and as a new concept, not an old palace or standard laboratory with or without chintz," *Art News* observed ("First View," 68).

36. "Most controversial" from Knox, "New Art Museum Opens on 5th Ave." "Immediate iconographic" from Perl, *New Art City,* 379. "Civilizations are" from Huxtable, "What Should a Museum Be?" "[The museum represented]" from Huxtable, *Frank Lloyd Wright,* 230.

37. Plaque from BBP, *Guggenheim Correspondence,* 285–86. "After some ninety" from Remarks of Robert Moses, 2.

38. BBP, *Crowning Decade,* 48.

FRANK LLOYD WRIGHT IN NEW YORK CITY: A CHRONOLOGY

1. Dolkart and Postal, *New York City Landmarks,* 172.

2. "National Register of Historic Places."

3. Dolkart and Postal, *New York City Landmarks,* 157.

4. "National Register of Historic Places."

5. "National Historic Landmarks Program."

6. Dolkart and Postal, *New York City Landmarks,* 351.

7. Hoffman, *Frank Lloyd Wright,* 55–57.

8. These exhibits represent a selected list. Generally, "Exhibits During Frank Lloyd Wright's Lifetime," 15; "Exhibit Model City," and Smith, "The Show to End All Shows," 13, 45.

9. Brock, "A Pioneer in Architecture"; and e-mail exchange with Margo Stipe, FLWA, April 11, 2006.

10. "Built in the USA." Built in USA: 1932–1944 was on exhibit May 24–October 22, 1944; Built in USA: Post-war Architecture, January 20–March 5, 1953.

11. Corrigan, "Fabric Houses." Schumacher called these rooms the "Taliesin Suite" in its official portfolio of the Wright lines.

12. "Home Show Opens Today for Nine Days."

13. "Wright's Plans for Baghdad Cultural Center Shown."

14. Knox, "Global Art Show Opens Here Today."

15. Preston, "Modern Architecture's New Look."

16. DeVree, "Highly Diverse."

BIBLIOGRAPHY

Abbott, Carl. *Urban America in the Modern Age: 1920 to the Present.* Arlington Heights, IL: Harlan Davidson, Inc., 1987.

"About Philip Johnson," The Pritzker Architecture Prize Web site: www.pritzkerprize.com.

"After Hours: Himself," *Harper's Magazine* (December 1953).

Ainsworth, Troy. "Modernism Contested: Frank Lloyd Wright in Venice and the Masieri Memorial Debate." PhD dissertation: Texas Tech University, Lubbock, TX, 2005.

Albrecht, Donald. *The High Style of Dorothy Draper.* New York: Museum of the City of New York and Pointed Leaf Press, LLC., 2006.

Alden, Robert. "Art Experts Laud Wright's Design," *New York Times,* October 22, 1959.

Alofsin, Anthony. *Frank Lloyd Wright: The Lost Years, 1910–1922: A Study of Influence.* Chicago: The University of Chicago Press, 1993.

———. "Pinwheel on the Prairie: An Overview of the Price Tower," in Alofsin, *Prairie Skyscraper.*

———, ed. *Prairie Skyscraper: Frank Lloyd Wright's Price Tower.* New York: Rizzoli International, Inc., 2005.

Ambassador Lodge Text, Guggenheim Museum Speech, October 21, 1959. The Solomon R. Guggenheim Foundation, New York.

Amon, Rhoda. "Legacy: William Zeckendorf: Planner, Dreamer," undated article, *Newsday* Web site: www.newsday.com.

"And Now, Frank Lloyd Wright Designs Home Furnishings You Can Buy!" *House Beautiful* (November 1955).

"Appreciation of Frank Lloyd Wright," *Architectural Design* (January 1960).

"Architect Models New Type of City," *New York Times,* March 27, 1935.

"Architect Opposes A Universal Style," *New York Times,* September 18, 1931.

"Art in Review: The Museum of Modern Art to Install a Department of Architecture as a Regular Feature," *New York Times,* July 3, 1932.

"Art: Museum à la Wright," *Time* (July 23, 1946).

"Art: Optimistic Ziggurat," *Time* (October 1, 1945).

Astragal Cable Reply, *The Architects' Journal* 106 (August 28, 1947).

"The Atomic Mr. Wright," *Newsweek* (May 15, 1955).

"Automobile Agency Leases on Park Avenue," *New York Times,* April 6, 1954.

Balch, David. "Wright's 'Fantasy' Sparks Controversy," *New York World-Telegram and Sun,* October 21, 1959.

Ballon, Hilary. "Frank Lloyd Wright and the Vertical Dimension," *Frank Lloyd Wright Quarterly* 15, no. 3 (Summer 2004).

———. "Frank Lloyd Wright's Plan for St. Mark's-in-the-Bowery." St. Mark's Historic Landmark Fund Lecture Series, St. Mark's Church, New York, April 20, 2006.

———. "From New York to Bartlesville, the Pilgrimage of Wright's Skyscraper," in Alofsin, *Prairie Skyscraper.*

Barney, Maginel Wright. *The Valley of the God-Almighty Joneses.* New York: Appleton Century, 1965.

Bender, Thomas. "Review: Scully's Way," *The Nation* Web site: www.thenation.com.

Benjamin, Philip. "City Wins Bravos on Architecture," *New York Times,* March 14, 1959.

Blake, Peter. "Critical Opinion: Peter Blake," *Museum News* 3 (January 1960); reprinted from *Architectural Forum* (December 1959).

———. *The Master Builders: Le Corbusier, Mies van der Rohe, Frank Lloyd Wright.* New York: W. W. Norton & Co., Inc., 1996; originally published in 1960.

Boddy, William. *Fifties Television: The Industry and Its Critics.* Urbana: University of Illinois Press, 1993.

Book Beat: Brendan Gill Interview with Don Swain. CBS Radio and WUOB Center for Public Media, Ohio University. *Wired for Books* Web site: www.wiredforbooks.org.

Boyd, Virginia T. "Designing an American Way of Living," *Frank Lloyd Wright Quarterly* 17, no. 1 (Winter 2006).

———. "House Beautiful and Frank Lloyd Wright," *Frank Lloyd Wright Quarterly* 8, no. 4 (Fall 1997).

———. "The House Beautiful: Frank Lloyd Wright for Everyone." Elvehjem Museum of Art Annual Report. University of Wisconsin–Madison, 1987–1988.

"Brains, Money and Imagination," unidentified publication, March 1958. The Frank Lloyd Wright Archives, Taliesin West, Scottsdale, AZ.

Breit, Harvey. "Talk with Frank Lloyd Wright," *New York Times,* July 24, 1949.

Brock, H. I. "Architecture Styled 'International'," *New York Times,* February 7, 1932.

———. "Le Corbusier Scans Gotham's Towers," *New York Times,* November 3, 1935.

———. "A Pioneer in Architecture That is Called Modern: Frank Lloyd Wright, Who Proposes a Glass Tower for New York, Has Adapted His Art to the Machine Age," *New York Times,* June 29, 1930.

Bryson, Lyman. "The Greatest Good—and Goods—for the Greatest Number," *House Beautiful* 95 (April 1953).

Buck, Thomas. "Sky City Plan No Idle Dream, Says Wright," *Chicago Daily Tribune,* October 17, 1956.

"Built in the USA," Museum of Modern Art DADABASE Web site: www.library.moma.org.

Burns, Ken, and Lynn Novick, directors and producers, *Frank Lloyd Wright.* Washington, D.C.: Florentine Films and WETA, The America Lives Film Project, Inc., 1998; DVD Warner Brothers and the Public Broadcasting Service: Paramount Home Entertainment, 2004.

Canaday, John. "Easy Does It," *New York Times,* July 31, 1960.

———. "Two Torch Bearers," *New York Times,* October 25, 1959.

———. "Wright Vs. Painting," *New York Times,* October 21, 1959.

Cannell, Michael. *I. M. Pei: Mandarin of Modernism.* New York: Carol Southern Books, 1995.

Caro, Robert. *The Power Broker: Robert Moses and the Fall of New York.* New York: Vintage Books, 1975.

Carrillo, René, interview with Indira Berndtson, July 18, 1996, copyright the Frank Lloyd Wright Foundation, the Frank Lloyd Wright Archives, Taliesin West, Scottsdale, AZ.

"The Caroline Wiess Law Building: About the Law Building." Museum of Fine Arts, Houston Web site: www.mfah.org.

Carter, Nick. *Alistair Cooke: A Biography.* New York: Arcade Publishing, 1999.

"Chronological Lists of U.S. Newspapers, 1940–1989." Library of Congress Web site: www.loc.gov.

"Closing the Poetry Gap," *Time* (November 7, 1960).

"The Clubhouse That was to Be Marilyn's Bunker," unidentified publication, September 13, 1998. The Frank Lloyd Wright Archives, Taliesin West, Scottsdale, AZ.

Cohen, Lizabeth. *A Consumers' Republic: The Politics of Mass Consumption in Postwar America.* New York: Vintage, 2003.

Cohn, Art. *The Nine Lives of Mike Todd.* New York: Pocket Books, Inc., 1959.

Condit, Carl W. *The Chicago School of Architecture: A History of Commercial and Public Building in the*

Chicago Area, 1875–1925. Chicago: The University of Chicago Press, 1964.

"A Conversation with Jed Perl," The Borzoi Reader Online Web site: www.randomhouse.com.

Cooke, Alistair. "Memories of Frank Lloyd Wright," *AIA Journal* 32 (October 1959).

Cooper, Lee E. "Offices Will Rise on Park Avenue Site," *New York Times,* March 29, 1953.

Corrigan, Faith. "Fabric Houses Unfold Fall Collections for Home," *New York Times,* September 22, 1956.

Crist, Judith. "Grass in the Street of N.Y. in 25 Years," *New York Herald Tribune,* May 14, 1953.

De Long, David G. "Frank Lloyd Wright and the Evolution of the Living City," in De Long, *Frank Lloyd Wright and the Living City.*

———, ed. *Frank Lloyd Wright and the Living City.* Weil am Rhein, Germany: Vitra Design Museum, 1998.

———, ed. *Frank Lloyd Wright: Designs for an American Landscape, 1922–1932.* New York: Harry N. Abrams, in association with the Canadian Centre for Architecture, the Library of Congress, and The Frank Lloyd Wright Foundation, 1996.

Derks, Scott. *The Value of a Dollar: 1860–2004.* 3rd ed. Millerton, NY: Grey House Publishing, 2004.

DeVree, Howard. "Highly Diverse," *New York Times,* May 31, 1953.

———. "Modern Movement," *New York Times,* February 8, 1953.

Dolkart, Andrew S., and Matthew A. Postal. *New York City Landmarks.* 3rd ed. Hoboken, NJ: John Wiley & Sons, Inc., 2004.

Douglas, Anne. "Frank Lloyd Wright Furniture on Display," *Chicago Daily Tribune,* November 13, 1955.

———. "Wright Furniture on View," *New York Times,* March 15, 1956.

Droste, Magdalena, Bauhaus Archiv. *Bauhaus: 1919–1933.* Köln, Germany: Taschen GmbH, 2006; originally published in 1990.

Dudley, Michael Quinn. "Sprawl As Strategy: City Planners Face the Bomb," *Journal of Planning Education and Research* 21: 52–63 (Association of Collegiate Schools of Planning, 2001): 56–57.

Dugan, Dennis. "Circular Layout Has Varied Uses," *New York Times,* October 28, 1962.

Easel, William, ed. *Russel Wright: Good Design is for Everyone . . . in His Own Words.* Garrison, NY: Manitoba/The Russel Wright Design Center; New York: Universe Publishing, 2001.

Eggener, Keith L., ed. *American Architectural History: A Contemporary Reader.* London: Routledge, 2004.

Engels, Mary. "They'd Rather Be Wrong Than Wright," *Daily News,* October 10, 1976.

Ennis, Thomas W. "'57 Set a Record for New Office Space, and '58 Will Top That," *New York Times,* January 5, 1958.

———. "Building is Designer's Testament," *New York Times,* November 10, 1957.

———. "Prefabrication Comes of Age," *New York Times,* May 13, 1956.

———. "Skyscraper Rises in Rural Setting," *New York Times,* February 12, 1956.

Esterow, Milton. "Curator Resigns from Guggenheim," *New York Times,* June 15, 1966.

"Evolution of a Museum," *Art in America,* no. 3 (June 1965).

"Exhibit Model City," *New York Times,* April 14, 1935.

"Exhibitions at Home and Abroad," *Frank Lloyd Wright Quarterly* 5, no. 1 (Winter 1994).

"Exhibits During Frank Lloyd Wright's Lifetime," *Frank Lloyd Wright Quarterly* 5, no. 1 (Winter 1994).

"4 to Make Theatres of Aluminum Domes," *New York Times,* December 11, 1957.

Farr, Finis. "Frank Lloyd Wright: Defiant Genius," *The Saturday Evening Post* (January 7, 1961).

"Fighting the Box," *The New Yorker* (July 5, 1952).

Filler, Martin. "Museums and the Maecenas Touch, *Architectural Record* (November 2005).

———. "Surveying a Century," *House Beautiful* (November 1996).

"First View of the Guggenheim," *Art News* 58 (November 1959).

Flanagan, Barbara. "Reproducing Wright," in *A House Beautiful Tribute to Frank Lloyd Wright and the Solomon R. Guggenheim Museum.* New York: The Hearst Corporation, 1992.

Fleischer, Leonore. "Letter From New York: 'Here, Ben, It's Yours,'" *The Washington Post,* July 2, 1978. The Frank Lloyd Wright Archives, Scottsdale, AZ.

Foreman, John, and Robbe Pierce Stimson, *The Vanderbilts and the Gilded Age: Architectural Aspirations, 1879–1901.* New York: St. Martin's Press, 1991.

Fowler, Glenn. "Wright Designs Pre-Fab Houses," *New York Times,* October 14, 1956.

Frankel, Stephen Robert, ed. *Frank Lloyd Wright's Guggenheim Museum: An Architectural Appreciation.* New York: Guggenheim Museum Publications, 2004.

"Frank Gehry: Architect." Guggenheim Museum Web site: www.guggenheim.org.

"Frank Lloyd Wright: 1869–1959," *Architectural Forum* 110 (May 1959).

"Frank Lloyd Wright, Architect: St. Mark's Tower," *Architectural Record* 67 (January 1930).

"Frank Lloyd Wright Day Proclaimed in Chicago," *Architectural Forum* 105 (November 1956).

"Frank Lloyd Wright Designs a Small Commercial Installation: A Showroom in New York for Sports Cars," *Architectural Forum* 103 (July 1955).

"Frank Lloyd Wright Dies; Famed Architect Was 89," *New York Times,* April 10, 1959.

"Frank Lloyd Wright on Restaurant Architecture: An Exclusive Interview," *Food Service Magazine* (November 1958), in Meehan, *Master Architect.*

Frank Lloyd Wright: The Mike Wallace Interviews. New York: Archetype Associates, 2001, DVD.

"Frank Lloyd Wright's Concrete and Copper Skyscraper on the Prairie for H.C. Price Co.," *Architectural Forum* (May 1953).

"Frank Lloyd Wright's Masterwork," *Architectural Forum* 96 (April 1952).

"Frank Lloyd Wright's Sole Legacy to New York," *Contract Interiors* 119 (December 1959).

"Frank Lloyd Wright's Work Is Carried On," *New York Times,* October 20, 1963.

Frazier, Nancy. *The Penguin Concise Dictionary of Art History.* New York: Penguin Reference, 2000.

Gathje, Curtis. *At the Plaza: An Illustrated History of the World's Most Famous Hotel.* New York: St. Martin's Press, 2000.

Gelernter, David. *1939: The Lost World of the Fair.* New York: The Free Press, 1995.

Gelernter, Mark. *A History of American Architecture: Buildings in Their Cultural and Technological Contexts.* Hanover: University Press of New Hampshire, 1999.

Genauer, Emily. "Guggenheim Museum is Ready for Public," *New York Herald Tribune,* October 21, 1959.

Gill, Brendan. *Many Masks: A Life of Frank Lloyd Wright.* New York: G. P. Putnam Sons, 1987.

Goldberger, Paul. "'Lost' Frank Lloyd Wright House is Found," *New York Times,* June 6, 1984.

———. "Philip Johnson Dead at 98," *New York Times* Web site: www.nytimes.com.

"'Golden Age' of Television Drama," The Museum of Broadcast Communications Web site: www.museum.tv.

Goodwin, George M. "Wright's Beth Sholom Synagogue." Questia Web site: www.questia.com.

Gordon, Elizabeth. "The Threat to the Next America," *House Beautiful* 95 (April 1953).

Gould, Jack. "Television in Review: Frank Lloyd Wright a Stimulating, Poetic Figure in the Latest of NBC's Conversation Pieces," *New York Times,* May 20, 1953.

Gropp, Louis Oliver. "A Salute to Genius," in *A House Beautiful Tribute to Frank Lloyd Wright and the Solomon R. Guggenheim Museum*. New York: The Hearst Corporation, 1992.

____. Foreword in Maddex, *Frank Lloyd Wright's House Beautiful*.

Guerrero, Pedro E. *Picturing Wright, An Album from Frank Lloyd Wright's Photographer*. San Francisco: Pomegranate Artbooks, 1994.

"Guggenheim Art Fascinates Nehru," *New York Times,* October 2, 1960.

"Guggenheim Chides Critics of Museum," *New York Times,* December 22, 1956.

"Guggenheim Fund to Build Museum," *New York Times,* April 17, 1951.

"Guggenheim Museum Progresses," *New York Times,* August 31, 1958.

"The Guggenheim Museum: Wright Has the Last Word," *Frank Lloyd Wright Quarterly* 3, no. 3 (Summer 1992).

"The Guggenheim Names Curator," *New York Times,* January 27, 1962.

Hall, Trish. "A Landmark 1959 Home with All the Wright Stuff," *New York Times,* October 24, 1999.

Hanks, David A. *The Decorative Designs of Frank Lloyd Wright*. Mineola, NY: Dover Publications, Inc., 1979.

Harris, Cyril M. *Illustrated Dictionary of Historic Architecture*. New York: Dover Publications, Inc., 1983; originally published by McGraw-Hill Book Company, 1977.

Haverstick, John. "To Be or Not to Be," *Saturday Review* (May 21, 1955).

Hill, John deKoven, interview with Janet Margolies for *House Beautiful,* Taliesin West, March 26, 1992, copyright The Frank Lloyd Wright Foundation, The Frank Lloyd Wright Archives, Taliesin West, Scottsdale, AZ.

———, oral history interview with Maggie Valentine, June 6, 1995. Copyright 1997 Regents of the University of California, The Frank Lloyd Wright Archives, Taliesin West, Scottsdale, AZ.

———, Papers #4032.369, The Frank Lloyd Wright Archives, Taliesin West, Scottsdale, AZ.

Hine, Thomas. *Populuxe*. New York: Knopf, 1987.

Hitchcock, Henry-Russell. "Editorial: Frank Lloyd Wright, 1867(?)–1959," *Art News* 58 (May 1959).

———, and Philip Johnson. *The International Style*. New York: The Norton Library, 1966. Original publication: *The International Style: Architecture Since 1922*. New York: W. W. Norton & Company, Inc., 1932.

———, and Vincent Joseph Scully. *Modern Architecture: Romance and Reintegration*. New York: Payson & Clark Ltd., 1929.

Hoffman, Donald. *Frank Lloyd Wright, Louis Sullivan, and the Skyscraper*. Mineola, NY: Dover Publications, Inc., 1998.

"Home Show Opens Today for Nine Days," *New York Times,* May 4, 1957.

Hoppen, Donald W. *The Seven Ages of Frank Lloyd Wright: The Creative Process*. Mineola, NY: Dover Publications, 1993.

"The Hot Cross Bun," *New York Times,* May 8, 1956.

"House of Wright is Previewed Here," *New York Times,* October 21, 1953.

Huxtable, Ada Louise. "Architecture: A Museum is Also Art, Exhibition Shows," *New York Times,* September 25, 1968.

———. *Frank Lloyd Wright*. New York: Penguin Group, Inc., 2004.

———. "Park Avenue School of Architecture," *New York Times,* December 15, 1957.

———. "That Museum: Wright or Wrong?" *New York Times,* October 25, 1959.

———. "What Should a Museum Be?" *New York Times,* May 8, 1960.

Illson, Murray. "Wright Gives List of What's Amiss," *New York Times,* January 10, 1958.

Iovine, Julie L. "Elizabeth Gordon, 94, Dies; Was *House Beautiful* Editor," *New York Times,* September 17, 2000.

"Iraq Halts Work on Royal Palace," *New York Times,* July 28, 1958.

Jackson, Kenneth, ed. *The Encyclopedia of New York*. New Haven, CT: Yale University Press, 1995.

James, Philip. "Wright on Fifth Avenue," *Motif,* no. 5 (Autumn 1960).

Johnson, Philip. *Philip Johnson: Writings*. New York: Oxford University Press, 1979.

———. "Letter to the Museum Director," *Museum News* 3 (January 1960).

Johnston, David Cay. "Ben Raeburn, 86, Publisher of the Known and the Aspiring," *New York Times,* April 23, 1997.

Kahn, Eve M. "One Wright Dream on Staten Island," *New York Times,* March 24, 1988.

"Kaiser Aluminum Dome." Promotional booklet by Kaiser Aluminum and Chemical Sales, Inc., 1957, in Sylvester Weaver Papers, Wisconsin Historical Society, Madison, Wisconsin.

Keeler, Robert F. *Newsday: A Candid History of the Respectable Tabloid*. New York: Arbor House/William Morrow, 1990.

Kellogg, Cynthia. "First Frank Lloyd Wright House in City to Go on View on Staten Island," *New York Times,* July 3, 1959.

———. "Frank Lloyd Wright's Mass-Produced House," *New York Times,* December 21, 1956.

Kentgens-Craig, Margret. *The Bauhaus and America: First Contacts 1919–1936*. Cambridge, MA: The MIT Press, 2001.

———. "The Search for Modernity: America, International Style, Bauhaus," in Eggener, *American Architectural History*.

Kirkham, Pat, and Scott W. Perkins. "Interiors, Furniture, and Furnishings," in Alofsin, *Prairie Skyscraper*.

Knox, Sanka. "Global Art Show Opens Here Today," *New York Times,* October 29, 1958.

———. "Guggenheim Museum Director Resigns in Difference of 'Ideals,'" *New York Times,* July 21, 1960.

———. "Guggenheim Picks Museum Director," *New York Times,* January 31, 1961.

———. "Moses Gets Prize from Art Society," *New York Times,* May 21, 1959.

———. "Museum Designed by Wright to Rise," *New York Times,* May 7, 1956.

———. "New Art Museum is Dedicated Here," *New York Times,* October 22, 1959.

———. "New Art Museum Opens on 5th Ave.," *New York Times,* October 21, 1959.

Krinsky, Carol Herselle. *Gordon Bunshaft of Skidmore, Owings & Merrill*. New York: The Architectural History Foundation; Cambridge, MA: The MIT Press, 1988.

Lanmon, Lorraine Welling. *William Lescaze, Architect*. Philadelphia: Art Alliance Press and London: Associated University Presses, 1987.

LaRusso, Carol. "Letters to the *Times*: Genius vs. Public," *New York Times,* November 8, 1959.

"Last Monument," *Time* (November 2, 1959).

Lawrence, Madge. "Letters to the *Times*: Guggenheim Museum Praised," *New York Times,* November 5, 1959.

Leach, William. *Land of Desire*. New York: Vintage Books, 1994.

Legler, Dixie, ed. "Architecture and the Automobile," *Frank Lloyd Wright Quarterly* 8, no. 2 (Spring 1997).

———. "Frank Lloyd Wright's Automobiles," *Frank Lloyd Wright Quarterly* 8, no. 2 (Spring 1997).

Lescaze, William. "Architect's History," *New York Times,* May 30, 1943.

"Letters," *New York Times,* October 27, 1957.

"Letters to the Times," *New York Times,* May 12, 1956.

Levine, Neil. *The Architecture of Frank Lloyd Wright*. Princeton, NJ: Princeton University Press, 1996.

Library of American Art: Georgia O'Keeffe, The. New York: Harry N. Abrams Inc. Publishers, 1991.

Louchheim, Aline B. "Development of the Skyscraper," *New York Times,* October 25, 1953.

———. "Museum in Query," *New York Times,* April 22, 1951.

———. "Newest Building in the Newest Style," *New York Times,* April 27, 1952.

———. "Wright Analyzes Architect's Needs," *New York Times,* May 26, 1953.

Lucie-Smith, Edward. "Pragmatists and Theoreticians," *Studio International* 172 (December 1966).

Ludvigsen, Karl E., "The Baron of Park Avenue," *Automobile Quarterly* X, no. 2 (Second Quarter 1972).

Lukach, Joan M. *Hilla Rebay: In Search of the Spirit of Art.* New York: George Braziller, Inc., 1983.

Luo, Michael, "New in the Showroom: Wright," *New York Times,* October 30, 2003.

Lupfer, Gilbert, and Paul Sigel, *Walter Gropius: 1883–1969.* Köln, Germany: Taschen GmbH, 2004.

Lyon, Herb. "Tower Ticker," *Chicago Daily Tribune,* September 12, 1955.

Maddex, Diane. *Frank Lloyd Wright's House Beautiful.* New York: Hearst Books, William Morrow and Co., Inc., 2000.

Margolies, Jane. "Meeting Mr. Wright," *House Beautiful* (November 1996).

———. "Remembering Mr. Wright," *A House Beautiful Tribute to Frank Lloyd Wright and the Solomon R. Guggenheim Museum.* New York: The Hearst Corporation, 1992.

"Marilyn's New Life," *Look* (October 1, 1957).

Martin, Douglas. "Home Sweet Landmark," *New York Times,* August 7, 1996.

Marty, Myron A., and Shirley L. Marty, *Frank Lloyd Wright's Taliesin Fellowship.* Kirksville, MO: Truman State University Press, 1999.

McAndrew, John. "Our Architecture is Our Portrait," *New York Times,* January 18, 1953.

McAucliffe, George. "The Guggenheim: Great Architecture, Difficult Installation," *Industrial Design* 6 (November 1959).

Meech, Julia. *Frank Lloyd Wright and the Art of Japan.* New York: Japan Society and Harry N. Abrams, Inc., 2001.

Meehan, Patrick J. *Frank Lloyd Wright Remembered.* Washington, D.C.: The Preservation Press, National Trust for Historic Preservation, 1991.

———, ed. *The Master Architect: Conversations with Frank Lloyd Wright.* New York: John Wiley & Sons, Inc., 1984.

———, ed. *Truth Against the World.* Washington, D.C.: The Preservation Press, 1992.

"Meeting of the Titans," *Newsday,* April 20, 1957.

"Memorandum of Understanding by The Frank Lloyd Wright Foundation/Henry J. Kaiser, Michael Todd and Pat Weaver," December 6, 1957. The Frank Lloyd Wright Archives, Taliesin West, Scottsdale, AZ.

Messer, Thomas M. "Editorial: Past and Future," *Art in America,* no. 3 (June 1965).

"Mike Todd Party: Cronkite Recalls Low TV," *All Things Considered,* National Public Radio Web site: www.npr.org.

Miller, Arthur. *Timebends: A Life.* New York: Penguin Books, 1995.

Mitgang, Herbert. "Sidewalk Views of That Museum," *New York Times,* October 12, 1958.

Moe, Doug, and Alice D'Alessio. *Uncommon Sense: The Life of Marshall Erdman.* Black Earth, WI: Trails Custom Publishing, 2003.

Mohl, Raymond. *New City: Urban America in the Industrial Age.* Wheeling, IL: Harlan Davidson, 1985.

Moholy-Nagy, Sibyl. "F.Ll.W and the Aging of Modern Architecture," *Progressive Architecture* 40 (May 1959).

"Mr. Arnold: Buildings and Botany," *New York Times,* January 6, 1960.

Mumford, Lewis. "Critical Opinion: Lewis Mumford," *Museum News* 3 (January 1960); reprinted from *The New Yorker* (December 5, 1959).

———. *Sketches from Life: The Autobiography of Lewis Mumford, The Early Years.* New York: Dial Press, 1982.

———. "The Sky Line: A Phoenix Too Infrequent-II," *The New Yorker* (December 12, 1953).

Muschamp, Herbert. *Man About Town: Frank Lloyd Wright in New York City.* Cambridge, MA: The MIT Press, 1983.

"Museum Building to Rise as Spiral," *New York Times,* July 10, 1945.

"A Museum Director Resigns," *New York Times,* July 22, 1960.

"Museum Opens Tribute to the Architect Today," *New York Times,* April 10, 1959.

"National Historic Landmarks Program," National Park Service Web site: www.tps.cr.nps.gov.

"National Register of Historic Places," National Park Service Web site: www.nr.nps.gov.

"Nautilus's Prune," *The New Yorker* (July 12, 1952).

NBC Collection. Library of Congress Web site: www.loc.gov.

Nelson, James, ed. *Wisdom: Conversations with the Elder Wise Men of Our Day.* New York: W. W. Norton Company, Inc., 1958.

"New Director Appointed by Guggenheim Museum," *New York Times,* October 15, 1952.

"New Era for Wright at 86: The Marketplace Redeemed?" *Architectural Record* 118 (October 1955).

"The New Museum," *Newsday* (Long Island Edition), October 22, 1959.

"News of TV and Radio," *New York Times,* March 1, 1953.

Nichols, Joe. "Belmont Park Shut; Track Held Unsafe," *New York Times,* April 11, 1963.

"N.Y. Opens Museum Built Like Corkscrew," *Chicago Daily Tribune,* October 22, 1959.

"Odd-Type Buildings to Overlook Church, *New York Times,* October 19, 1929.

Okrent, Daniel. *Great Fortune: The Epic of Rockefeller Center.* New York: Viking, 2003.

"On Radio," *New York Times,* May 9 and June 6, 1956.

Opening day news footage, the Solomon R. Guggenheim Museum, October 21, 1959, CBS Archives, New York.

"Our Company/History," F. Schumacher & Co. Web site: www.fschumacher.com.

"Outside the Profession," *The New Yorker* (September 26, 1953).

"Paint Company to Hold Tour of New Office," *Chicago Daily Tribune,* December 30, 1956.

Patterson, Jerry E. *Fifth Avenue: The Best Address.* New York: Rizzoli International Publications, Inc., 1998.

Peatross, C. Ford. "Symbol and Catalyst: The Automobile in Architectural Representation Before 1930," in De Long, *Frank Lloyd Wright: Designs for An American Landscape.*

Pepis, Betty. "Conventional Furniture by Frank Lloyd Wright," *New York Times,* October 18, 1955.

———. "Home Design Held of Social Import," *New York Times,* May 8, 1953.

Perl, Jed. "Art at Mid-Century in New York." Lecture, October 11, 2005. The Metropolitan Museum of Art, New York.

———. *New Art City.* New York: Alfred A. Knopf, 2005.

Peter, John. "The Clichés Are His Own," *New York Times,* February 15, 1959.

———. *The Oral History of Modern Architecture: Interviews with the Greatest Architects of the Twentieth Century.* New York: Harry N. Abrams, Inc., 1994.

Peters, William Wesley, video interview with Indira Berndtson, September 24, 1989, copyright the Frank Lloyd Wright Foundation, the Frank Lloyd Wright Archives, Taliesin West, Scottsdale, AZ.

Petersen, Anna. "Museums Visited by Royal Sisters," *New York Times,* November 16, 1960.

Pfeiffer, Bruce Brooks. "Exploring Wright Sites in the East," *Frank Lloyd Wright Quarterly* 7, no. 1 (Spring 1996).

———. *Frank Lloyd Wright: The Crowning Decade, 1949–1959*. Fresno: The Press at California State University–Fresno, 1989.

———. *Frank Lloyd Wright: The Guggenheim Correspondence*. Carbondale: Southern Illinois University Press, 1986.

———, selected and with commentary by. *Frank Lloyd Wright: His Living Voice*. Fresno: The Press at California State University, Fresno, 1987.

———. "Frank Lloyd Wright in Manhattan," *Frank Lloyd Wright Quarterly* 7, no. 2 (Spring 1996).

———. *Treasures of Taliesin: Seventy-Seven Unbuilt Designs*. Rohnert Park, CA: Pomegranate Communications, Inc., 1999.

———, ed. *Frank Lloyd Wright Collected Writings, Volume 5, 1949–1959*. New York: Rizzoli, in association with The Frank Lloyd Wright Foundation, 1995.

———, ed. *Frank Lloyd Wright: Letters to Architects*. Fresno: The Press at California State University, Fresno, 1984.

———, and Yukio Futagawa, eds. *Frank Lloyd Wright Monograph: 1951–1959*, vol. 8. A.D.A. Edita Tokyo, 1988.

———, and Robert Wojtowicz, eds. *Frank Lloyd Wright and Lewis Mumford: Thirty Years of Correspondence*. New York: Princeton Architectural Press, 2001.

"Philip Johnson on Frank Lloyd Wright, an Interview," *An American Genius, Frank Lloyd Wright*. New York: Philosophical Library, 1986.

Pickrel, Debra. "Encore: Frank Lloyd Wright," *House Beautiful* (August 2002).

Pittel, Christine. "What Style Reveals," *House Beautiful* (November 1996).

"Prefabricated House Bears Unmistakable Stamp of Frank Lloyd Wright," *New York Times,* July 5, 1959.

"Prefabricated Housing," *New York Times,* January 2, 1941.

Preston, Stuart. "Modern Architecture's New Look," *New York Times,* June 21, 1959.

———. "Museum Review," *New York Times,* August 17, 1958.

"The Private Residences at the Plaza," *Robb Report* (June 2004).

"Published Comments on the United Nations Headquarters," *Journal of the American Institute of Architects* 8 (October 1947).

Raeburn, Ben, video interview with Indira Berndtson and Greg Williams, July 21, 1991. Copyright The Frank Lloyd Wright Foundation,

The Frank Lloyd Wright Archives, Taliesin West, Scottsdale, AZ.

Ramírez-Montagut, Mónica. "Exhibition Catalog," in Alofsin, *Prairie Skyscraper*.

———. "The Tower Rises, A Chronology," in Alofsin, *Prairie Skyscraper*.

Rattenbury, John. "Living with Frank Lloyd Wright." Lecture, June 18, 1996. Sims Hemicycle House, Waimea, Hawaii.

"Real Estate: Prairie Skyscraper," *Time* (May 25, 1953).

Reed, Peter, and William Kaizen, eds. *The Show to End All Shows: Frank Lloyd Wright and The Museum of Modern Art, 1940*. New York: The Museum of Modern Art, 2004.

Remarks of Robert Moses at the Opening of the Solomon R. Guggenheim Museum, Fifth Avenue, New York City, October 21, 1959. The Solomon R. Guggenheim Foundation, New York.

Reynolds, Donald Martin. *The Architecture of the City of New York*. New York: MacMillan Publishing Company, 1994.

Riis, Jacob. "How the Other Half Lives," in *New York, New York: The City in Art and Literature*. New York: The Metropolitan Museum of Art/Universe, 2000.

"Rudolph M. Schindler." Great Buildings Web site: www.greatbuildings.com.

"600 an Hour See Guggenheim Museum," *New York Herald Tribune,* October 22, 1959.

Saarinen, Aline B. "Lively Gallery for Living Art," *New York Times,* May 30, 1954.

———. "Pioneer of Modern Architecture," *New York Times,* October 28, 1956.

———. "Tour with Mr. Wright," *New York Times,* September 22, 1957.

"Sally Victor Hats for Spring Reflect Manhattan's Changing Face," *New York Times,* January 5, 1960.

Saxon, Wolfgang. "Empress Visits 2 Museums Here," *New York Times,* April 16, 1962.

Schulze, Franz. *Philip Johnson: Life and Work*. Chicago: The University of Chicago Press, 1994.

Scully, Vincent, Jr. *Masters of Architecture: Frank Lloyd Wright*. New York: George Braziller, Inc., 1960.

Secrest, Meryle. *Frank Lloyd Wright: A Biography*. Chicago: The University of Chicago Press, 1998; originally published in 1992.

Shabad, Theodore. "Russians Lecture N.Y.U. on Education," *New York Times,* January 31, 1960.

Slavin, Richard E. *Opulent Textiles, The Schumacher Collection*. New York: Crown Publishing Group, 1992.

Smith, Kathryn. *Frank Lloyd Wright, America's Master Architect*. New York: Abbeville Press, 1998.

———. "The Show to End All Shows: Frank Lloyd Wright and The Museum of Modern Art, 1940," in Reed and Kaizen, eds. *The Show to End All Shows*.

Solomon R. Guggenheim Foundation Press Release, October 21, 1959. The Solomon R. Guggenheim Foundation, New York.

Solomon R. Guggenheim Museum, New York City Landmarks Preservation Commission Designation, List 226, LP-1774, August 14, 1990.

Speech of Harry F. Guggenheim at Formal Opening of the Solomon R. Guggenheim Museum, October 21, 1959. The Solomon R. Guggenheim Foundation, New York.

Statement by Mr. Guggenheim, October 21, 1959. The Solomon R. Guggenheim Foundation, New York.

Steinberg, Cobbett. *TV Facts*. New York: Facts on File, 1985.

Stern, Robert A. M., Gregory Gilmartin, and John Massengale. *New York 1900: Metropolitan Architecture and Urbanism, 1890–1915*. New York: Rizzoli, 1983.

———, Gregory Gilmartin, and Thomas Mellins. *New York 1930: Architecture and Urbanism Between the Two World Wars*. New York: Rizzoli, 1987.

———, Thomas Mellins, and David Fishman. *New York 1960: Architecture and Urbanism Between the Second World War and the Bicentennial*. 2nd ed. New York: The Monacelli Press, 1997.

Stern, Walter H. "Dramatic Buildings Are Legacy of Frank Lloyd Wright," *New York Times,* April 12, 1959.

Stoller, Ezra, photographs by; and Neil Levine, introduction by. *Frank Lloyd Wright's Taliesin West*. New York: Princeton Architectural Press, 1999.

———, photographs by; and Jane C. Loeffler, introduction by. *The United Nations*. New York: Princeton Architectural Press, 1999.

Stone, Edward Durell. "Hero, Prophet, Adventurer," *Saturday Review* 42 (November 7, 1959).

Storrer, William Allin. *The Frank Lloyd Wright Companion*. Chicago: The University of Chicago Press, 1993.

"The Story of the United Nations Headquarters," The United Nations Web site: www.un.org.

Sweeney, James Johnson. "Chambered Nautilus on Fifth Avenue," *Museum News* 3 (January 1960).

Sweeney, Robert L. *Frank Lloyd Wright: An Annotated Bibliography*. Los Angeles: Hennessey and Ingalls, Inc., 1978.

"Sweeney to Head Houston Museum," *New York Times,* January 10, 1961.

"21 Artists Assail Museum Interior," *New York Times,* December 12, 1956.

Tafel, Edgar, FAIA. *About Wright: An Album of Recollections by Those Who Knew Frank Lloyd Wright.* New York: John Wiley and Sons, Inc., 1993.

———. *Apprentice to Genius: Years with Frank Lloyd Wright.* New York: McGraw-Hill Book Company, 1979.

———. *Frank Lloyd Wright: Recollections of Those Who Knew Him.* Mineola, NY: Dover Publications, Inc., 1993.

"Taliesin to the Trade," *Contract Interiors* 115 (October 1955).

"Theatre of the future (?) . . . and three who have visions," *Honolulu Star-Bulletin,* November 5, 1957. Henry J. Kaiser Papers, The Bancroft Library, University of California–Berkeley.

"Throngs Inspect Wright's Exhibit," *New York Times,* October 23, 1953.

Thurman, Christa C. Mayer. "'Make Designs to Your Heart's Content': The Frank Lloyd Wright/Schumacher Venture," in *The Prairie School: Design Vision for the Midwest.* Chicago: The Art Institute of Chicago, 1995.

Tisch, Alice and Tom. *Max Hoffman House.* Brochure, September 2002.

Today, May 17, 1953, NBC News Archives, New York.

"Today's Prefabs: A Challenge to *All* of Home Building" in "Here is Prefabrication's Biggest News for 1957," *House & Home* (December 1956).

Todd, Michael, Jr., and Susan McCarthy Todd. *A Valuable Property: The Life Story of Mike Todd.* New York: Arbor House, 1983.

Trachtenberg, Marvin, and Isabelle Hyman. *Architecture from Prehistory to Postmodernity.* 2nd ed. New York: Harry N. Abrams, Inc. and Upper Saddle River, NJ: Prentice-Hall, Inc., 2002.

Trager, James. *The New York Chronology.* New York: Harper Resource, 2003.

Twombly, Robert C. *Frank Lloyd Wright: His Life and His Architecture.* New York: John Wiley & Sons, Inc., 1979.

"Typical Plans of Solomon R. Guggenheim Museum," *Architectural Forum* (January 1948).

Tyrnaeur, Matt. "Forever Modern," *Vanity Fair* (October 2002).

"Ultra-Modern Museum to Rise in 5th Ave. to House Non-Objective Art Collection," *New York Times,* March 21, 1944.

Unger, Irwin, and Debbie Unger. *The Guggenheims: A Family History.* New York: HarperCollins, 2005.

"The United Nations at 50: The Zeckendorf Connection," *Real Estate Weekly* Web site: www.highbeam.com.

"Unwrap New Museum, Find It's All Wright," *New York Daily News,* October 22, 1959.

The Usonian House: Souvenir of the Exhibition: 60 Years of Living Architecture, the Work of Frank Lloyd Wright, 1953. New York: The Solomon R. Guggenheim Museum, 1953.

"A Visit with Frank Lloyd Wright," *Look* 21, no. 19 (September 17, 1957).

Wallace, Mike, interview with Jane King Hession and Debra Pickrel, November 12, 2003, CBS Studios, New York.

Wallace, Mike, and Gary Paul Gates. *Close Encounters.* New York: Berkley Books, 1985; originally published by New York: William Morrow and Company, Inc., 1984.

Watterson, Joseph, AIA. "The Editor's Page: The Guggenheim Museum," *AIA Journal* 33 (January 1960).

Weaver, Pat, with Thomas M. Coffey. *The Best Seat in the House: The Golden Years of Radio and Television.* New York: Alfred A. Knopf, 1984.

"What Architects are Talking About," *American Architect* 136 (December 1929).

What's My Line? CBS, June 3, 1956. In the collection of the Museum of Television and Radio, New York.

White, E. B. *Here is New York.* New York: The Little Bookroom, 2005; originally published by New York: Harper and Bros., 1949.

White, Norval, and Eliot Willensky. *AIA Guide to New York City: The Classic Guide to New York's Architecture,* 4th ed. New York: Three Rivers Press, 2000.

Wisdom: A Conversation with Frank Lloyd Wright. In the collection of the Museum of Television and Radio, New York.

The *Wisdom* Collection, Library of American Broadcasting, University of Maryland, College Park.

Wood, Francis. "At Guggenheim Museum," *Newsday,* October 21, 1959.

Woolf, S. J. "A Pioneer in Architecture Surveys It," *New York Times,* January 7, 1932.

"Working Display Opens at Gallery," *New York Times,* March 7, 1946.

"Wright, 88, to Design Iraqi Cultural Center," *New York Times,* June 8, 1957.

"Wright Building Saved: Zeckendorf Will Pay $125,000 for Doomed Robie House," *New York Times,* December 21, 1957.

Wright, Frank Lloyd. *An Autobiography.* New York: Duell, Sloan and Pearce, 1943; originally published by London: Longmans, Green, 1932.

———. "Frank Lloyd Wright Speaks Up," *House Beautiful* 95 (July 1953).

———. *The Future of Architecture.* New York: Horizon Press, 1953.

———. Interview with Newt Mitzman, "The Changing Face of Park Avenue," CBS Television Archive, New York.

———. *The Living City.* New York: Horizon Press, 1958.

———. "Mass Media, Technology and Nature Study," Talks to the Taliesin Fellowship, #200, September 29, 1957. The Frank Lloyd Wright Archives, Taliesin West, Scottsdale, AZ.

———. *The Natural House.* New York: Bramhall House, by arrangement with Horizon Press, 1954.

———. "The Shape of the City." Address to the American Municipal Association, November 26, 1956, in Meehan, *Frank Lloyd Wright: Remembered.*

———. *The Story of the Tower.* New York: Horizon Press, 1956.

———. *A Testament.* New York: Horizon Press, 1957.

———, ed. *Frank Lloyd Wright on Architecture.* New York: Duell, Sloan and Pearce, 1941.

———, and Edgar Kaufmann, ed. *An American Architecture.* New York: Horizon Press, 1955.

"Wright Going to Iraq to Design Opera House," *New York Times,* January 27, 1957.

Wright, John Lloyd. *My Father, Frank Lloyd Wright.* New York: Dover Publications, Inc., 1992.

Wright, Olgivanna Lloyd. "Our House," *Madison Capital-Times,* May 3, 1958.

———. *Our House.* New York: Horizon Press, 1959.

———. *The Shining Brow.* New York: Horizon Press, 1960.

"Wright Plans a Mile-High Building Here," *Chicago Daily Tribune,* August 26, 1956.

"Wright Retreats on Museum Plans," *New York Times,* July 29, 1953.

"Wright Revisited," *The New Yorker* (June 16, 1956).

"Wright Says Problems are Solved for the New Guggenheim Museum," *New York Times,* July 22, 1954.

The Wright Stuff: The Television Interviews of Frank Lloyd Wright. Museum of Television and Radio (MTR) Seminar. In the collection of MTR, New York.

"Wright to Design Dome Theater for Mike Todd," *Architectural Forum* (February 1958).

"The Wright Word," *Time,* August 2, 1954.

"Wright's Plans for Baghdad Cultural Center Shown," *New York Times,* May 3, 1958.

Zeckendorf, William. *Autobiography.* New York: Holt, Rinehart and Winston, 1970.

CREDITS

AP/Wide World Photos, 46, 86, 105

The Art Archive/Culver Pictures, 7, 96

Avery Architectural and Fine Arts Library,
Columbia University, 67

© BBC/Corbis, 84

© Bettmann/Corbis, 9, 14, 49, 72, 73, 83,
114-115

© Philip Gendreau/Bettmann/Corbis, 97

Ezra Stoller © Esto, 3, 29, 33, 36, 40 right,
43 bottom, 51, 100 top

Photographs courtesy The Frank Lloyd Wright
Archives, Taliesin West, Scottsdale, AZ, 20
bottom, 21, 23, 28, 31 (John deKoven Hill
Collection), 45, 52, 55, 56 left (John
deKoven Hill Collection), 65, 74, 80, 95 bottom, 98, 104, 108, 111 (photograph by John
Engstead), 113

Drawings of Frank Lloyd Wright are © 2007
The Frank Lloyd Wright Foundation,
Taliesin West, Scottsdale, AZ, 22 top, 24, 38,
39, 40 left, 41 bottom, 42, 44, 70-71, 74-75,
76-77, 81, 95 top, 102-03, 106

FremantleMedia, 89 right

From the collection of Curtis Gathje, 20 top

Photograph © Pedro E. Guerrero, 25, 26, 37, 53,
63, 64, 68, 99, 100 bottom

Photograph by David Heald © The Solomon R.
Guggenheim Foundation, New York, 119

Photograph by Robert E. Mates © The Solomon
R. Guggenheim Foundation, New York, 112,
116-117, 118, 120-121

Photograph by William Short © The Solomon
R. Guggenheim Foundation, New York.
Courtesy The Frank Lloyd Wright Archives,
Taliesin West, Scottsdale, AZ, 93

Hulton Archive/Getty Images, 89 left

Photograph by Halley Erskine/Time & Life
Pictures/Getty Images, 123

Photograph by Andreas Feininger/Time & Life
Pictures/Getty Images, 12

Photograph by Lisa Larsen/Time & Life
Pictures/Getty Images, cover, 22 bottom

Photograph by John Loengard/Time & Life
Pictures/Getty Images, 79

Photograph by Frank Scherschel/Time & Life
Pictures/Getty Images, 34

Used with permission, Henredon Furniture.
Courtesy The Frank Lloyd Wright Archives,
Taliesin, West, Scottsdale, AZ, 57

Used with permission, *House Beautiful.* Courtesy
The Frank Lloyd Wright Archives, Taliesin
West, Scottsdale, AZ, 56 right

Library of American Broadcasting, University of
Maryland, 85

Courtesy of Mercedes-Benz USA, 50

Museum of the City of New York, Print
Archives, still from an unidentified film, 18

Museum of the City of New York, The Byron
Collection, (93.1.1.6480), 19

Museum of the City of New York, The Byron
Collection, (93.1.1.6493), 30

NBC News Archives, 88

The New York Times/Redux. General Research
Division, The New York Public Library,
Astor, Lenox and Tilden Foundations, 76

Sam Falk/The New York Times/Redux, 109

Copyright 2007, Newsday, reprinted with permission, 101

Courtesy of Photofest, 2, 10, 13, 17, 69, 87

Photographs by Joe Price, (Price Tower Arts
Center 2003.16.215) 41 top, (Price Tower
Arts Center 2003.16.293) 43 top

Courtesy of the Hilla von Rebay Foundation, 94

Photograph by Ben Schnall, 15

© Schumacher. Reprinted with permission. All
rights reserved. Courtesy The Frank Lloyd
Wright Archives, Taliesin West, Scottsdale,
AZ, 59, 60

© The Sherwin-Williams Company. Used with
permission. Courtesy The Frank Lloyd
Wright Archives, Taliesin West, Scottsdale,
AZ, 58

United Press International/Seagram Building
Fonds, Collection Centre Canadien
d'Architecture/Canadian Centre for
Architecture, Montreal, 35

Courtesy of Mike Wallace, 90 top, 90 bottom, 91

The authors have made all reasonable efforts to
find and secure permissions and reproduction
rights. Any omissions or errors are inadvertent.

INDEX

A

Aalto, Alvar, 76, 131

ABC (American Broadcasting Company), 89–90, 91

Abraham & Straus (New York), 61

Abramovitz, Max, 34

Abstract Expressionist movement, 11

accessories (wood), 57

Adler and Sullivan, 131

"Aerotors," 42

affordable housing, 63–64

AIA Journal, on Guggenheim Museum design, 114

Air House Exhibit, 125

Alfa automobile, 52

All About Eve, 68

Alloway, Lawrence, 144

Alumination Magazine, 138

America House (New York), 135

American Academy of Arts and Letters, 125

American Architecture, An, 28

American Federation of Arts, 125

American Forum of the Air, 78, 80

American Institute of Architects, 32, 86

American Institute of Decorators, 136

American Optical Company, 137

American Small House Exhibition, 125

Anderton Court Shops (1950, Beverly Hills, California), 133

Architectural Forum: on Price Tower, 43; on Hoffman Automobile Showroom, 52; on Guggenheim Museum construction delay, 97; on Guggenheim art displays, 116; issues dedicated to Wright, 143

Architectural League of New York, 45, 125, 132

Architectural Record: 61–62; on Wright's design for St. Mark's-in-the-Bouwerie, 39

architecture: post World War II growth of New York and, 8–12; Wright on collaboration in, 34; influence of nature in Wright's, 35–36; Wright's organic principles, 35–36, *37,* 47

Aristophanes, 121

Aronin, Jeffrey Ellis, *28*

Around the World in 80 Days, 73

"Art and Craft of the Machine, The," 131

Art Deco, 20, 34

Art News: on Guggenheim art displays, 116; on museum as art, 144

Arts and Crafts movement, 54

Asian art collection, Wright's: 24–27, *28, 100,* 129–30, 141; Japanese prints, 14, *28*

Astoria Hotel (New York), 18, 129

Ausgeführte Bauten und Entwürfe von Frank Lloyd Wright, 44

Autobiography, An, 28, 50

automobiles: 50–54, 88, 132; growing U.S. ownership of, 134; of Frank Lloyd Wright, 134

"automotive row" (New York), 50

B

B. Altman & Company (New York), 61

baby boom, 11

Baghdad, Iraq: Wright's designs for, 76–77; plan for Grand Opera, 76, 125; King Faisal Esplanade, 77; plan for Greater Baghdad, *76–77;* Hashim Hilli, *76;* 125

Bailleres House (project, Acapulco, Mexico), 71

Ballon, Hilary, on Wright's television talent, 91

Barney, Maginel Wright: on Wright living in the Plaza Hotel, 14, 30; on Wright's love of the piano, 27

Bartlesville, Oklahoma, 40

Bauhaus, 32, 45, 133

Baxter, Anne, *23,* 68

BBC Television, *84*

Beaton, Cecil, 19, 129

Belmont Park, New York, 103

Bender, Thomas: on International Style, 32; on Modern Architecture: International Exhibition, 45

Bergdorf Goodman, 18

Berlin, Germany, 44, 119

Birgitta and Désirée, Princesses of Sweden, 116, 143

Bitter, Karl, 18

Blake, Peter: on Guggenheim art displays, 116; on Guggenheim Museum, 121; on Broadacre City, 132

Blondell, Joan, 137

Bloomingdale's (New York), 61

BMW, 50, 52

Bogk House (1916, Milwaukee, Wisconsin), 59

Boyd, Virginia T., on failure of Taliesin furniture line, 62

Brady, "Diamond" Jim, 16, 21

Bramlett Enterprises, Motor Hotel for (project, 1956, Memphis, Tennessee), 78

Breuer, Marcel, 55, 119, 133

Brevoort House (New York), 128

Broadacre Cathedral, 124

Broadacre City: 40, *42,* 46, 132–33; "Broadacres Countryside," *42;* model display, 125; Peter Blake on, 132

Brock, H. I., on European modernists, 45

Bronfman, Samuel, 34–*35*

Built in USA: 1932–1944 (exhibition), 125

Built in USA: Post-War Architecture (exhibition), 125

Bunshaft, Gordon, 34, 37

"Burberry, The." *See* Heritage-Henredon

Business Week, on growth of New York, 32

C

Caedmon Records, 28, 130

Cain Hoy Stables, South Carolina, 103

Calatrava, Santiago, 119

Canaday, John, on Guggenheim art displays, 114–16

carpet, 58

Carrère and Hastings, 18

Carrillo, René: 58, 62, 135; Wright criticizes, 61

cars. *See* automobiles

Carson & Lundin, 37

Cass House (1957, Staten Island, New York), *63–64,* 124, 134–35, 137

Cass, William and Catherine, 64, 136

CBS, 44, *88*

Central Park (New York), *14, 16–17,* 18, 31, 47, 95, 107–8, 142

Chase Manhattan Bank (New York), 37

Cheney, Mamah Borthwick, 14, 29, 128

Chicago Arts and Crafts Society, 131

Chicago Daily News, on Taliesin Line, 59

Chicago Daily Tribune, on Taliesin Line, 59

Chicago Furniture Mart, 59

Chicago School of Architecture, 131

Chicago Theological Seminary, 79

Chicago, 21, 34, 37–38, 47–48, 58–59, 79–80, 85, 131, 133, 136

Chicago's Armour Institute, 133

Chrysler Automobile Salon (New York), 134

Chrysler Building (New York), 34, 78, 134

cities: Wright's hatred of, 8; Wright's views on expanding, 78; Wright's interest in planning, 132

Citroen, 51

Cohen, Barbara, 130

Cohen, George, 19, 102, *104*

Colette, 130

Colgate-Palmolive Building (New York), 37

Columbia University, 66–67

Consolidated Edison Company, 12

Contemporary Arts Center (Cincinnati, Ohio), 119

Conversations with Elder Wise Men, 85, 87, 139

Cooke, Alistair, 23, *72*

Coonley House (1907, Riverside, Illinois), 58

Cormier, Ernest, *34*

Corning Glass Building (New York), 37

"Crimson Beech, The." *See* Cass House

Cronkite, Walter, on Mike Todd, 73

Crystal Heights (project, 1939, Washington, D.C.), 133

Culwell, Haskell, *31*

Cummings, e. e., 130

curtain wall technology, 34, 131

D

d'Harnoncourt, René, 23

Dakota Apartments, The (New York), 18

Daly, John, 88–*89*

Dark Star, 103

de Kooning, Willem, 11, 106

De Long, David, on term Usonia, 135

de Wolfe, Elsie, 129

Delahaye automobile, 50

Delson, Morton, 64

Dick, Virginia Connor, 61

Dietrich, Marlene, 19

DiMaggio, Joe, 68

Dior, Christian: 19; Plaza suite designed by, *20, 21, 27, 29*

Disappearing City, The, 42

Downs, Hugh, 85–86, *87*

Draper, Dorothy, 58, 135

Drexel Furniture Company, 62

DuBois, Natalie, 37

Dudley, Michael Quinn, 132

Duell, Sloan and Pearce, 130

E

East Wing, National Gallery of Art (Washington, D.C.), 119

Eisenhower, Dwight D., 19, 110, 113

Elad Properties, 129–30

Elizabeth II, television coverage of coronation, *83*

Ellis Island (New York), 119

"Eloise," 19

Emerson, Ralph Waldo, 35

Emery, Roth & Sons, 37

Empire State Building (New York), 10–*11*, 47, 82, 129

Ennis, Thomas W., on Mies van der Rohe's career, 36

Erdman & Associates, Marshall, *63*–64, 136

Essex Hotel (New York), 135

Euclid Contracting Corporation, 102

exhibitions, Wright's work on, 125

F

fabric, 57–59, 124, 136

Fabris, R. Joseph, 24

Faisal II, King of Iraq: 76; assassination of, 77

Falaise (Sands Point, New York), *101*

Falkenburg, Jinx, 84

Fallingwater. *See* Kaufmann House

Falstaff Press, 130

Farah, Empress of Iran, 116, 143

Ferriss, Hugh, 84, 104, 141

Fields, W. C., 68, 137

Fifth Avenue (New York): 8, *12*, 14, 16–*17, 18*, 92, 95, *97–98*, 104, 109, 113, 116, *119–21*, 128, 140; Guggenheim Museum on, 6, 50; Plaza Hotel on, 8, 14, *17*; skyscrapers on and around, 37

Filler, Martin, 119

Fitch, James Marston, 56

Fitzgerald, F. Scott and Zelda, 19

Flemming, Arthur S., 113

Form Givers at Mid-Century (exhibition), 125

"Four Square, The." *See* Heritage-Henredon

Francis, Arlene, 88

Frank Lloyd Wright . . . on Record, 28

Frank Lloyd Wright: A New Theatre (exhibition), 125

Frank Lloyd Wright: American Architect retrospective (exhibition), *7, 124*

Frank Lloyd Wright: Buildings for the Johnson Wax Company (exhibition), 125

Frank Lloyd Wright: Work from 1893 to 1930 (exhibition), 45, 125

French and Company (New York), 128

Frick Collection (New York), 16

Fry, Maxwell, 133

Fuller, R. Buckminster, 73–74, 138

furniture: designed by Wright for Plaza suite, 24;

Wright designs, *57*–58, 124; in Taliesin Line, 59, 62

Future of Architecture, The, 28, 37

G

Gannett, William C., 54

Garbo, Greta, 19

Garroway, Dave, 87–*88,* 139

Gathje, Curtis, on Plaza Hotel, 18, 20

Gehry, Frank, *119,* 144

Gill, Brendan: 23; on interviewing Wright at the Plaza, 30–31, 128; on Arthur Miller's impression of Wright, 68; on Wright and the Chicago Theological Seminary; 79; on Wright's love of publicity, 91

Gimbel's, 99

Giotto, 142

"glass box boys," 32, 35, 47, 133

glass boxes, 37, 40, 55, 131

Goff, Bruce, 132

"Golden Age," of television, 11, 128

Golden Beacon (project, 1956, Chicago, Illinios), 79, 133

Gordon, Elizabeth: 23, 54–*55,* 56, 61–62, 134; anti–International Style sentiments, 55; launches Taliesin Ensemble, 57–58; memorial tribute of, 112

Gould, Jack, 87

Grady Gammage Auditorium, Arizona State University (1959, Tempe, Arizona), 77

Grand Army Plaza (New York), *18*

Grand Canal, Venice. *See* Masieri Memorial

Grand Waikapu Country Club (Maui, Hawaii), 137

Greater Baghdad, plan for. *See* Baghdad, Iraq

Griffith, D. W., 125

Gropius, Walter: 32, 45, 55, 133, 139; on Wright's international influence, 44; Wright's relationship with, 46; invited to design buildings for Baghdad, 76; excluded from UN commission, 131

Guernica, 142

Guerrero, Pedro, 29, 130

Guggenheim Collection, 114

Guggenheim Museum Bilbao (Spain), *119*

Guggenheim, Harry F.: 23, *72,* 98, *101–3, 112, 114–15,* 128; oversees Guggenheim Museum construction, 101–2, 107, 140; attends Guggenheim Museum opening, *112–13, 114–15;* on Guggenheim Museum visitors, 118; on Guggenheim museum interior, 141;

Falaise, the Long Island estate of, *101;* New Sports Pavilion for, *102–3*

Guggenheim, Irene, 94

Guggenheim, Solomon R. Foundation, 94, 98, 113, 118–21, 128, 140, 142–43

Guggenheim, Solomon R. Museum (1943–1959, New York): 6, 8, 11, 14–*15,* 16, 45, 47, 50, *68, 91, 93, 97, 104, 108, 113, 119, 120–21,* 124; Wright with model of, *15, 96;* Wright on site, 92–*93, 104;* Wright accepts commission for, 94–95; "The Modern Gallery," *95;* announced to the press, *96–97;* site of, *98;* delays and changes in, 98–101; Robert Moses gets permit for, 102; construction begins on, 102–4, 141; construction and art displays of, 104–7, *108;* artists' protest of design, 106; "Middle of the Road," *106–7;* atrium, 107, 113, *114–15, 143;* completion of and reactions to, 107–8, *109;* visitors to, *109,* 116–*17, 118;* opening of, *112–13, 114–15, 116–17,* 142; descriptions of, *113;* descriptors of, Wright, public, and press, 113; controversy surrounding completed, 113–14; ramp, 114, 143; interior of, 114–16, *118,* 142; art display method in, *118,* 143; influence of, 119, 143; aerial view of, *120;* observations on, 121; annex, 124; Harry Guggenheim on interior of, 141; leadership changes at, 144

Guggenheim, Solomon R.: *96,* 101, 113, *141;* suite at Plaza Hotel, 14, *94,* 128; death of, 98

Guthrie, William, 38–39, 131

H

Hadid, Zaha, 119

Hanks, David, on Taliesin Line furniture, 59

Hardenbergh, Henry, 14, 18–19, 128

Haroun al-Rashid, 76

Harper's, 86, 99

Harrison, Abramowitz & Abbe, 37

Harrison, Wallace K., 34, 138

Harvey, Henry Blodgett, 54

Hawaiian Village Hotel (Honolulu, Hawaii), 73

Hearst Corporation, 134

Hearst Magazines, 54

Hearst, William Randolph, 134

Hellman, Geoffrey T., 30

Henken, David, 140

Henredon Furniture Industries, Inc., 62, 135

Heritage-Henredon: 23–24, *25,* 27, *100;* "The Honeycomb," "The Burberry," "The Four Square," Wright's furniture lines for, *57,* 59,

61–62; *100,* 124, 130, 135

Hildegarde, 19

Hill, John deKoven: *31, 56,* 58, 62, 130, 135, 141; on Wright's Plaza Hotel suite, 27; on buying flowers for Wright, 29; Wright refers Hoffman to, 53; fills position at *House Beautiful,* 56; handles Wright's belongings, 110

Hilli, Hashim, 76

Hilton, Conrad, *20–21,* 27, 129

Hitchcock, Henry-Russell, 32, 45, 110

Hoffman Automobile Showroom (1955, New York), 50–*51, 52–*53, 54, 65, 124, 134

Hoffman House (1955, Rye, New York), 53–54

Hoffman, Maximilian, 23, *50,* 51–54, 130

Hofmann, Hans, 11

Holden, McLaughlin & Associates, 102

Home Fashions League, 55

Home Insurance Building (1885, Chicago, Illinois), 34

"Honeycomb, The." *See* Heritage-Henredon

Hood, Raymond, 45

Hoover, Herbert, 85, 101

Hoppen, Donald, on Mile High "Illinois," 47

Horizon Press, 28, 130

House & Garden, 135

House & Home, 136

House Beautiful, The, 54–55

House Beautiful: 27, 54–55, *56,* 65, 99, 135, 141; cover of, *56;* issues dedicated to Wright, *56,* 112; Taliesin Ensemble featured in, 57, *60–61,* 62; Usonian Exhibition House covered by, 99; licensee partnerships promoted by, 124

House on the Mesa (project, 1931, Denver, Colorado), *45*

Howe and Lescaze, 45

Howe, George, 45, 131

Howland, Dr. Joseph, *56*

Hughes, Charles Evans III, 37

Hunt, Richard Morris, 18

Husser House (1899, Chicago, Illinois), 59

Huxtable, Ada Louise: on Park Avenue transformation, 35; on Guggenheim Museum, 114, 121; on Guggenheim art displays, 116; on disagreement between Sweeney and Guggenheim Foundation, 118; on museums as art, 119; on Wright's age, 139

I

"I'll Take Manhattan," 87

Impellitteri, Vincent, on growth of Manhattan, 32

Imperial Hotel (1913–1923, Tokyo): 22, 68, 129;

annex, Wright's apartment in, *21*

Industrial Arts Exposition, 125

interior design, 62, 136

International Home Building Exposition, 125

International Style: 8, 32–35, 40, *43,* 45, 56, 114, 134; Wright's criticism of, 44–46; waning popularity of, 47; Elizabeth Gordon's attitude toward, 55; Guggenheim Museum and, 114

Internationale Architektur, 32

Iraqi Consulate (New York), *76,* 125

Iraqi Development Board, 76

Islamic architecture, 76

J

Jaguar, 50–52, 134

Jeanneret, Charles-Edouard. *See* Le Corbusier

Jenney, William Le Baron, 34

Johnson Wax Company, 125

Johnson, Philip: 23, *33–*34, *35,* 47, 132–33, 143; collaborates on Seagram Building, 34; on Wright as greatest architect of the nineteenth century, 45, 133; Wright's relationship with, 46; recommends Wright to Maximilian Hoffman, 50–51, 53; memorial tribute of, 112; on Guggenheim Museum atrium, 113–14; uses spiral design, 119; on Guggenheim Museum, 121; commissions Mies van der Rohe to design apartment, 131

Johnson, S. C. and Son Administration Building (1936, Racine, Wisconsin) and Research Tower (completed in 1950), 39, *40,* 45, 125

Jones, Jennifer, 21

K

Kahn & Jacobs, 34, 37

Kaiser Aluminum Dome, 73–75, 137, 138

Kaiser, Henry J., 23, 73–*74, 75,* 138

Kandinsky, Vasily, 107

Karastan, 57, 124

Kaufmann House, "Fallingwater," (1937, Mill Run, Pennsylvania), 45, 125

Kaufmann, Arthur, 99

Kaufmann, Edgar Sr., 99, 132, 133

Kennedy, John F. and Jacqueline, 19

Kentgens-Craig, Margret, on Wright's international influence, 44

Kentucky Derby, 103

Khomeini, Ayatollah, 139

Kilgallen, Dorothy, 88, 89

kinescopes, 139

Kitt, Eartha, 19

Klapp, Eugene, 54
Kline, Franz, 106
Knight, Hilary, 19

L

Ladies' Home Journal, 134
Lambert, Phyllis, 34–*35*
Larkin Company Administration Building (1903, Buffalo, New York), *44*
Lawford, Peter, 88
Lawson, Jean, *56*
Le Corbusier: 132; International Style and, 32; collaborates on UN complex, *34;* Modern Architecture: International Exhibit and, 45; Wright's relationship with, 46; *House Beautiful* and, 55; Villa Savoye, 55; invited to design buildings for Baghdad, 76; National Museum of Western Art, 119; excluded from Seagram Building commission, 131; machines and, 131; uses spiral design, 140
Lee, Sheila, 30
Leerdam Glass Company, 134
Lescaze, William, 45–46, 131, 133
Lever House (New York), 32–*33,* 34–35, 131, 142
Levine, Neil: on Wright's vision of the unity of living and working, 22; on influence of nature on Wright, 35; on Wright's reinvention, 45; on Wright's fame, 66; on the design development of the Guggenheim Museum, 140
Liang, Ssu-ch'eng (Yen), *34*
Liberace, 89
Lie, Guri, 138
Lie, Trygve, 138
Lieber Meister. See Sullivan, Louis
Lincoln Center (New York), 119
Lindbergh, Charles, 101
Living City, The, 28, 42
Lloyd Jones family, 86, 142
Lodge, Henry Cabot, 113, 142
Loeb, Gerald, 23
Loewy, Raymond, 58
Longmans, Green, 130
Look, 70
Louchheim, Aline B.: 140, visits Wright at Plaza Hotel, 23; on growth of New York, 35; on waning popularity of International Style, 47; censure of Rebay, 98; tour of Guggenheim Museum with Wright, 107–9; marriage of, 131
Ludvigsen, Karl, on Hoffman House, 53
Lukach, Joan, 140

Luxfer Prism Office Building (project, 1895, Chicago, Illinois), 131

M

Macy's (New York), 48–*49, 64
Maddex, Diane, on relationship between Wright and Gordon, 55
Madison Avenue (New York), 11, 27, 29, 116, 140
Madison Square Garden (New York), 73
Manhattan: *10*–11, 43, 47, 66, 68, 72, 87, 95–96; Vincent Impellitteri on growth of, 32; skyscrapers in, *39*–40; automobile sales venues in, 50; Iraqi Consulate in, 76; Rockefeller Center in, 82
Manufacturers Trust Company (New York), 37
Marconi, Gioia, 138
Markelius, Sven, 34
Martin, Tony, 87
Martin-Senour Company, 57–*58,* 61, *65,* 124, 136
Masieri Memorial (project, 1953, Venice, Italy), 130
Masselink, Eugene, 112
Maugham, Somerset, 129
McAndrew, John, on UN buildings, 35
McBride, Mary Margaret Show, 84
McCrary, Tex, 84
McKim, Mead and White, 129
media, 11. *See also* radio, television
Meech, Julia: on Wright's Plaza suite, 14; on Wright's Japanese collection, 27; on Wright's career as art dealer, 129
Meet the Press, 90
Mercedes-Benz, 50, *52,* 130, 134
Merman, Ethel, 19
Messer, Thomas M., 119, 121, 144
Metropolis of Tomorrow, The, 84
Metropolitan Museum of Art (New York), 16, 96–*97,* 112, 140
Mies van der Rohe, Ludwig: curtain wall technology and, 34; Seagram Building, 34–*35,* 131; Thomas W. Ennis on, 36; on Wright's international influence, 44; featured in Modern Architecture exhibit, 45; Wright's relationship with, 46; Tugendhat House, 55; memorial tribute of, 112; New National Gallery (Neue Nationalgalerie), 119; excluded from UN commission, 131; influence of Wright on, 132; receives AIA Gold Medal, 133
Mike Wallace Interview, The, 6, 64, 70, 82, *90,* 110, 113

Mile High "Illinois" (project, 1956, Chicago, Illinois), *46*–47
Miller House (project, 1957, Roxbury, Connecticut), *70*–71
Miller, Arthur: 23, *69,* 137; on Wright's fame and stature, 68; Wright designs house for, 68–69, *70*–*71,* 72
Miller, Morton A., 137
"Millionaires' Row" (New York), 16
Minic Display, 57, 124
Mitzman, Newt, 44
Modern Architecture: International Exhibition. *See* Museum of Modern Art
Modern Architecture: Romanticism and Reintegration, 32
Mondrian, Piet, 107
Monitor, 84
Monroe, Marilyn: 19, 23, *69;* meeting with Wright at the Plaza, 68; *70*–72, 137. *See also* Miller, Arthur
Morgan Library (New York), 140
Moser, Robert, *56*
Moses, Robert: *95,* 140; visits Wright's Plaza suite, 23; New York City Parks Commissioner, 23, 88, 94; Wright's cousin by marriage, 88; New York decentralization and, 88; construction of Guggenheim Museum and, 94; on Alicia Patterson, 101; gets Guggenheim permit, 102; tribute to Wright at Guggenheim Museum opening, 113; on Wright, 121; helps negotiate UN complex, 138; museum locations and, 140; criticizes Wright, 142
Motherwell, Robert, 106
Mumford, Lewis: visits Wright at Plaza, 14, 23, 30; on Guggenheim atrium, 114; on Guggenheim Museum design, 114; on Guggenheim interior, 116; stands up for Wright, 133; on Lever House, 142
Municipal Art Society, 142
Murray, Carolyn, *56*
Muschamp, Herbert, on Wright's relationship with New York, 13
museum as art, 119, 144
"Museum Mile" (New York), 140
Museum of Fine Arts of Houston, 144
Museum of Modern Art (MoMA) (New York): *7,* 35, 46, 105, 124, 140; Modern Architecture: International Exhibit, 44–*45,* 125; memorial tribute of, 110; Model House for, 124; Wright exhibits at, 125; Philip Johnson and, 132–33; visitors to, 143

Museum of Non-objective Painting (New York), 94, 97–98, 140

Museum of the City of New York, 140

N

National Alliance of Art and Industry, 125

National Distillers Building (New York), 37

National Historic Landmark, 124

National Institute of Arts and Letters Gold Medal for Architecture, 125

National Life Insurance Company (project, 1924, Chicago, Illinois), 37, *38–39*

National Register of Historic Places, 124

National Republican Club (New York), 59, 61, 125

National Trust for Historic Preservation, 138

Natural House, The, 28

NBC (National Broadcasting Company): 73, 78, 82, 84–85, *87–88;* executives of, *85*

NBC Lecture Hall, 84

Nehru, Jawaharlal, 85, 116, 143

Neue Nationalgalerie (New National Gallery, 1968, Berlin, Germany), 119

Neutra, Richard, 133

New Country House by Frank Lloyd Wright, A, (exhibition), 125

New House by Frank Lloyd Wright on Bear Run, A, (exhibition), 125

New Motor Hotel for William Zeckendorf (project, 1957, New York), 78, 80–*81,* 124

New Sports Pavilion, The (project, 1956, Belmont, New York), *102–3*

New York Building Commission, 101

New York City Landmark, 124

New York City: *2, 10, 12–15,* 16–17, *18, 33, 36, 83,* 92, *98*–99, 101, *108–9,* 116–*17, 120–21;* Frank Lloyd Wright on, 6, 8, 13, 48, 56, 88, 113; Wright establishes home and office in, 8, 92; status in postwar years, 8–12; Wright's views on 8, 78; as artistic center, 11; as epicenter of consumer explosion, 11; as media nexus, 11, 86; television industry in, 11, 82–83, 128; taxicab service inaugurated in, 19; growth of, 32–34; skyscrapers in, *33–*34; radio and television appearances of Wright's in, 84–85, *87–91;* as publishing center, 86; overcrowding in, 132

New York City's Board of Standards and Appeals, 142

New York Daily Mirror, 114

New York Daily News, 101

New York Herald Tribune, 87, 114, 142

New York Home Fashions League, 55

New York Racing Association, 103

New York State Pavilion, 143

New York State Theater (New York), 119

New York Times: increases coverage of architecture, 11; Wright's pronouncements in, 32; on International Style buildings, 34; on growth of New York, 35; on St. Mark's-in-the-Bouwerie, 39; on European modernists, 45; announcement of design for Hoffman Automobile Showroom, 51; on Taliesin Lines, *59–61;* description of the Cass House in, 64; announcement of production of aluminum dome theaters, 74; announcement of Zeckendorf purchase of Robie House, 79; coverage of Wright on television, 87; reports on Wright's New York office, 92; announcement of Wright's commission to design museum, 95; censure of Rebay, 98; on Guggenheim permit, 102; coverage of Guggenheim Museum construction tour, 107; on reactions to Guggenheim Museum, 108; memorial tribute of, 110; covers Guggenheim Museum opening, 114; on Guggenheim art displays, 114–16, *118,* 141; on Guggenheim visitors, 116; on Sweeney resignation, 118; on museums as art, 119; on Guggenheim Museum, 121

New Yorker, The: Wright's pronouncements in, 13, 27, 30, 134; writers from, 30; on Wright, 66; on Usonian Exhibition House, 99

Newsday: praise of Guggenheim Museum, 101; on Guggenheim art displays, 114; on Guggenheim Museum design, 114

Newsweek, on growth of New York, 32

Niemeyer, Oscar, 34

Nixon, Richard, 19

Noel, Miriam. *See* Wright, Miriam Noel

Noguchi, Isamu, 13

non-objective art, *94,* 128, 140

Norcross, Carl Hafey, 134

O

O'Dell, Herman, 74

O'Dwyer, William, 138

O'Keeffe, Georgia, 27

Oak Park, Illinois: 14, 35, 72, 128, 134; Wright's home in, 21, 54

Obolensky, Colonel Serge, 21

Olmsted, Frederick Law, 18

Omnibus, 72

organic architecture, 35–36, 47

Oriental Art Gallery (New York), 27, 130

P

paint, 57–58, 124

Paris Exposition of 1900, 129

Park Avenue: 140; Lever House on, *32–33;* Seagram Building on, *36;* skyscrapers on and around, 31, 37; transformation of, 35, 131; Wright criticizes skyscrapers on, 44; Hoffman Automobile Showroom on, 50–*51,* 52, 54

Park Fifty-ninth Street Corporation, 129

Park, Ben, 85

Parker, Ann, *56*

Parker, Maynard, *56, 135*

Parole Board in Washington, D.C., 130

Patterson, Alicia, 23, 72, *101–2*

Patterson, Joseph Medill, 101

Pei, I. M., 119

Pelvis with Shadows and the Moon, 26–27

Pepsi-Cola Building (New York), 37

Perl, Jed: on New York as artistic center, 11; on Guggenheim Museum, 121

Persian Room, Plaza Hotel, 19

Peter, John, 42

Peters, William Wesley: *31;* as Taliesin apprentice on Guggenheim Museum, 8; meets Marilyn Monroe, 69; attends Guggenheim Museum opening, 112; leads Taliesin Associated Architects, 142; on Guggenheim Museum location, 142

Pfeiffer, Bruce Brooks: on Wright's feelings about the Plaza Hotel, 16; on buying flowers for Wright, 29; on Wright's daily life in the Plaza Hotel, 29–30; on Wright's international influence, 44; on Guggenheim Museum, 92; on Wright supervision of Guggenheim Museum construction, 102–4

Pfeiffer, Carl, 129

Philip Morris Company, 90

Picasso, Pablo, 142

plasticity, 36

Plaza Hotel: 6, *9, 14,* 16–*17, 18–20, 37,* 90, 112, 129; as Wright's home, *3, 6,* 12–14, 86, 101–2; Wright moves to, 8; view from, 16, 18; design and surroundings of, 18; high reputation of, 18–19; Wright's attitude toward, 19–20, 31, 128; Edwardian Room in, 19, 30–*31;* Oak Room in, 19–20, *30–*31, 128; Palm Court in, *19–*20, 30, 129; Christian Dior suite in, *20;*

key to Wright's suite, *20;* Wright's suite in, 20–21; Wright's suite, redesign of, *22–23, 24–26,* 27, *29,* 124; daily life in, *28–29;* Wright's credit with, 29–30; "Taliesin East" in, 29; Oak Bar in, 30; Marilyn Monroe and Arthur Miller at, 68–72; Solomon R. Guggenheim's suite in, *94;* Guggenheim Museum plans unveiled at, 96–97; Olgivanna settles bill at, 110;

Po, Ling, 136

Poiret, Paul, 58

Pollock, Jackson, 11

Ponti, Gio, 116

Pop Art, 92

Pope, Loren, on Wright's Plaza Hotel suite, 27, 129

"Populuxe," 48

Porsche, 50–53

Post, George B., 18

Povlika, Dr. J. J., 103

Prairie houses, 35

prefabricated housing, 42, 63–64, 134, 136

Press Building (project, 1912, San Francisco, California), 131

Price House, "Grandma House" (1954, Paradise Valley, Arizona), 132

Price Tower (1952–56, Bartlesville, Oklahoma): *31,* 40–*41,* 42–*43,* 89, *104,* 132; floor plan of, *41;* office in, *43;* model of, 104–*5*

Price, Harold C. Sr., 40, 43, 132

PSFS Building (Philadelphia), 131

Public Service Company of Oklahoma, 41

Pulitzer Fountain (New York), 18, *19,* 129

Pulitzer, Joseph, 129

Puttnam, Tony, on Wright in New York, 31

Q

Quadracci Pavilion at the Milwaukee Art Museum, 119

R

radio, 84–85

"Radio City," 82–*83,* 138

Raeburn, Ben, 23, 28, 102, 130

Ralph M. Chait (New York), 128

Rattenbury, John, 69, 130, 137

Rattenbury, Kay. *See* Schneider, Kay

Rayward House (1955, New Canaan, Connecticut), 62

RCA (Radio Corporation of America), 82, 139

RCA Building (New York), 82

Rebay, Baroness Hilla, 23, 94, *96*–97, 98, 102, 113, 128, 140, 142

Rebhuhn House (1937, Great Neck, New York), 28

Rebhuhn, Ben, 130

Rembrandt, 142

Richardson, H. H., 35, 131

Riis, Jacob, on lure of New York, 11

Riley, Terence, on Wright and television, 91

"Road Machines," 42

Robie House (1906, Chicago, Illinois), 58, 79–*80,* 138

Rockefeller Center (New York), 42, 82–*83,* 84, 87, 125, 138, 140

Rockefeller, John D., Jr., 78, 138

Rockefeller, Nelson, 138

Rogers Lacy Hotel (project, 1946, Dallas, Texas), 133

Rolls-Royce, 50

Roney, Marianne, 130

Rooney, Andy, 129

Roosevelt, Franklin D., 84

Rose, Henry, 58

Rubicam, Ray, 23

rugs, 57, 124

Russell, Bertrand, 85

S

Saarinen, Aline B. *See* Louchheim, Aline B.

Saarinen, Eero, 23, 112, 131

Saint-Gaudens, Augustus, 18, 129

Sandburg, Carl, 23, *72,* 85

Sarnoff, "General" David, 84–*85*

Sarnoff, David, *85*

Sarnoff, Robert, *85*

Schindler, Rudolph, 133

Schneider, Kay: 130; on life in Wright's Plaza suite, 29; on Wright's ability to handle stress, 29; on Wright's relationship with the Millers, 69

Schumacher & Company, F.: 57–58, *59–60,* 61; "Taliesin Line," 58–*59,* 62, 139

Schumacher & Son, F., 124

Schumacher's Taliesin Suite, 125

Scully, Vincent, 116, 143

Seagram Building (New York), 34–*35, 36*–37, 46, 125, 131

Secrest, Meryle: on Wright's clothing, 68; on Wright's stubbornness, 86

Self-Service Garage for Edgar J. Kaufmann (project, 1949, Pittsburgh, Pennsylvania), 133

Selznick, David O., 21

"shelter" magazines, 54

Sherman, General William Tecumseh, statue of (New York), 18

Shining Brow, The, 78

Shinn, Everett, 30, 130

Shore, Dinah, 87

Short, William, 102, *104,* 110, 113–14

Silsbee, J. Lyman, 142

Sixty Years of Living Architecture, exhibition (1953, New York), 24, 56, *68, 99,* 104–*5,* 124

Skidmore, Owings & Merrill, 34, 37, 131

Skyscraper Regulation, 124, 132

skyscrapers: 124; increased popularity of, 32–34; Wright on, 35; on and around Fifth Avenue and Park Avenue, 37; designed by Wright, 37–39; Wright's opinions on, 40, 44–46, 132

Slavin, Richard, 58

Small Exhibit of Organic Architecture, 125

Spero, Charles W., *104*

Spivak, Lawrence, 90

St. Mark's-in-the-Bouwerie (project, 1929, New York), 38–*39,* 40–41, *42,* 124, 128, 131, 133

Steel Cathedral, 124, 131

Steichen, Edward, 85

Steinway & Sons, 23, 27, 130

Stewart, Countess Castle, 113

Stewart, Earl Castle, 140

Stokowski, Leopold, 23, 104

Stoller, Ezra, 29, 135

Stone, Edward Durrell, 23, 47, 112–13, 131

Stonorov, Oskar, 99

Story of the Tower, The, 28, 41

Stravinsky, Igor, 85

Streamline Moderne, 34, 40–*41*

Strong Automobile Objective and Planetarium, Gordon (project, 1924, Sugarloaf Mountain, Maryland), 96, 133, 140

Sullivan, Louis, 35, 37–38, 101, 131

Sweeney, James Johnson: 101–2 104–*5,* 140, 144; replaces Rebay, 98; on disagreement with Wright on Guggenheim art display, 104–7; on Guggenheim atrium, 114, 143; on Guggenheim interior, 116; resignation as Guggenheim director, 116, 118–21

Sweeney, Robert L., on Wright's self-promotion, 86, *118*

T

Tafel, Edgar, 29

Taliesin (begun in 1911, Spring Green,

Wisconsin): Wright saves, from foreclosure, 14; as Wright's primary residence, 8, 16, 22; Wright with Mercedes at, *52;* definition of term, 128

Taliesin Associated Architects, 112, 137, 142

Taliesin East. *See* Plaza Hotel

Taliesin Ensemble: 57–59, 135–36; press reactions to, 59–61; retail sales of, 61–62; Wright's reasons for launching, 62–65

Taliesin Fellowship, 85, 13

"Taliesin Line." *See* Schumacher & Company, F.

"Taliesin the Third," 130

Taliesin West (begun in 1937, Scottsdale, Arizona): *55,* 74, 77, 125; as Wright's primary residence, 8, 16, 22; *House Beautiful* recognizes, 55

"taproot" structural system, 37–38, *40*

Taylor, Elizabeth, *73–74,* 75, 138

Teague, Walter Dorwin, 134

television: Golden Age of, 11; in New York, 11, 128; Wright's appearances on, 80, 84–91, 138–39; broadcasts coronation of Elizabeth II, *82;* as new medium, 82–84; television set sales, 84; BBC television, *84*

Testament, A, 28

Tex and Jinx Show, The, 84, 138

Thiele, Albert, 142

Thomas, Dylan, 130

Thompson, Kay, 19

Thoreau, Henry David, 35

Thousand and One Nights, 76

Time: on growth of New York, 32; on Guggenheim Museum, 113; on Price Tower, 132; on Henry Kaiser, 137

Times Square (New York), *13*

Today, 73, 87–88, 138–39

Todd Universal Theater, Mike (project, 1958), *74–75*

Todd, Mike, Jr., 74–75, 137–38

Todd, Mike: 23, *73–74,* 75, 137–38; Universal Theater for, *74–75;* death of, 75

Todd-AO, 73, 137

Tonight, 73

Trillora Court (Sands Point, New York), 94

Truman, Harry, 19

Tugendhat House (Brno, Czechoslovakia), 55

Twain, Mark, 68, 137

Two Great Masters: Frank Lloyd Wright and D. W. Griffith (exhibition), 125

U

U.S. Rubber Corporation, 125, 136

Union Carbide Building (New York): 37; office in, *43*

Unitarian Meeting House (1947, Shorewood Hills, Wisconsin), 63–64

United Nations International Festival Exhibit, 125

United Nations: Organization (New York): 11, 78, 79; headquarters, *10–11,* 131; Secretariat, *10,* 51; complex, 34, 35; design committee: *34,* 131; Secretariat, Wright's description of, 131

Unity Chapel (near Spring Green, Wisconsin), 142

Unity Temple (1908, Oak Park, Illinois), 72

Universal Portland Cement Company, 50, 124

University of Chicago, 138

Urban, Joseph, 20

Usonian Exhibition House (1953, New York), 24, 56, 99–*100,* 124, 135, 140

V

Van Noppen, Donnell, 62

Vanderbilt, "Commodore" Cornelius, 18

Vanderbilt, Cornelius II, mansion of, *18*

Vanderbilt, Mr. and Mrs. Alfred Gwynne, 18–19

Vaux, Calvert, 18

V. C. Morris Gift Shop (1948, San Francisco, California), 133

Vertes, Marcel, 27

Villa Savoye (Poissy, France), 55

Volkswagen, 50

W

Wagner, Robert F., *112–13*

Wainwright Building (St. Louis, Missouri), 37

Waldorf Hotel (New York), 18, 129

Waldorf-Astoria Hotel (New York), 75, 129, 136

Wallace, Mike: foreword, 6; on television as new medium, 82; on Wright's appearance on *The Mike Wallace Interview,* 89–90, *91;* on Wright's as interview subject, 139. *See also Mike Wallace Interview, The*

wallpaper, 57–58, 124, 136

Wanamaker, John, 50

Wasmuth monograph or portfolio, *44*

Wasmuth, Ernst, 44

Weaver, Sylvester, 23, 73–74, 75, *85,* 138

Webb and Knapp, 78, 79

What's My Line? 88, 89

When Democracy Builds, 42

White, E. B., on New York, 11–12

Whitney Museum of American Art (New York), 119, 140

Wieland Motor Hotel (project, 1955, Hagerstown, Maryland), 78

Williams, Tennessee, 130

Wilson, T. Henry, 136

Winchell, Paul, and Jerry Mahoney, 88

Windfohr House (project, 1949, Fort Worth, Texas), 71

Windsor, Duke and Duchess of, 19

Winslow, William H., 54

Wisdom. *See* Conversations with Elder Wise Men

World War I, 32

World War II: 50, 62–63, 92, 95, 116, 128, 143; postwar prosperity and growth in United States, 8, 11, 48

World's Fair, 1939 (New York), 84, 140, 143

Wright, Anna Lloyd Jones, 27

Wright, Catherine Lee Tobin, 21, 129

Wright, Eric Lloyd, 23

Wright, Frances, 135

Wright, Frank Lloyd: *110,* 122–*23;* **Career:** Museum of Modern Art exhibits of, *6,* 45; dislike of cities, 8; as collector of Asian art, 14, 24; with model of Guggenheim Museum, 14–*15, 96;* Sixty Years of Living Architecture (exhibition), 24, *68, 99, 105;* Usonian Exhibition House, 24, 99–*100;* writing career of, 28; on International Style buildings, 32, 44–46; on skyscrapers, 32, 35, 40; difficulty working with, 34; Prairie houses, 35; influence of nature on work of, 35–36; principles of organic architecture, 35–36, *37,* 47, 54; skyscraper designs of, *37–39;* builds Price Tower, 40–43; international influence of, 44–46; design for Mile High "Illinois," 46–47; retail spaces designed by, 48–50; design for Hoffman Automobile Showroom, 50–*51, 52*–54; Taliesin Ensemble, 57–59, 61–62; promotion of Martin-Senour paint line, 57–*58,* 61, *65;* Taliesin Line of, 62–65; construction of Cass House, 63–64; celebrity of, 66–*67, 68,* 73, 76; at Columbia University, *67;* design for Miller House, 68–69, *70*–71, 72; design for Mike Todd Universal Theater, *73–74, 75;* admiration of Islamic architecture, 76; design for Grand Opera and Civic Auditorium for Baghdad, *76–77;* design for New Motor Hotel for William Zeckendorf, 78; self-promotion, 86; opinion of television, 90–91; Museum of Non-objective Painting, 92, 94–97; construction of Guggenheim Museum, *92,* 102, *104;*

Guggenheim Museum, 96–98, 101–2; design of New Sports Pavilion, *102–3;* completion of Guggenheim Museum, 107–9; descriptions of Guggenheim Museum, 113; success, Wright on, 122; executed works and projects of, 124; exhibitions and awards of, 125, 133, 141; unexecuted tower commissions of, 131; on crowding in New York, 132; automobile designs of, 134; prefabricated housing concepts of, 136–37; **Contemporaries:** *23, 28, 31, 76, 111, 123;* Mike Wallace on, 6, 89–90, 139; relationship with Philip Johnson, 46, 112; relationship with *House Beautiful* and Elizabeth Gordon, 54–*55, 56;* criticism of René Carillo, 61; house design for Miller and Monroe, 68–*69, 70–71,* 72; on Marilyn Monroe as architecture, 70; relationship with Carl Sandburg, *72;* relationship with William Zeckendorf, 78–80, 138; relationship with Robert Moses, 88, *95,* 102; Alicia Patterson, *101;* relationship with Harry Guggenheim, 101–2; disagreements with Sweeney 104–7; on relationship with Aline (Louchheim) Saarinen, 107; influence on Mies van der Rohe, 132; **Media:** interviews, 28–29; *Newsday* interview with Carl Sandburg, *72;* appearance on BBC television, *84;* radio interviews with, 84–85; appearance on *Conversations with Elder Wise Men,* 85, *87;* with reporters, *86;* self-promotion of, 86; appearance on *Today,* 87–*88;* appearance on *What's My Line?* 88–*89;* appearance on *The Mike Wallace Interview,* 89–*90, 91;* attitude toward television of, 90–91; television appearances of, 138–39; **Personal life:** establishes home and office in New York, 8, 34; residences of, 8, 14, *21–22,* 129; Plaza Hotel as home of, 12–14, 128; dining at "21" restaurant, 13; Plaza suite of *20–21, 22, 24–26,* 27, *29,* 30–31, 129; Imperial Hotel annex, Wright apartment in, *21;* combines living and work spaces, 21–22; love of music, 27; daily life at Plaza Hotel of, *29;* finances, 29–30, 48; preference for Old Bushmills, 30–31; Unitarian roots, 35; automobiles of, 51–*52,* 134; clothing and personal style, 68; death of, 110–12; on success, 122; on overcrowding in New York, 132; art preferences of, 142

Wright, Iovanna, 51, 112, 142

Wright, John Lloyd, 62

Wright, Lloyd, 23

Wright, Miriam Noel: on Wright's Imperial Hotel residence, 22; marriage to Wright, 129

Wright, Olgivanna (Olga) Lazovich Hinzenberg: 8, *31, 100, 112,* 128, 136; on Wright designing Plaza Hotel suite, 22; on Wright's apprentices, 24; on Plaza living spaces, 27; on television interviews, 29; at National Republican Club, 61; on meeting Marilyn Monroe, 69; on relationship between Wright and Zeckendorf, 78; *The Shining Brow, 78;* at Usonian Exhibition House, *100;* settles Plaza bill, 110; attends Guggenheim Museum opening, *112, 142;* on Guggenheim interior, 116; books published by, 130; letter to Kaiser Aluminum, 138; appearances on *Tex and Jinx Show,* 138

Wright, Russel, 135

Z

Zeckendorf, William, Jr., 138

Zeckendorf, William: *79;* visits Wright at Plaza Hotel, 23; on New York's post–World War II economic boom, 48; as New York realtor, 78–79; saves the Robie House, 79–*80,* 138; New Motor Hotel for, 78, *81,* 124; Wright plans to design restaurant for, 138; sells lot to Guggenheim Foundation, 140

ziggurat, 96, 140, 143